"This work not only captures the history of HR but offers a unique and powerful way HR may shape our planet for decades to come. A must read, learn, and do for all of us."

David Ulrich, HR Academic, Professor of Business, University of Michigan

"Thought provoking and challenging – a call to action for the HR profession."

Leena Nair, CHRO Unilever

"Who dares to read must act. This book will provoke you to start leading into a better future like nothing else you have ever read."

Kate Brown, Group People Director, Specsavers

"Hugely empowering research and thinking on the evolution of the HR function, and its role in society to help change the way we work for the better. We need to be Transformers rather than Robots in this evolving world!"

Catherine Lynch, Former CHRO Virgin Media

"Join the disruption and be part of reshaping the future of HR – this compelling book outlines the path and provides hard evidence of what's to come and how to prepare for it. A must read."

Beth Clutterbuck, CPO Cloudreach

"A rare look at the complete evolution of HR, demonstrating how HR professionals have always reactively adapted to the world at the time. A thought-provoking insight into the future of HR and a comprehensive offering on how HR leaders can be instrumental in leading the transitions."

Natasha Adams, CPO Tesco

"Watkins and Dalton offer a compelling alternative future pathway. A tsunami of thought-provoking narrative where positive organisational and societal transformation are inextricably linked and where all people truly are at the heart of this seismic and (r)evolutionary change."

Nathan Clements, HRD Boots UK

"Thought provoking read on HR evolution to shape the future for us – HR leaders, for our people, for companies, for communities and for the PLANET. What we will do with this understanding is entirely up to us? Let's shape the future now!"

Karel Foltyn, Head of HR Amazon Europe

"The book is a must read for business leaders. A compelling case is made for a leap forward and for HR to step up. The golden triangle – CEO, CFO and CHRO – will drive together the change of the workplace to change the world!"

Martin Booisma, CHRO AkzoNobel

"A thought provoking read that encourages HR professionals to reflect on whether our role should be to purely react to the social and political environment or to take a lead in the response that businesses take as they evolve through the 'Waves' of change."

Vicky Wallis, CHRO Santander UK

"This book is an essential read for leaders, and those developing tomorrow's leaders, faced with the challenges of both defining and delivering sustainable value in not just a digital economy but a world within which social equality and environmental concerns are paramount."

Keith Jones, COO Halfords

"A compelling and exciting view on the lessons of the past and how that shapes the future for individuals, business and the world around us. It's the call to action that both HR professionals and business leaders need. Change is not coming – it's here. It is now up to us to show that we cannot only learn from it, but develop and lead the next wave."

Elaine Thomas, Global Head of People Solutions Refinitiv

"A call to arms for all HR professionals to start thinking ahead and influencing their business to change – it's no longer about evolution but revolution. An interesting perspective on the future of work, the authors help us to understand the past, in order to work out what we must do differently to survive the future."

Jenn Barnett, Head of D&I, Wellbeing Grant Thornton

"This book should be read by all students of HR as well as CEOs and their CHROs."

Jo Ferris, CPO, Alter Domus

"An indispensable guide which equips HR to lead through disruption to create sustainable workplaces of the future. The authors steer the reader through the 'Seven Waves of Change' to develop organisations which deliver benefits to both business and society. A great read."

Andrea Eccles, HRD City HR

"A thought-provoking call to action for any business leader/People professional. Historical fact and logic inspire to disrupt the present to create the future – workplace and world. Recommended!"

Hayley Tatum, SVP People Asda

"This book illuminates why we in HR do what we do. It calls for leaders and the HR profession to think again and prepare themselves for an unfamiliar future. It offers concrete advice on how leaders and the HR profession should evolve if they wish to change the world for the better."

Jo Dunne, HRD, Church of England

"As well as giving a considered and compelling perspective on the forces that have changed the workplace and the role of HR in the past, the authors of this book also challenge us all – HR professionals, business leaders, employment lawyers, policy makers – to revolutionize our thinking to ensure that through the next HR wave, we enable a philosophy and approach which is not only sustainable but delivers benefits for all. A must read for every one of us who is up for that challenge!"

Janette Lucas, Partner, Labour & Employment, Squire Patton Boggs

"We are in times of great change and the opportunity and need for HR to step up and lead to impact positive organisational as well as societal outcomes has never been clearer. This book signposts the direction, building on historical context and inspiring HR practitioners to challenge and lead for a better future for all."

Peter Cheese, CEO CIPD

"This is for leaders that are committed to putting people strategy ahead of all else. The authors not only provide a concise and in depth analysis of the evolution of HR but more importantly this book offers a thought provoking glimpse of what most probably will be. I love the P-Wave and its limitless possibilities."

Txabi Aboitiz, CHRO Aboitiz Equity Ventures

"Watkins and Dalton provide context for where HR functions find themselves today and bring insight to the challenges now faced which ultimately impacts the way people think and wish to engage with work. Well worth reading for those looking to the future."

Fiona Claybrook, HR Director, The Ardonagh Group

"A fascinating read, this book tells the story of the evolution of HR and has inspired me to have real confidence and excitement that in this VUCA world, we can create a future workplace where people can flourish and be happy and healthy. In fact, for businesses to succeed this will be the only way!"

Louise Rich, Global Head HR, Mayborn

"A book that should be read by all business leaders not just CHRO's. It offers a history of HR but also invites CHRO's to look at the role they can proactively take in the future of leadership ensuring they are proactively meeting business challenges and staying ahead of the game."

Jacky Simmons, CPO VEON

The HR (R)Evolution

Many observers have suggested that capitalism is fast destroying our planet, concentrating power in a few big companies. Excessive short-termism, leveraged debt, digitisation, and disruption are the new normal. We stand at a critical juncture where the two paths ahead could lead to very different futures. One route could take us back to the harshest days of the early Industrial Revolution and the Great Depression. The other could lead to a world of abundance, equality, inclusivity, and prosperity for all. Which future awaits us will largely be determined by business, and HR (Human Resources) in particular.

Books on HR tend to focus on HR practices and potential interventions, but they rarely look at the profession, how it evolved, and how and why those people practices were created. *The HR (R)Evolution: Change the Workplace, Change the World* describes the "Seven Great Waves" of change and explains how each wave impacted business. It explains how some companies are stuck in the past and how HR can break the deadlock if it understands what the future holds. This book is meant for senior business leaders or anyone currently working in HR who are grappling with the paradoxes of business today. It's for leaders who recognise that people issues are the central challenge of our time. Whether we embrace the waves yet to come will determine whether we survive or regress, whether we flourish or flounder. The future is in our hands.

Alan Watkins is the CEO and Founder of Complete, a consultancy specialising in developing enlightened leaders, teams, and organisations. He has written several books, including *Coherence: The Secret Science of Brilliant Leadership*, *4D Leadership*, *Wicked and Wise: How to Solve the World's Toughest Problems*, co-authored with Ken Wilber, and *Crowdocracy: The End of Politics*, co-authored with Iman Stratenus.

Nick Dalton is Executive Vice President HR for Unilever. He has been in HR for over 30 years, working globally, regionally, and locally. He has also worked in all areas of HR, from leading international negotiations with trade unions to managing senior leadership development and enabling organisational change.

The HR (R)Evolution

Change the Workplace, Change the World

Alan Watkins and Nick Dalton

Routledge
Taylor & Francis Group

LONDON AND NEW YORK

First published 2020
by Routledge
2 Park Square, Milton Park, Abingdon, Oxon OX14 4RN

and by Routledge
52 Vanderbilt Avenue, New York, NY 10017

Routledge is an imprint of the Taylor & Francis Group, an informa business

British Library Cataloguing-in-Publication Data
A catalogue record for this book is available from the British Library

Library of Congress Cataloging-in-Publication Data
Names: Watkins, Alan, 1961- author. | Dalton, Nick, 1963- author.
Title: The HR (r)evolution : it's time to change the workplace and
change the world / Alan Watkins, Nick Dalton.
Description: First Edition. | New York : Routledge, 2020. | Includes
bibliographical references and index.
Identifiers: LCCN 2019033706 (print) | LCCN 2019033707 (ebook) |
ISBN 9780367348137 (hardback) | ISBN 9780429328190 (ebook)
Subjects: LCSH: Personnel management. | Work environment. |
Organizational change.
Classification: LCC HF5549.A7 W38 2019 (print) |
LCC HF5549.A7 (ebook) | DDC 658.3–dc23
LC record available at https://lccn.loc.gov/2019033706
LC ebook record available at https://lccn.loc.gov/2019033707

ISBN: 978-0-367-34813-7 (hbk)
ISBN: 978-0-429-32819-0 (ebk)

Typeset in Bembo
by Swales & Willis, Exeter, Devon, UK

 MIX
Paper from
responsible sources
FSC
www.fsc.org FSC™ C013985

Printed in the United Kingdom
by Henry Ling Limited

Contents

About the authors

Alan Watkins is the CEO and Founder of Complete – a consultancy that specialises in developing enlightened leadership through individual and team development.

Alan is unusual in that he advises completely different businesses in totally different market sectors and in different geographies, and works with many different types of businesses, from start-ups to FTSE 100 giants. He consults with them on how to grow their revenues, transform their strategy, step change their leadership capability, and develop their culture. He is a disruptive thinker and a modern business innovator.

Alan has written several books, including:

- *Coherence: The Secret Science of Brilliant Leadership* (Kogan Page, 2014);
- *Wicked and Wise: How to Solve the World's Toughest Problems*, co-authored with Ken Wilber (Urbane Publications, 2015);
- *4D Leadership* (Kogan Page, 2016);
- *Crowdocracy: The End of Politics*, co-authored with Iman Stratenus (Urbane Publications, 2016); and
- *Our Food Our Future: Eat Better, Waste Less, Share More*, co-authored with Matt Simister (Urbane Publications, 2017).

Nick Dalton is Executive Vice President HR for Unilever.

Nick has been in HR for over 30 years, working globally, regionally, and locally – living and working in three countries, experiencing life from Grimsby to Zurich (with many places in between). Nick and his wife Diane have managed a house move ten times and counting!

He has worked in all areas of HR, from leading international negotiations with trade unions, managing senior leadership development, enabling organisational change, introducing HR shared service organisations, setting up new companies from scratch, and project-managing the implementation of HR information systems. Nick describes his purpose as "bringing creativity from conflict." His life's work has been to change the workplace, to change the world.

Nick is well known in HR circles internationally, having presented to various HR conferences and networks. He is an acknowledged global thought leader on industrial/employee relations and has an extensive HR and business network. Nick has written the book directly to appeal to people like himself. He sees the book as a manual for change that will be insightful for HR practitioners, particularly those working in large multinational companies.

Disclaimer. Nick has written this book in a personal capacity, and views expressed represent his personal "world view," and not the view of his employer or any other organisation.

Acknowledgements

Alan Watkins

Writing a book is both joyful and hard work. The pleasure is not just in convolving ideas in a new way for the modern age to help address an issue humanity is currently grappling with, although the act of offering something that might help people bravely toiling at the coalface of human relationships in organisations around the world is fulfilling. A big part of the pleasure is the privilege of working with exceptional people to create the offering.

So, I would like to humbly acknowledge Nick, my co-author, for his tireless effort, rich experience of the world of HR, and relentless good humour, although being a Tottenham Hotspur fan means his humour is necessarily tinged with doubt! Writing with Nick has been a tremendously enjoyable experience, and I am deeply proud of what we have managed to create together.

I would also like to acknowledge the numerous HR professionals that I have had the pleasure of working with over the last 22 years, some of whom very kindly agreed to provide a quote of support for this book. This book is really for you. Since leaving medical practice, I have worked across hundreds of companies in multiple markets and multiple geographies, and this has provided me a privileged view of the patterns that human beings create when they work together in pursuit of their goals. These patterns are often difficult to see when your experience is restricted to a career in a couple of companies. I hope our observations of these patterns illuminate your journey and may provide some food for thought. I further hope the suggestions offered may help you accelerate development and reduce the suffering that sometimes happens inside companies.

I would also like to acknowledge Karen McCreadie for her unrivalled editorial prowess. Karen has again been absolutely invaluable in reconciling the differences that Nick and I inevitably created at times, ensuring the narrative arc flowed in a coherent way, and helping us to produce something that was complete without being overwhelming.

I would like to acknowledge Rebecca at Routledge for her responsiveness and encouragement in the production of the manuscript and the freedom she provided in helping Nick and I to get out what we wanted to say.

Finally, I would also like to acknowledge my wife, Sarah. I simply couldn't complete such a work without the sacrifices and unwavering support that Sarah provides. You role-model some of the greatest qualities we talk about in this book with grace and ease.

Life is so much about the people with us on the journey, and this particular journey has been illuminated by some exceptional lights.

Nick Dalton

My thanks to my parents, Joan and Kieran, for encouraging me to believe that the world can be made better. To my wife, Diane, and my "children," Maria and Michael, for being who they are.

To my many bosses and peers in Unilever over the years, who have given me confidence, inspired me, and always challenged me to be my better self.

Preface

Something is happening out there.

Until fairly recently, if you asked any CEO or C-suite leader the question "What is the purpose of your business?" once the ubiquitous platitudes about how people are "our most important asset" had been trotted out, they would almost certainly have added something along the lines of "to deliver shareholder value," "to deliver exceptional customer service and generate profit," or "to grow market share." These imperatives have been so thoroughly baked into the corporate mindset that no one questioned their ongoing validity.

Until now.

Today, CEOs often sound more like priests. Their mission statements sound almost biblical. Nike states, "Our mission is what drives us to do everything possible to expand human potential." Proctor & Gamble suggest, "Our purpose unifies us in a common cause and growth strategy of improving more consumers' lives in small but meaningful ways each day." Increasingly, senior executives are keen to emphasise that their business is about more than just making money.[1]

The 1980s Tears for Fears anthem suggested that "everybody wants to rule the world"; in modern business, it would appear that everyone wants to change the world. Mission statements increasingly talk in "grandiose, world-saving terms" in the hope of attracting more customers and talented new recruits keen to work for a business with heart. Such missionary zeal has become especially important for millennial employees. Caterpillar don't just build equipment, they "help our customers build a better world." Cisco pulls no punches – they want to "change the world" via a list of values including "win together" and "always do the right thing." Walgreens Boots Alliance says it is "caring for people and communities around the world" and Chevron talks of "enabling human progress by developing the energy that improves lives and powers the world forward."[2] I wonder how many customers knew that when they filled up their tank?

Whether this trend is authentic or little more than "greenwashing" is up for debate. What is not up for debate is the trend in organisations to embrace purpose, which suggests that more people realise we are at a tipping point for business, society, and our planet. We have surely reached a significant milestone when the CEO of one of the largest asset management firms in the world (BlackRock) sends a letter to chief executives urging them to deliver not just financial performance, but a positive contribution to society to benefit customers and communities as well as shareholders.[3] Something is in the air. Something has got to give. We know business must change.

Our current configuration of the "best, worst system" of capitalism is fast destroying our planet and leading inexorably to a concentration of fewer, bigger companies. New digitally enabled companies are disrupting and destroying established businesses, evolving forms of "surveillance capitalism"[4] – finding novel ways to monetise data acquired through surveillance and use it to sell more stuff to the few of us who may still have a job once artificial intelligence (AI) has automated the rest of us out of the workplace.

We stand at a critical juncture in human history where the two paths ahead could lead to two very different places. One route could take us back to the harshest days of the early Industrial Revolution and the Great Depression. We can't allow that future to happen. The other, which we must embrace, could lead us to a world of abundance, equality, inclusivity, and prosperity for all.

In this book, we will outline how society, instead of regressing to a replay of the 1890s or the 1930s, could evolve to a higher level of being, thinking, and doing.

We believe the accumulation of social capital, rather than financial capital, will provide the heartbeat for a better future. This will mean that people *really* will be our most important asset, rather than simply referred to as such on a mission statement. The effectiveness of people practices in the workplace and the quality of leadership development practices will be fundamental to this future, in the same way that financial practices are the core fundamentals of business practice today.

If this change is to happen, the HR profession needs to seize the initiative and become *the* key enabler. This is a radical departure from how leaders currently view HR. But we believe and will seek to demonstrate in this book that HR could hold the key to business choosing the right path, the new HR mission being no less than "to change the workplace, to change the world."

The chapters that follow are structured around the past, present, and future of society, business, and what that has meant – and continues to mean – for people practices in the workplace (HR).

We will describe "Seven Great Waves" – or "P-waves" of change (see Figure 0.1). Five P-waves have emerged since the first Industrial Revolution. Right now (2020), the "leading edge" is HR 5.0, although a handful of thinkers have gone further. The leading edge of any evolutionary change means a sizeable minority have consolidated around a significantly more inclusive, more advanced, conscious and sophisticated way of thinking.

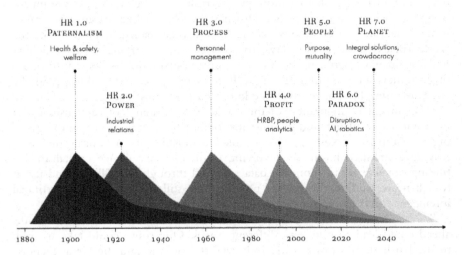

Figure 0.1 The "Seven Great Waves"

However, the leading edge is not the reality for most workers. But it does represent the emergence of the next step in our evolutionary path. A step that can help us out of our current predicament. Beyond HR 5.0 we foresee two more P-waves that will emerge more fully over the next couple of decades, assuming we course correct and survive until then!

As this book is about HR, we label each P-wave according to the people practices of the time. Each wave correlates to Clare Graves' values evolution and illuminates the dominant "world view" available at that time in history.

As a psychology professor in New York in the 1950s, Graves noticed that when he asked his students to write an essay, they tended to take just one of four world views, depending on what they valued most. Over time, expanding his population beyond students, Graves defined six, and subsequently eight, levels or world views. Each view related to an individual's value systems, and each emerged to transcend and include the previous level.

These value systems are not mere variations of each other; they are evolutions that expand up a vertical hierarchy, with the focus switching from the individual to the collective and back again. As we grow up and mature through these levels, we can't skip forward or jump to more advanced world views; we must evolve through every level if we are to develop as adult human beings.

Graves' work has been transformational in our ability to understand how our values evolve. The evolutionary dimension helps to explain and contextualise the world we see around us, as well as the people practices in each P-wave.

What we value changes and evolves over time if we mature and develop. As we evolve, we don't lose appreciation for the things we valued at earlier levels; we simply transcended our interest in those things. Our interest becomes more sophisticated, subtle, and nuanced as we become more sophisticated, subtle, and nuanced. What we value determines our actions, and this can be seen very clearly in business. Values are critically important in business because they provide direction to our actions, individually and collectively. Our values are also key building blocks of corporate culture.

Bearing this in mind, we will describe how every wave to date has delivered considerable benefits to business and society at large. Unfortunately, progress is always accompanied by some negative and unintended consequences that can exacerbate the problems we face and create new issues. Ironically, it is the problems generated by progress, which we will outline, that always trigger the next evolutionary leap forward, or occasionally the downside of each level heralds the collapse or regression to earlier, simpler times.

Genuine progress and elevated capability can only come from positive forward evolution. But sometimes when things become especially chaotic and uncertainty is rampant, it can be tempting to retreat and regress to an earlier time guided by a nostalgic illusion that life used to be better "back in the day." It rarely was – at least not for the vast majority of the population.

Our journey starts in the early days of the Industrial Revolution with the first people practices of HR 1.0, which were paternalistic. Factory and mill owners viewed their workforce as family. The emergence of the "factory system" meant that large workforces gathered in one place for the first time. Factory bosses felt workers needed to be controlled for their own good. Conditions were usually extremely harsh. The workforce, on the other hand, recognised there was "strength in numbers," so they began to challenge the paternalistic approach. As a result, HR 2.0, with its emphasis on Power, began to emerge. Trade unions emerged to try to even the odds between owners and workers, with mixed results. After the First World War, a monumental power battle erupted, and only ended when the Second World War broke out.

With the advent of war, there was a strong need to establish a new order, come together for the good of the country, and put in place a new set of rules to help win the war. HR 3.0, the Process wave, emerged. Factories were repurposed and women entered the workforce in much greater numbers as the men went to fight – changing the nature of work completely. Rules, regulations, and procedures were established to help everyone navigate this exceptional time. They were also used to kick-start business again after the war, reduce the risk of further power battles, and acknowledge the considerable contribution made by working-class men on the battlefield. There was a push for greater efficiency on top of the previous focus on productivity. That effort took decades, reaping significant benefit, but by the mid-1970s the inevitable downside of the Process wave started to emerge. Business complained about a lack of flexibility, adaptability, and entrepreneurialism. Too much process and too many rules were hindering progress. Lumbering bureaucracies and excess regulation were stifling growth.

Once again, that downside triggered the next evolutionary jump up to HR 4.0 – the Profit wave – where "shareholder value" became king. Greed was good. To parody the culture of the time, comedian Harry Enfield created a character called "Loadsamoney." Although the obsession with money had been bubbling away in the background for decades, it wasn't until the 2000 dot-com crash and then the 2008 global financial crisis that the negative elements of HR 4.0 came into sharp focus. Greed, hubris, fraud, and escalating inequality triggered the emergence of the next wave, HR 5.0 – People. With the emergence of this P-wave, leading-edge businesses sought to pursue a wider, more purpose-driven remit, rather than define their *raison d'être* as simply to make more money for their shareholders.

The Introduction sets the scene for the book and makes the case for urgent action. Although pockets of purpose-driven thinking now exist in businesses around the world, profit-driven thinking still remains the dominant mindset and the main economic model. The Introduction explores the consequences and implications of that obsession – both positive and negative – and invites HR professionals to consider their role in the resulting reality.

Chapters 1–5 look back at history and examine how the people practices (HR) of each wave have always adapted and reacted to the political, societal, and business changes experienced at that time. These chapters offer a whistle-stop "history of HR," but no ordinary history. We will show that HR is contextual and situational, not a set of objective static standards like financial or engineering standards. HR is an ever-fluid collection of activities reflecting the needs of the time. HR is, at its core, the story of people, their politics, their dreams, and their frailties. We will show how, up to now (2020), HR practices in the workplace have simply reflected the political and commercial norms of the day – whether HR professionals have realised it or not.

We believe that HR must stop evolving reactively to suit only the masters of that time or the prevailing political and economic climate, but instead take a revolutionary stance to ensure that business chooses the right path into a better future for all.

This book is therefore a call to arms for all HR professionals to stop reacting and start leading. It is a manifesto for revolution and radical change designed to move from the world of today, predominantly HR 4.0 – Profit – with a leading edge of HR 5.0 – People – to HR 6.0, where HR practitioners embrace Paradox, polarities, and complexity. But we should not stop there. We can accelerate forward to Planet-focused HR 7.0, where we prosper alongside other species and the planet, not at their expense. Chapters 6 and 7 explore the possible future outcomes and interventions of these P-waves yet to emerge. Chapter 8 unpacks how to transition from one P-wave to the next and prevent a regression to an earlier P-wave.

We hope to see the more inclusive and elevated P-waves of HR 6.0 and HR 7.0, but we will only witness them if we spark an HR revolution now.

Notes

1 Bartleby (2018) Mission Implausible: Beware Corporate Expressions of Virtue, *The Economist*, www.economist.com/business/2018/08/02/mission-implausible
2 Bartleby (2018) Mission Implausible: Beware Corporate Expressions of Virtue, *The Economist*, www.economist.com/business/2018/08/02/mission-implausible
3 Fink L (2018) *Letter to CEOs: A Sense of Purpose*, www.blackrock.com/corporate/investor-relations/2018-larry-fink-ceo-letter
4 Zuboff S (2015) Big Other: Surveillance Capitalism and the Prospects of an Information Civilization, *Journal of Information Technology*, 30: 75–89.

Introduction
The case for revolution

We are vampire finches.

Charles Darwin's detailed observations of various animal and bird species on the Galapagos Islands profoundly altered the way we understand the world. His original insights explained for the first time how change and adaptation occur.

For example, Darwin discovered that there are 15 species of finch in the Galapagos, each evolving from a single common ancestor species to exploit an environmental or ecological niche and increase its likelihood of survival.

Invariably, the evolutionary adaptations that allow the species to flourish also cause unintended, often negative, consequences. For example, the vampire finch's adaptation to a shortage of fresh water on Wolf and Darwin Islands means that it has a sharp beak which penetrates the skin of other local birds so it can drink their blood.[1] They do groom the other birds first to remove parasites, which is helpful, but the downside is an increased risk of infection in the host bird.

It is these negative consequences of evolutionary change that, over time, cause more complex or pressing problems than the original evolutionary adaptation was designed to solve. Taken to its logical conclusion, the vampire finch's adaptation could spell the end for the finch and the Nazca booby birds that it feeds from, especially as the finch also eats their eggs. If an adaption eventually leads to a species extinction, it's hardly a roaring success.

Today, business is like the vampire finch – delivering marginal benefit to some while systematically sucking the life out of others, society, and the planet. C-suite leaders, including HR professionals, have had a hand in creating this reality, and if we don't make an evolutionary correction to a new, more inclusive, cooperative, and sustainable world view, then human extinction is a very real possibility.

The progress humanity has experienced over the last few hundred years has been extraordinary. From the media, it's easy to assume that poverty is increasing, but actually over the last 30 years, the number of people living in absolute poverty, defined as living on less than $1.25 per day, has declined from 53 per cent of the global population to 17 per cent. Global literacy has increased from around 10 per cent to close to 100 per cent in the last 500 years.[2] Despite the war and unrest of the twentieth century, infant mortality has decreased by 90 per cent and the human lifespan has increased by more than 100 per cent. The cost of food has dropped 13-fold, the cost of energy 20-fold, and the cost of transportation 100-fold.[3]

The chance of dying a violent death has dropped 500-fold since the Middle Ages.[4] Despite the panic, doom, gloom, and mayhem the nightly news prefers to share, progress has improved the length and quality of most of our lives.

But this progress has come at a cost. Everything always does. Each new evolutionary P-wave brings positive progress and unlocks a new level of prosperity. But those benefits are always accompanied, over time, by some negative consequences or disadvantages. In fact, the process of evolution occurs because, for whatever reason, there is a need for change. Something isn't working, so a new adaptation emerges to solve that issue.

It is increasingly clear that our current economic system isn't working, and we risk a major regression unless we can make an evolutionary leap forward to a more inclusive, sustainable economic model and mindset in business and beyond.

Weapons of mass disruption

According to Richard Wolff, Professor of Economics Emeritus, University of Massachusetts, until the 1970s, capitalism in the US delivered a real rise in wages for its workforce year after year for 100 years. Consistently escalating wages allowed the American working class to achieve a standard of living unheard of anywhere else in the world. This increasing prosperity was at the very heart of the "American Dream."

Wolff goes further, and even suggests that the rise of the US as the dominant capitalist power in the world was built on constantly raising wages. In other words, "The way we [the US] became a rich, powerful, capitalist country in the 100 years before the 1970s was by providing workers with rising wages."[5]

Today that approach is the very antithesis of modern business.

Today businesses push toward continuous cost-cutting, year on year. Every business sector today, whether in energy, transportation, retail, or consumer packaged goods/fast-moving consumer goods (CPG/FMCG), reports unprecedented levels of disruption, or anticipates it, in the not too distant future. Low-cost ideas such as lean methodology, agile technology, roboticised factories, AI, and machine learning (ML) are having, or will have, an impact.

Many established businesses are in a "race to the bottom" that no one will win. The old "barriers to entry," painstakingly built by established business over decades, are fast disappearing.

The digital age is decimating long-standing industries, and with it our assumptions about business and capitalism. We have already seen this phenomenon at work in the highly lucrative (and protectionist) world of publishing.

Would-be authors, not accounting for the time they may spend writing a book, can now publish and sell their book on multiple online platforms for next to nothing. Few of us buy daily newspapers; we read our social media feeds and get our information from various other online platforms. People resent paying for content, and journalism has been decimated. The same is true in the communications industry. When was the last time you schlepped to the post office to pay to send a telegram, for example? More than likely, you chose to send an email, which was free and didn't require you to leave the house. Or maybe you used one of the countless "free" encrypted messaging apps that allow for private instant communication.

And, as we know, it has not just stopped at publishing. Very few of us visit a music store – certainly not a bricks-and-mortar one – where we would happily wile away a morning browsing physical products. People are watching less TV now, other than sport or the odd set-piece programme; we "Netflix" and we "stream." Advertising companies, the "Mad Men" of Madison Avenue, are now simply mad – incandescent and powerless as they watch their once billion-dollar businesses dwindle and die.

Advances in and the accessibility of technology mean that new businesses and individuals can compete on a near level playing field with existing, well-established brands. Whole industries are being upended. Airbnb, the home-sharing business, is now valued at more than the Hyatt hotel group, and yet they don't own a single property.[6] Uber is an extremely valuable transport company, and yet it doesn't own a single vehicle.

These innovations will impact us all. Most businesses are already in the grip of massive and perpetual revision, and this means modes of employment and ways of working will also radically change over the next few years. Technology and automation will mean fewer jobs in virtually every industry and market sector, and the casualties of this technological unemployment will not just be the low-paid repetitive roles. Digital disruption has already moved from the information industries to the real economy of real physical things. CPG/FMCG and retail are at the very start of major disruption, and this will have major societal impact, as factory workers, cashiers, shop assistants, office workers, even marketing executives all start to be replaced by cobots (machines that interact with human beings), scanning machines, and algorithms.

Take voice technology as another example of disruptive change. Voice is set to decimate many consumer goods retailers. For generations, large manufacturers, from FMCG to furniture to cars, have created a product, sought to differentiate those products through a brand proposition, and then invested heavily in advertising to cement the brand message of superiority in the mind of the customer. And it worked.

Then along came voice. According to Scott Galloway, Professor of Marketing at NYU Stern School of Business, "Voice is the Grim Reaper of brands." The number of people who can name their favourite brand has declined between 20 and 40 per cent in the last three years. Customers can now buy things by talking to the Google Home device or Amazon's Echo at the exact moment they realise they need it. Imagine a consumer with an Echo who gets up in the morning and goes to the bathroom to brush their teeth, using the last of the toothpaste in the process. They go downstairs to make breakfast, and en route say, "Alexa, buy toothpaste."

One short, market-decimating sentence on the way to the kitchen!

The problem for Colgate is that their customer didn't say, "Alexa, buy Colgate Sensitive 75 ml." As a result, Amazon will sell the customer whatever toothpaste *it* wants and ship it. And this will happen across markets and industries as products are once again commodified. All the effort building a brand, all the billions invested in advertising over countless decades, will disappear almost overnight.[7]

Greater technological advance and automation, together with consolidation and extreme innovative market disruption, mean that many businesses and jobs, including well-paid jobs, are facing rapid extinction.

New entrants are constantly nipping at the heels of the old incumbents and often surpassing them. These new entrants are like speedboats – light, lean, and nimble – which means they can adapt faster to an ever-changing commercial environment. The existing businesses are more like an ocean liner – heavy, bloated, and clumsy. Their size, which used to be their biggest asset, is now their biggest vulnerability. This highly competitive market spawns more disruption and pushes down prices still further. Galloway explains how General Motors, a titan of the Process wave, employed 215,000 employees, with a market cap per employee of $231,000. Facebook, by contracts, employs just 17,048 employees, with a market cap per employee of $20.5 million.[8]

Through it all, what is HR doing? How many HR executives have stepped forward and warned of the dangers? How many of us are simply towing the corporate line, continuing to implement ineffective people policies we have no hand in discussing or agreeing?

Is HR anticipating these changes and the ramifications on business and the workforce?

Do we seek to institute people practices and development protocols that would help employees and business leaders get ahead of these and other game-changing shifts?

How many of us are pushing for a strategic role at the decision-making table so we can influence business strategy mindful of its impact on people and planet, not just profit?

Industry consolidation and the disappearing profit margin

John Hagel, a Silicon Valley futurologist, reminds us, "All of our businesses are built for predictability, efficiency and to maintain the status quo, not for disruption."[9] And yet disruption is the new normal. Serial entrepreneur and angel investor David S. Rose went further when he said, "Any company designed for success in the twentieth century is doomed to fail in the twenty-first."[10]

According to Galloway, in the West, we are already operating in a business world of almost zero growth, adjusted for inflation. We can seek to consolidate, where the winners gobble up the losers until there are only a handful of companies left. In the West, Facebook, Apple, Amazon, Netflix, and Google (FAANG) are likely to be the winners, and in Asia Tencent and Alibaba.

History tells us that when markets mature and businesses compete on price, their margins are squeezed as the competition drives prices lower and lower to attract customers. If such businesses can hold out during a period of stagnant or even negative growth while its competitors go bankrupt, they can consolidate their market, and the companies that are left can mop up their competitors' customers until a monopoly or oligopoly is created.

We have also witnessed something like this cycle in the airline industry. Do we really have a choice for many routes? Despite the bad service and our vowing never to fly with that company again, the lack of available alternative means invariably we do. And those companies know it – hence why they don't spend money to fix the delays or bad service!

As digital barriers to entry fall, as the likes of Amazon or Alibaba apply their seemingly endless capital and clout, we will simply have more mergers and acquisitions, more desperate projects to identify synergies and eliminate duplication. And less companies, fewer alternatives, fewer jobs, and in the end almost certainly less choice, poorer quality, and worse service.

Driving costs to the bone in the hope to outlast the competition is a twentieth-century strategy, but it certainly doesn't always work in the twenty-first century. Relying on old-world strategies in a new world condemns us to failure and equates to corporate suicide.

Where is HR in all of this?

Near zero marginal cost

Take these and other considerations to their logical conclusion, and eventually we will arrive at a point where business is operating at near zero marginal cost. In other words, the cost of producing each additional unit once the fixed costs are covered is nearly zero.

To make profit, something must be sold for an amount greater than the cost of supplying or delivering that item. So, what happens to business when the goods and services that are offered in the marketplace are free or nearly free? What happens when the costs to produce those products and services are so low, due to the technological advance, reduction in labour costs, or industry consolidation, that there are no longer any barriers to entry into that market?

What happens when the economies of scale, which business has relied upon for centuries to increase efficiency and keep competitors out of the market, evaporate?

Where is the profit then?

We are already seeing this phenomenon appear in renewable energy, where the cost to install your own power system has plummeted, and 3D printing is changing the face of manufacturing – even beyond the changes that are happening with automation. There is now a 3D printer on the International Space Station creating spare parts that are "Made in Space"! These are the first man-made objects not created on Earth.[11] Relatively cheap 3D printers can print just about anything using a variety of recycled "foodstuffs." In the not too distant future, when we need a new desk, we won't be visiting Officeworks; instead, we will download a free specification on a table we like and visit an out-of-town upcycling centre for the printer "foodstuffs." We will purchase recycled plastic, steel, paper, wood, or glass for next to nothing and go home and print our table using energy from solar panels on our house with zero waste.

Where's the profit in that model?

Even old bastions of society such as Ivy League universities are having to adapt to a monumental shift in education – massive open online courses (MOOCs). As of 2018, some 101 million people had enrolled in a MOOC, with over 900 universities offering about 11,400 courses to students for free.[12] In addition, many of these courses are now being taught by some of the most distinguished professors in the world. Just imagine – world-class education from the comfort of your own home with zero student debt.

Where's the profit in *that* model?

There is now an abundance of solutions, providers, and competitors, but if they are all providing free or nearly free products and services, then the whole capitalist edifice starts to crumble. Alfred Marshall's long-standing economic principles of supply and demand, marginal utility, and costs of production no longer apply. We will need new models of business, and quickly.

What is the HR point of view on the new models that must emerge?

Planetary limits

> Anyone who believes exponential growth can go on forever in a finite world is either a madman or an economist.
>
> Kenneth Boulding, economist

In addition to the economic realities of modern business that herald a "changing of the guard," there are also practical environmental realities that signal the urgent need for a change of direction. If we value the planet we live on and would like to maintain a home for our children and grandchildren, then modern business must evolve.

Business requires growth. It needs to achieve growth year on year in order to be considered successful. But a system that requires growth cannot last forever on a planet with finite resources. Business, as we currently understand, is therefore fundamentally unsustainable – sooner or later, it will run up against a variety of planetary limits that will prevent the system from functioning. We are already seeing this reality play out.

We are rapidly increasing our use of planetary resources as we make more "stuff" so we can sell more "stuff" and business can make more money. This "stuff" is created in what is known as the materials economy, which consists of extraction, production, distribution, consumption, and disposal.

But each of these stages is already hitting planetary limits.

In the past three decades alone, we have used up one-third of the planet's natural resources. In the US, for example, there is less than 4 per cent of original forests left, and 40 per cent of the fresh waterways have become undrinkable. The US has 5 per cent of the world's population but uses 30 per cent of the world's resources while also creating 30 per cent of the world's waste. If everyone consumed at the rate of the US, we would need three to five planets. We have one.[13] But it's by no means just the US – all the developed countries use more than their fair share of global resources.

We are currently locked into an economic model that is killing itself and the planet, and the vast majority of the global population will end up no better off, with many considerably worse off.

So, what is HR doing to counter these challenges? Are we driving the human development of the leadership cadre to ensure that senior executives are capable of viewing business from a more expanded perspective where they value and pursue objectives beyond simply profit?

The time for change is now

Thankfully, as depressing as this picture is, it doesn't have to be like this. We are entering an age of potential abundance, despite all these challenges.

Technological advance, alternative energy sources, and accessibility mean that amazing things are also happening.

Princeton graduate Marcin Kakubowski and his team identified 50 machines and tools that were instrumental in creating a sustainable and decent quality of life. The idea was to create open-source specifications of these ideas so that people in poor communities could download them for free and print them on 3D printers from locally available feedstock such as scrap metal or plastic, thus giving these communities a "global village construction kit." Eight prototypes were created, including a bulldozer, rototiller, and micro-tractor. But how can poor communities possibly afford a 3D printer or have access to sufficient energy to operate it? Considering how fast technology costs plummet once the technology is available, it's only a matter of time before 3D printers are affordable for even the poorest people on the planet. There are already free specifications that would allow a 3D printer to print another functional 3D printer.[14]

Couple that innovation with localised power generation and the possibilities are endless. In 2012, social entrepreneurs Yashraj Khaitan and Jacob Dickinson created Gram Power and set up India's first smart microgrid in a remote village. A bank of solar panels is connected to a brick substation that houses batteries that allow the village to store power during the evening or when there is cloud cover. The microgrid provides green energy to more than 200 residents far cheaper and cleaner than traditional sources.[15] Imagine what will be possible when those villages can also purchase a 3D printer and download free specifications for the tools and equipment they need to prosper. Mass production will shift into production by the masses. Real social change and lifting millions of people out of poverty becomes probable, not just possible.

Although a few thinkers ahead of their time, including Adam Smith, John Maynard Keynes, Karl Marx, and John Stuart Mill, could see the writing on the wall if the system was taken to its logical conclusion, their insights were swept aside in the enthusiasm of a booming economy and rising living standards. What makes the situation a little different now is that there are many people in business, academia, and beyond who not only see the writing on the wall, but appreciate its threat *and* opportunity. The need for change is not political or ideological or even moral; it's practical. We need a new economic model because the current one is gradually destroying us. If we want a place to live and a planet for our grandchildren to enjoy, then it's absolutely essential that we find and move to a new economic model. And HR must be at the forefront of that revolution.

To access abundance, to address planetary limits, to glory in human potential and live in a world of meaningful relationships, we need new ways of leading, thinking, being, and doing.

The existing scarcity model and mindset of late capitalism is redundant. Accumulation of financial capital is no longer the purpose of business. The future, in a world of zero marginal costs, could be about "us," not just about money. Organisations could exist to serve us, to really help to make our lives better, rather than those sentiments being empty words on a mission statement. Organisations and customers could coexist in mutually beneficial symbiotic relationships, rather than the vampire finch approach, where business seeks to take as much money from us as possible, regardless of the consequences. Perhaps, as investment banker and politician Baroness Shriti Vadera suggests, the key indicator of business success in the twenty-first century should be the level and quality of wages and household incomes.[16]

Economic and social theorist Jeremy Rifkin talks about a "collaborative commons," a sharing society where well-being is our primary economic goal. In 1848, John Stuart Mill talked about something similar when he predicted that once the work of economic growth was done, a "stationary" economy would emerge in which we could focus on human improvement:

There would be as much scope as ever for all kinds of mental culture, and moral and social progress ... for improving the art of living and much more likelihood of it being improved, when minds cease to be engrossed by the art of getting on.[17]

In other words, when we were no longer consumed by making a living, we could be liberated to make a life. We could enter a world where we measured gross national happiness more than gross national product – something already being done in Bhutan.

As Scott Galloway suggests, we must now invest in "organic intelligence." People still want to interact with people; a robot may do the job in a factory that builds iPhones, but will it do the job when that iPhone isn't working and you want to speak to someone about it?

The companies that will thrive in this disruptive market are the ones that are investing in people, and that's where HR comes in. It may seem unfair to question HR's role in the profit-obsessed corporate culture of today, but every department in business must take responsibility – especially HR. HR is, after all, the department that provides the knowledge, necessary tools, training, administrative services, coaching, talent management, and legal advice that a business needs for successful operation. And yet, so far, HR has been almost exclusively reactive. That must change.

We have two paths ahead of us.

One leads "back to the future": consolidation of industry, less employment, greater inequality, social unrest, and at worst a decimated ecosystem.

The other leads to a new paradigm: a world where social capital counts more than financial capital, a world where sustainability matters, and potentially we can all enjoy an abundance and move beyond scarcity. Our data, the new gold of the twenty-first century, could become a collaborative data commons for the collective good of everyone, where individuals are paid by companies for the use of their data. There are already initiatives seeking to achieve this.[18] There is only one logical path. As Gandhi pointed out, "Earth provides enough to satisfy every man's need but not enough for every man's greed."[19]

HR must step forward to take an active role in facilitating this new inclusive mindset in business – from the shop floor to the board room. To understand what we can do differently today in the workplace, we must first understand the past, starting with pre-1920 and the Industrial Revolution. Conditions were, in many ways, similar to today, with massive amounts of technological, social, and business upheaval.

As we consider the P-waves of Paternalism, Power, Process, Profit, and People, we will call out the similarities to today and the associated risks of regression. We will highlight the learnings from the past so we don't regress, but instead move forward into a better future where the next waves of change – Paradox and Planet – open up a myriad of possibilities.

Notes

1 Kareus M, Five Astounding Animal Adaptations in the Galapagos Islands, *Natural Habitat Adventures*, www.nathab.com/articles/galapagos-islands/animal-adaptations/

2 Diamandis PH (2016) Why the World Is Better Than You Think in 10 Powerful Charts, *SingularityHub*, https://singularityhub.com/2016/06/27/why-the-world-is-better-than-you-think-in-10-powerful-charts/#sm.00011vjz8z1d8peu7wujbpiws7vlw

3 Diamandis PH and Kotler S (2014 Updated) *Abundance: The Future Is Better Than You Think*, Free Press, New York.

4 Pinker S (2011) *The Better Angels of Our Nature: The Decline of Violence in History and Its Causes*, Penguin, London.

5 KPFA: Richard Wolff – Capitalism Hits the Fan, *YouTube*, www.youtube.com/watch?v=GJc5g5bgPm4

6 Ismail S (2014) *Exponential Organizations: Why New Organizations Are Ten Times Better, Faster, and Cheaper Than Yours (and What to Do about It)*, Diversion Books, New York.

7 Galloway S (2017) Winners and Losers in the Age of Amazon, *YouTube*, www.youtube.com/watch?v=R8HPnysZ3us

8 Galloway S (2017) *The Four: The Hidden DNA of Amazon, Apple, Facebook and Google*, Bantam Press, New York.

9 Hagel J and Seely Brown J (2014) *Shift Happens: How the World Is Changing, and What You Need to Do about It*, Idea Bite Press, New York.

10 Ismail S (2015) Exponential Organisations Talking at USI, *YouTube*, www.youtube.com/watch?v=FNQSM4ipZog&t=1810s

11 Ismail S (2015) Exponential Organisations Talking at USI, *YouTube*, www.youtube.com/watch?v=FNQSM4ipZog&t=1810s

12 Shah D (2018) By the Numbers: Moocs in 2018, *Class Central*, www.class-central.com/report/mooc-stats-2018/

13 Leonard A (2007) The Story of Stuff, *The Story of Stuff Project*, https://storyofstuff.org/movies/story-of-stuff/

14 Rifkin J (2014) *The Zero Marginal Cost Society: The Internet of Things, the Collaborative Commons, and the Eclipse of Capitalism*, Palgrave Macmillan, London.

15 Rifkin J (2014) *The Zero Marginal Cost Society: The Internet of Things, the Collaborative Commons, and the Eclipse of Capitalism*, Palgrave Macmillan, London.

16 Vadera S (2018) Oliver Wyman Forum: Leadership Disrupted at Tate Modern, www.oliverwyman.com/our-expertise/events/2018/nov/oliver-wyman-forum-leadership-disrupted-uk-event.html#OliverWymanTeam

17 Mill SJ (1848) *Principles of Political Economy*, John W. Parker, London.

18 Solid website, https://solid.inrupt.com/

19 Pyarelal (1956) *Mahatma Gandhi: Poornahuti vol 10: The Last Phase, Part 2*, Ahmedabad, India: Navajivan Trust.

1 HR 1.0

The Paternalism wave (pre-1920)

It all started with Mrs E.M. Wood.

In 1896, Rowntree appointed Mrs Wood as the first "welfare officer," essentially the first HR manager (HR 1.0). She was charged with ensuring the welfare of women and children working at the Rowntree factory in the UK.

The "factory system" emerged in Britain during the Industrial Revolution in the late eighteenth century. For the first time in modern history, labour required organisation. The majority of factories, like the "dark satanic"[1] cotton mills of Lancashire, were powered by water or steam, and only later by electricity. The factory system completely changed the economy. It shifted the production of items such as shoes and muskets away from skilled craftsmen, who made entire products, to unskilled labour, who only made part of the product. Such changes in the way people worked ushered in a brutal time for many employees as they entered factories and mills in their thousands. Men, women, and children were expected to toil for long hours in dingy, often toxic environments on dangerous machinery. It was the emergence of the factory system and the gathering together of large groups of people in the mills that eventually led to welfare concerns and the emergence of Paternalism.

Paternalism, in this context, is a system or practice of managing and governing individuals in business like a father figure dealing with his children. At best, this meant a benevolent authority imposing restriction on his subordinates "for their own good," and at worst a harsh, punitive, and cruel disciplinarian flexing his will and whim. As factories become more commonplace, the smarter and more perceptive owners realised that there may be some advantage to managing the workforce rather than just bullying them.

On 6 June 1913, the Welfare Workers' Association (WWA) was formed at an employee conference in York. Thirty-four employers in attendance, including Rowntree, Boots, and Cadbury, declared the WWA as an "association of employers interested in industrial betterment and of [the] welfare [of] workers engaged by them."[2] With the formation of the WWA just over 105 years ago, the discipline of HR management emerged. In fact, the WWA is now known as the Chartered Institute of Personnel and Development (CIPD), which will be familiar to many HR professionals today.

Before the factory system, work used to be "put out." Weavers would work from home. Families would work together to ensure delivery of weaved cloth, organising themselves around the rhythm of their daily lives. Guilds of apprentices, journeymen, and masters would provide services such as weaving, dying, bookbinding, painting, masonry, baking, leatherwork, embroidery, cobbling, and candle-making. None of them had any need for an HR function. They were their own HR department.

All this changed when Richard Arkwright built his first cotton mill in Nottingham, first using horses to power spinning machines, which he held the patent on, and then switching to water power. Along with partners, Arkwright went on to build several factories, eventually moving to steam power. By 1833, his mill complex in Belper, seven miles south of Cromford, Derbyshire, employed 2,000 people. Several factories in Manchester employed over 1,000 workers. Although still the exception, the giant factory had arrived,[3] and with them a growing need for people such as Mrs Wood and associations such as the WWA.

But factories were not all doom and gloom. They produced a boom in productivity. The "social science" of economics emerged around the same time to explain the relationships between individuals within a society as a result of shifting financial patterns. Adam Smith, largely seen as the father of economics, and Alfred Marshall's contributions were immense during this time. Smith's "division of labour" described how dividing the production process into different stages enabled workers to focus on specific tasks. If workers could concentrate on one small aspect of production, it would increase overall output – so long as there was sufficient volume and quantity produced.[4] Marshall, one of the founders of neoclassical economics, brought the ideas of supply and demand, marginal utility, and costs of production to business for the first time.[5] Together, Smith and Marshall were instrumental in explaining how specialisation of task and increased scale, enabled by mechanisation, reduced marginal costs and increased profits. It made complete sense for businessmen to build for scale.

The impact on productivity and society was revolutionary. According to historian and author Joshua Freeman:

> The average annual per capita growth of global economic output from the birth of Jesus to the first factory was essentially zero. After the introduction of the factory system, in the eighteenth century it approached 1 per cent per annum, from the mid twentieth century 3 per cent per annum.[6]

Of course, this advance was welcomed, and seen rightly as genuine progress that would, or at least could, benefit all. For the vast majority of the global population prior to the early stirrings of the Industrial Revolution in the eighteenth century, human endeavour was focused on eking out a living in rural areas or small settlements. Work was sporadic and life was precarious, plagued by hunger and disease. The Industrial Revolution offered alternative employment, and people flooded to the factories in the hope of a better life as towns and cities sprang up around them.

In the UK, the birthplace of the Industrial Revolution, the government was keen to encourage industrialisation. People were getting rich; an empire was being built.

Perhaps unsurprisingly, the UK government cleared the way for the mill owners to proceed without hindrance. The Combination Acts of 1799 and 1800 made it illegal for people to "enter into contracts for the purpose of improving conditions of employment or calling or attending meetings for that purpose and of attempting to persuade another person not to work or refuse to work with another worker."[7] In other words, it was illegal for workers to strike or even discuss the possibility of seeking improved safety, conditions, or welfare. Punishment was jail time, hard labour, and even transportation to Australia for those leading such action. Anyone contributing to the expenses of a person convicted under the Acts was also subject to a fine, and defendants could be forced to testify against each other. Collectively, the Combination Acts drove labour organisations underground. Ironically, this effort to combine into groups, tribes, or gangs is a defining characteristic of the emergence of the Paternalistic wave. Individual survival in the harsh conditions of the mills and factories of the time was tough. The family unit is the first tribe we belong to, but that sense of "us" will eventually push out to include other groups, including co-workers banding together to improve working conditions and safety and reduce exploitation. Collaboration provides strength in numbers, at least in principle, and the factory owners recognised it and sought, with government help, to diminish that strength.

The Masters and Servants Act of 1823 went even further in favour of employers, and was designed to discipline employees and prevent workers from working together to press for better conditions – actions viewed at the time as a "restraint of trade." Permitted punishment under the law included up to three months' hard labour for an employee who missed any days of service before the end of their contract. Between 1858 and 1875, there were 10,000 prosecutions under the Act.[8]

The leading edge of Paternalism was, however, waking up to what was going on in the factories and mills and the brutal and unjust realities facing the vast majority of workers. Remember, the "leading edge" of any evolutionary change represents the most inclusive, most advanced, and most sophisticated thinking at that time. It doesn't represent the majority, but it encapsulates a potentially "better way" that emerges from the negative realities of the current way.

And Freeman paints a very bleak picture of the current way at that time:

> the noise and motion of the machinery; the stifling air, full of cotton dust, in many mills kept oppressively warm to reduce breakage; the pervasive stench from whale oil and animal grease used to lubricate the machinery … and the sweat from hundreds of labouring people, the pale countenances and sickly bodies of the workers; the fierce demeanour of the overseers, some of whom carried belts and whips to enforce their discipline.[9]

Or, as William Blake more poetically put it:

> And did the countenance divine
> Shine forth upon our clouded hills?
> And was Jerusalem builded here
> Among those dark Satanic Mills?[10]

Every evolution, every advance, has an upside and a downside. The large factories of the Industrial Revolution made many people very wealthy. They were viewed as the pantheons of human achievement. However, that success came at a cost – significant human suffering.

The first glimmers of Paternalism

Paternalistic concern drove the UK government to intervene. Sir Robert Peel MP, whose son would later become Prime Minister, initiated the Health and Morals of Apprentices Act of 1802. Ironically, Peel, who was also a wealthy factory owner, had been instrumental in starting the practice of employing "pauper apprentices." Poor children or orphans, often under the age of 10, were "employed" as unpaid, bound apprentices until the age of 21. Needless to say, their free contribution significantly boosted mill owner profits. The children usually boarded on an upper floor of the building and were locked in. Shifts were typically 12 hours long after allowing for a meal break, and the children "hot-bunked" – where one child who had just finished a shift would sleep in a bed recently vacated by another child about to start a shift.

However, Peel's emerging Paternalistic concerns turned to action after an outbreak of a malignant fever at one of his cotton mills caused most of the children to die. The Manchester Board of Health investigated the employment of children in all Manchester factories, taking evidence from Peel among others. Seeking to address the issue, Peel introduced his bill in 1802. In doing so, he said that he was convinced of the existence of gross mismanagement in his own factories, and having no time to set them in order himself, was getting an Act of Parliament passed to do it for him.

In 1831, the Truck Act was passed to outlaw truck systems, also known as "tommy shops." "Truck" was the collective term used for company tokens, company currency, or credit. The Act prevented factory owners from paying their workers in tokens or credit that could then only be used in the mill store with vastly inflated prices. The Truck Act required workers to be paid in cash. In 1833, the first meaningful Factory Act was introduced, directly targeted at improving the conditions for children in factories.

In relation to the world view of today, it is illuminating to revisit the provisions made in the Factory Act of 1833:

- No child workers under the age of nine.
- Children 9–13 to work no more than nine hours a day.

- Children 13–18 to work no more than 12 hours a day.
- No child to work at night.
- Two hours' schooling each day for children.
- Four factory inspectors appointed to enforce the law.

Even though children as young as 9 were explicitly permitted to work nine hours a day, still considered brutal by today's standards, the process of ensuring the effective welfare and management of people had begun. Prior to these provisions, children as young as 5 had been apprenticed to mills, providing free labour to mill owners. This development was an important nod to the need for schooling and the beginnings of standard-setting, albeit with a limited number of inspectors and minimal enforcement.

"HR management" got its foothold through these early safety and education provisions. As Freeman noted, "the giant cotton factory had led to new ways of organizing production, new sets of social relations, and new ways of thinking about the world."[11]

It was increasingly clear that the factory system needed to develop a people management system not only to coordinate vast workforces, but also to get the most out of those workforces to maximise productivity. Child labour may have been free, but it wasn't always efficient, especially when those children were sickly. They were also unskilled and uneducated. The primary HR challenge for the early mill owners was recruitment and, according to Andrew Ure, an early business theorist, "training human beings to renounce their desultory habits of work, and to identify themselves with the unvarying regularity of the complex automation."[12]

Apprentices, journeymen and master craftsmen didn't want to lose their autonomy – at least until the factory system put them out of business. Male workers, especially skilled workers, used to their own paternalistic superiority in the home, resented the loss of freedom and imposition of rules. Although an appreciation of the value of training to change behaviour may have arisen during this time, it was achieved via discipline rather than actual training.

Women and children, already more familiar with subservience in the home, were easier to constrain and cheaper, so they often made up the vast majority of the workforce in the early textile mills. And yet the use of child labour became increasingly distasteful to polite society.

As large-scale mills and latterly iron and steel factories became common, workers would often have to walk many miles to work, depleting their energy reserves before their shifts even began. This led to the building of housing and mill villages by some of the early mill owners such as Richard Arkwright. Not only did this bring the workforce closer to the factories, preventing the wasted energy on their daily commute, but the mill villages also made provision for the creation of community, with schools, shops, churches, etc. This then encouraged wider Paternalistic interventions. Initially driven to ensure greater oversight of the workforce and better productivity, Paternalistic interventions also brought prestige to the mill owner. In the UK, for example, such Paternalism could mean elevation to the House of Lords, or at least a knighthood.

The famous Lowell mills in the US established boarding houses in the mid-1800s to house their female workers, although the accommodation did come with "morality" policing. Elaborate company rules, perhaps the forerunner of today's company codes or value statements, sought to regulate workers' activities in work and outside. For example, the company "would not employ anyone who is habitually absent from public worship on the sabbath, or whose habits are not regular and correct."[13] Workers couldn't smoke or drink. If they didn't have family nearby, they had to live in the boarding houses, where the house matron would enforce another set of rules, including a 10 o'clock curfew. Anyone caught breaking the rules was fired and effectively blacklisted. Of course, these Paternalistic rules were viewed as being "for their own good."

These early glimpses of Paternalism were not just regulatory and punitive. The Lowell mill village was a carefully planned town, with brick houses, tree-lined streets, and provision for social interactions. Protection against disease was also provided as everyone in the boarding house was vaccinated for smallpox, paid for by the company. The women came to the mill of their own accord for the educational opportunities offered in Lowell or to earn supplementary income. Although their wages were half that of the men, many of the "Lowell mill girls" were able to attain economic independence for the first time, thus challenging gender stereotypes.

In 1893, George Cadbury, a temperance Quaker, built the Bournville village close to the factory on the south side of Birmingham in the UK. The village was built at his own expense to "alleviate the evils of modern, more cramped living conditions." Over time, the estate included 313 cottages and houses set on 330 acres of land. The houses were designed by resident architect William Alexander Harvey, and included large gardens, where residents were encouraged to grow their own fresh food. Concerned with the health and fitness of the workforce, Cadbury incorporated park and recreation areas into the Bourneville village and encouraged swimming, walking and all forms of outdoor sport.[14]

The Lever Brothers, William and James, planned, designed, and built Port Sunlight village along the same lines. Having taken over the small grocery business started by their father, they entered the soap business in 1885, although it was older brother William who was the driving force. James never took a very active part in running the business due to ill health (diabetes). Built to accommodate workers in its factory, now part of Unilever, work started on the village in 1888, and it was named after their popular product Sunlight soap. Port Sunlight was declared a conservation site in 1978, and you can still walk around it today. Although the hospital and swimming pool have long gone, its twee mock Tudor houses, huge war memorial, theatre, and art gallery must have felt like heaven compared to the slums of Liverpool just a few miles down the road.

Despite such shining examples of employer benevolence, most cases of Paternalism were more about oversight and the imposition of authority than care. Thus, there were two sides of the Paternalistic coin: excessive "fatherly" dominance "for their own good" being the less mature expression, often driven by fear, and "fatherly" care being the more mature, inclusive expression.

During the Industrial Revolution, the former was more prevalent, often emanating from a dominant father figure (leader or owner) bent on flexing their "muscle." How Paternalism manifests in a business, even today, is therefore largely dictated by the maturity and sophistication of the leader. A leader who sees the world as full of risks will seek to protect their business and fend off any real or perceived threat. This type of Paternalism is defensive by nature; it spawns different types of people practices to the ones embraced by a more mature, caring, and expansive Paternalistic leader.

Alternatively, Paternalistic businesses were also sometimes ruled by Power-based HR 2.0 owners, with the more enlightened owners moving on into the HR 3.0 Process mindset, in the same way today that most of business is operating at HR 4.0 Profit, with HR 5.0 People being the leading edge and a few visionaries going still further to HR 6.0 Paradox.

Paternalistic-based leadership

Paternalistic leaders operate as though they were the paternal head of the family, only in this case the family is the business and all the workers are their own children. Often this is an easy assumption to make as the business is founded by a sole individual or a husband-and-wife team. The first employees of the business might be children, relatives, or family friends who are known to the founder before the venture starts. Interestingly, the medieval idea of a company revolved around a family business. The founders were people who "took bread together," hence the term *cum panis*.[15] This "head of the family" role is therefore logical and tends to determine the mindset in the business moving forward. For example, the original John Lewis store was opened by John Lewis as a draper shop on Oxford Street, London, in 1864. The business even took the family name, and it's likely that his wife and children worked in the store as it became more and more popular.

The main driver for a Paternalistic leader is the protection and welfare of the family, which makes them very tuned into threats that could negatively impact the business. Their ultimate goal is safety – safety for the business and the workforce – so that the family or tribe can survive and flourish. This type of leader has a thinking style that is very literal. The Paternalistic leader is vigilant, assessing risk and erring on the side of caution to work together and look after the "family."

With this type of mindset, it is easy to see why John Lewis took 41 years to acquire a second store. He almost certainly chose safety over the potential upside the expansion could deliver. A new store would also mean that the workforce would be split up and wouldn't be working together anymore. Lewis therefore preferred the reassurance of the single store. This type of leader tends to view the business as an extension of themselves, and this is especially relevant to the countless founders who name their business after themselves, such as John Lewis. They are the business – literally and meta-phorically – and they exert the same sense of ownership over the staff. Paternalistic leadership is not very sophisticated. The assumption is one of external danger from which the family must be protected. They see themselves as the father figure who knows best, and everyone is expected to fall in line behind them for the greater good of the family unit.

Of course, it is easy to see where this "I know best" mindset, emerging from Paternal oversight, can slip into the Power-based leadership of "I'm in charge." If workers are forced to slavishly follow the Paternalistic leader, that leader could increasingly slip into the Power dynamic, even though the intention was protectionism and defending the business family or tribe, rather than power or control.

As for those working under a Paternalistic leader, they tend to operate with an "us versus them" mindset. Initially, the dynamic is likely to be us (the workers) versus them (the leader). But if the Paternalistic leadership is effective, the leader develops a sense of belonging within the business, and the "them" becomes the competition, although the danger is that a tribal mentality establishes itself inside the business, and the "us versus them" morphs into interdepartmental spats, cliques, and factions.

At this stage of economic development, the commonest outcomes were for different "tribes" of employees to congregate together, resulting in organisational silos. Each type of worker viewed themselves as part of a small sub-tribe, and they would look out for each other without any consideration for their fellow workers or the operation of the wider business tribe. Each departmental tribe would use their understanding of their role in the process to create choke points to defend territory. For example, the process of puddling was one of the most important processes in making iron and steel. It was tough, dangerous work that required physical strength and concentration. Although puddlers rarely lived past 40 years old, they were the aristocracy of the workforce. Their status made them proud and clannish, and they would often seek to exploit that status and gain privilege by deliberately slowing production. These early turf wars often created tit-for-tat battles between silos, which we still see in business today. They created an in-crowd and an out-crowd – where professions such as the puddlers were the in-crowd and everyone else was the out-crowd. Often these factions or subtribes will have their own rituals, which may involve initiation ceremonies or hazing. We still see this today in university fraternities, where there is some sort of rite of passage for entry into the tribe.

Considering that protection is key in this P-wave, it actually makes sense that smaller subcultures emerge from the larger business tribe, but this is part of the pathology that ultimately makes Paternalism fail. Constant tensions emerge from the various cliques and factions, causing ongoing rumbling as each clique gains the upper hand and then loses it again to another clique. Paternalistic leadership therefore often degrades into little more than managing those tensions to maintain peace, not rock the boat too much, and ultimately keep the family together. The cliques and bubbling tensions are Paternalism's fault line into which the seeds of Power-based leadership are planted. Eventually, someone steps forward to lead the crowd out of inward-facing Paternalism to the world view of Power, which started to emerge after 1890.

At one level, Paternalistic policies are clearly about dominating a population "for their own good," underpinned by a belief that a Paternalistic leader will look after and protect that workforce and keep them safe. In the US, for example, this argument is still used as a way to purposefully avoid unionisation. Employees of companies are told, "Don't worry about joining the union, we will look after you," and often companies deliver on that promise. But when growth is under pressure or profits are not as rosy as hoped, best intentions can falter. On the upside, such a Paternalistic approach engenders a sense of belonging and tradition; workers feel as though they have found their tribe, and work together as a result.

Many factory owners in the age of Paternalism contented themselves with doing the minimum needed to attract workers and maintain order. Typically, supervision or micromanagement of concentrated groups was used as a way to make employees work longer and harder than dispersed workers. However, the coherent people management systems developed by the likes of Owen and Lever went further. They saw the organisation as a living whole, a group of people working together to look after each other (the family), which would in turn have a positive impact on the world, reaching beyond simply making a profit.

Teams at HR 1.0: talented individual family members

In practice, teams don't exist in Paternalistic business. This P-wave is pre-team, partly because the business is seen as a family, and therefore the family *is* the team.

At best, it is a collection of talented individuals who are gathered together under a single Paternalistic leader for organisational reasons. The only reason talented individuals come together as a team is for the convenience of the leader who wishes to maintain organisational structures and spans of control, as well as keeping wider power hierarchies in place. There is usually no clear team purpose beyond the safety and security of the family and little commitment to a team agenda. Groups of talented individuals are not necessarily dysfunctional, because there is little reason for the individuals involved to disagree as there is little overlap in accountabilities. If there is overlap, then this type of "team" is nearly always dysfunctional. Such "teams" are best run as organisational forums rather than a team, and are represented metaphorically as a flotilla rather than a single boat.

Emerging HR and people practices

Henry Ford was a leader who definitely preferred dominant Paternalism. It was a precursor to his eventual move to HR 2.0 Power. When his car plant was suffering workforce attrition, this posed a threat. He therefore introduced his famous $5 a day wage in 1913 to halt that attrition, as it was considerably more than any of the surrounding factories. Although this action appeared caring and progressive, it was actually about removing the threat and increasing profit and dominance. The wage increase helped convert Ford workers to Ford customers, making a car within their financial reach. Workers also had to pass a set of moral standards to be eligible for the day rate, including being married, maintaining "good conditions" at home, and showing thrift and sobriety.

Ford's "sociological department" was the HR department of its day, where employee performance was assessed against an agreed standard. Fifty investigators were employed in the sociological department to make home visits and ensure each worker was meeting the moral standards.

In addition, reward policies were introduced and linked to piece rates during the Paternalistic wave. In other words, how much someone was paid was dependent on how many units they completed in their shift rather than the hours they worked. This was the start of people being paid directly in relation to their individual or team productivity. Again, this may sound progressive, but often these early examples of performance-related pay were actually another form of risk management, as employers paid their workers via "truck" – tokens or credit. Small cash denominations were in short supply in the early market capitalist economy, so wages were often paid in the form of rent for housing or credit for company shops. However, this shortage of cash also meant that unscrupulous employers could exert even more influence over workers, restricting what they could then do with their "wages" while also exploiting them through higher rent or more expensive goods in the company shop. Factory overseers or supervisors had tremendous influence over the workforce, often being able to arbitrarily determine the piece payout and administer harsh discipline.[16]

The distinction between craft or trade jobs versus unskilled roles began to emerge. Craft or trade roles required an apprenticeship. Everything else was viewed as "unskilled," even though many involved working complex machinery without safety considerations. Training for anyone but a craftsman was captured by the phrase "sitting by Nellie." In other words, you learned on the job, watching someone who was more experienced, and you were incentivised by your piece rate to learn quickly. This practice is also still common today.

Although the Factory Act of 1833 stated that children working in the factories were to receive two hours of schooling, Frederik Engels, the cofounder of Marxist theory, observed that this was often provided by a spare worker, not by qualified teachers.

Thankfully, there were a few more enlightened employers who operated from a more mature, expansive Paternalistic perspective and who moved ahead of the government. They took their safety and education requirements seriously and built a coherent approach to people management in factories, thus establishing the first HR school of thought – the Paternalistic approach to people management.

Welshman Robert Owen, born in 1771, could easily be called the father of HR, although if alive today he would have probably hated the phrase "human resources." Famous for his employment practices at the New Lanark mill in Scotland, which employed 1,700 people at its height, Owen applied Enlightenment principles directly to the workplace. He captured his system in a series of articles and published his ideas in a book entitled *A New View of Society* (1813).[17]

His fundamental belief was that a person's character was shaped by their environment. With the correct environment, character would change for the better. By 1812, Owen was sure a good working environment and good living conditions for his workforce would result in a more moral, humane, kind, active, and educated workforce, and that those traits could be nurtured from childhood onwards. His view could be seen as the basis for the first ever purpose of a function called HR, although there is no record of him actually having a "people" function in his factory.

Work performance was evaluated regularly and communicated via the "silent monitor," a wooden block above a workplace painted in colours reflecting performance standards. Like the Lowell Initiative in the US, Owen ensured moral standards applied in the village, enforcing cleanliness and curfews. However, at New Lanark, compliance was supervised by committees elected by villagers themselves rather than company assessors. Such an approach could possibly be the first example of works councils – "shop floor," or in this case "village floor," organisations representing the workers.

In 1806, when production stopped due to an American embargo, Owen even paid his employees full wages. This would be an unprecedented step now, never mind in 1806. He promoted educational initiatives for children. He saw it as essential for social harmony and productivity in his mills. His educational system emphasised kindness, patience, and the need to make people happy.

Owen was a driving force behind the first Factory Acts. In his own essay about Owen's new view of society, William Hazlitt said that Owen was "the first philosopher we ever heard of, who recommended himself to the great by telling them disagreeable truths."[18] Today we call it "speaking truth to power."

He significantly improved education, provisions for those who were sick, and pension welfare funds at New Lanark. However, individual behaviour still determined who benefited from the interventions. Owen's New Lanark experiment lasted 25 years and its influence was profound. Although the last mill closed in 1968 and the village is now a UNESCO World Heritage site, his ideas provided inspiration for later educators, public health reformers, trade unionists, politicians, and, whether they know it or not, HR professionals!

But Owen was not alone; Rowntree, Cadbury, Wedgewood (who also inoculated his workforce against smallpox), the Lever brothers, and a few others – more often than not Quakers – followed in his footsteps.

These mill owners treated their employees like "family." Getting a job with Lever, for example, was life-changing. It still is today, where getting a job with Unilever in, say, Pakistan can provide long-term stability. For example, after the appointment of 250 people to permanent roles in a factory in Khanewal, there was a baby boom in the village nine months later. One of Lever's early HR measures in Port Sunlight was to measure life expectancy or morbidity of his workers – having a job was literally a matter of life or earlier death.

William Lever, like Owen, was a man with a world view ahead of his time. He served as a Liberal MP briefly and was keen to allow residents of Port Sunlight a degree of democratic control, so much so that he held a referendum in the village to decide if the dry pub should be allowed to serve alcohol, allowing men and women to vote. Although he hoped they would vote against the change, when they didn't, he let the decision stand.

Lever foresaw many of the people practices that would emerge in the future, and we will review those as we explore the HR upgrades – pensions, profit-sharing, and the shorter working week that is yet to come. Interestingly, Lever was one of the first to advocate a six-hour day, something today's tech revolution may bring, along with a four-day working week.

The fundamentals of Lever's Paternalistic system were clear – education and safety. The "people departments" in the best Paternalistic companies were educators and safety and welfare officers such as Mrs E.M. Wood. Rowntree's welfare officers and Ford's sociological department started to form only from the end of the first decade of the twentieth century.

Global competition brought new pressure to improve and become more efficient. Greater competition meant a greater need for organisational discipline. A clearer sense of direction and a more assertive and rigorous approach were required if a factory was to seize the opportunity offered by an expanding marketplace.

HR 1.0 Paternalism today

Despite the fact that there was no HR organisation in the factories of the nineteenth century, at least not as we know it today, the best of this first wave of Paternalistic HR practice is still evident, particularly in the developing world. As waves evolve, we don't lose the insights and capabilities we developed in a previous wave, in the same way that we don't lose the ability to walk when we learn how to run. With the emergence of each new wave of development, we are better placed to take the good ideas of the past and leave the unhelpful practices behind.

So, the Paternalistic approach to HR is still alive and well today. It is not just a relic from the past. Mature expressions of Paternalism still have their place in modern business. Family businesses, many of them very large and highly successful, still operate from a Paternalistic world view.

Specsavers is a classic example. Started in 1984 by husband-and-wife team Doug and Mary Perkins, Specsavers is still family-owned, and all three of their children work in the business in senior roles. However, it's worth pointing out that these types of Paternalistic family-run businesses usually only stay that way when they remain in private hands. As soon as they are taken public, the Paternalism gives way to different drivers.

Less integrated, more dominant versions of Paternalism are also still present in certain parts of the world, particularly in Asia and the Middle East. If you were to visit Dubai, you would find countless boarding houses built close to factories or hotels, providing accommodation to migrant workers from South Asia and the Philippines – often three people to a room.

Today, in Unilever's tea plantations, management of housing, safety (including social safety), schooling, and medical facilities is the primary task of local HR management. Currently, 30,000 people live on Unilever's tea plantation in Kericho, Kenya. A focus on education provision remains in factories in South Asia, and many factory workers still receive a rice allowance in South and South East Asia.

The authors have seen first-hand employee accommodation such as the newly built workers villages near the copper mines of Mauritania and Zambia or the tin huts for employees scattered across the mountainside of New Caledonia. Today, Asian electronic plants far exceed the scale and size of the early iron, steel, and textile mills. Even Ford's River Rouge factory, the biggest factory in the world in its heyday, would be dwarfed by some of the modern Asian factories. It is therefore perhaps inevitable that *their* people issues often echo the needs that the Paternalistic school of HR aims to address.

For example, Foxconn, the largest electronic contract manufacturer in the world, has Foxconn City. Manufacturing electronic products for major US, Canadian, Chinese, Finnish, and Japanese companies, Foxconn manufactures an estimated 40 per cent of the consumer electronics sold worldwide, including, iPhone, iPad, Kindle, PlayStation, Wii, and Xbox (today's consumer equivalent of wearing cotton clothes 200 years ago). Foxconn City is home to the biggest factory in recorded history. Some accounts claim the Shenzhen facility employs in excess of 500,000 people. Like the early mills, they have attracted migrant workers. Boarding houses accommodate the workforce in the same way the Lowell complex and model villages did in the nineteenth century, complete with a downtown, swimming pool, shops, and fire department (as Lever had in Port Sunlight).

Foxconn has developed the same primary focus on welfare following a spate of suicides and protests against working conditions. Like Henry Ford, Foxconn raised basic wages in 2010, set up a counselling service, and arranged social events and parades – all "back to the future" initiatives that remind us of the people practices of Ford's sociological department, Lowell mills, Lever and Cadbury, etc. In a further practical effort to stop the suicides, Foxconn installed netting around their dormitory buildings to catch any jumpers.[19]

In many of these environments, the "latest" thinking in HR is not necessary. Applying the basics of HR 1.0 is what is required. Each culture or business must evolve through the various P-waves – they can't skip waves or jump ahead. Embracing each wave will deliver real benefits to the workforce right now. But like all benefits delivered by every P-wave, eventually employees start to experience the downside of that wave, which triggers the evolution to the next P-wave.

We can see an apparent Paternalistic style in some of the largest and most powerful companies in the world. If we look at some of the "perks" Facebook, Amazon, Apple, Netflix, and Google (FAANG) provide for their key employees, they appear Paternalistic. For example, Google employees:

- get access to free gourmet food and never-ending snacks;
- are allowed to bring their dog to work;
- get free transport to the Mountain View campus;
- get free massage credits;
- receive extended parental breaks;
- receive death in service benefit of up to 50 per cent of 10 years' worth of salary;
- can use a free gym and get access to fitness classes; and
- are allowed to use the 80/20 rule, where 20 per cent of their time can be spent on their own projects.[20]

However, these interventions are almost certainly emerging from the more pragmatic Profit driver of HR 4.0, where such interventions encourage employees to stay at work for longer and help to inspire greater productivity. Alternatively, they emerge from the People-centric world views of HR 5.0, where employees are inspired by a purpose of being part of that company, both of which we will unpack in more detail in Chapters 4 and 5, respectively. Remember, we don't lose access to various world views as we evolve through them; they just become a bit more sophisticated as we integrate each wave and derive the value at each level. So, where Foxconn's intention is still largely welfare-focused (HR 1.0), the tech giants of the developed world are employing tactics that have emerged from a more integrated world view. They may look similar, but the intention or driver is different. As such, they are an echo of the earlier wave, with additional sophistication built in.

Evolution from HR 1.0 to HR 2.0

The factory system and Paternalistic wave drove unprecedented productivity through the application of scale – lots of people gathered in one place and organised around modern technology to deliver a collective output. This was its strength. It was also its greatest weakness.

Both were significant. The sheer numbers of workers transformed productivity, but people are hard to manage. Large groups of people can easily form a herd, with its corresponding herd mentality or groupthink, which is not always useful. Equally, the herd or tribe can subdivide into smaller factions or cliques that can be distracting. Such outcomes can easily trigger an HR 2.0 Power leader to step forward and seek to instil order and control through force.

From the worker's perspective, the disadvantages of the factory system were profound. Workers were not seen as individual people with aspirations and abilities, but expendable tools in the production process. They did not use the machines; machines used them. According to poet Robert Southey, even at its best the factory system destroyed individuality of character and domesticity, and at its worst it was outright devilish. Little wonder that workers treated badly would flock to those who treated them better.

Workers also discovered that if they could gang together and stop progress, there was strength in numbers. In 1810, there were the first substantial walkouts by workers, involving thousands of cotton spinners.[21] In 1811, the "Luddites" attacked textile machinery, mills, and mill owners in the north of England, claiming they were acting under the command of General Ludd. Today, the term "Luddite" is still used to describe someone resisting change, but the word originates from disgruntled workers who, prevented by law from collaborative effort, broke machines as a protest against the new mills and the detrimental impact they had on the old ways. Historian Eric Hobsbawm called it "collective bargaining by riot."[22] The 1820s also saw a wave of strikes. In 1842 in England, there was widespread strike action by mill workers and miners, called the plug riots (because vital components – "plugs" – were removed from the steam engines, rendering them inert).

This accumulating collective unrest sent alarm bells ringing for mill owners and gave hope to the collective, which together ushered in the age of "Power," and the birth of an HR function as we would recognise it today.

Notes

1 Blake W (1808) Second verse of a poem called "And Did Those Feet in Ancient Time," which appeared in the preface of his epic poem "Milton."
2 Leopold J (2002) *Human Resources in Organisations*, Pearson Educational/Financial Times Press, London.
3 Freeman JB (2018) *Behemoth: A History of the Factory and the Making of the Modern World*, W.W. Norton & Company, New York.
4 Smith A (1776) *The Wealth of Nations*.
5 Marshall A (1890) *Principles of Economics*; Marshall A (1892) *Economics of Industry*.
6 Freeman JB (2018) *Behemoth: A History of the Factory and the Making of the Modern World*, W.W. Norton & Company, New York.
7 Craig R (2007) *The History of Employment Law in England and Northern Ireland Business Law*, 8th edition, http://cws.cengage.co.uk/abbott8/students/ni_supp/employ_law/hist_of_employ_law.pdf
8 Craig R (2007) *The History of Employment Law in England and Northern Ireland Business Law*, 8th edition, http://cws.cengage.co.uk/abbott8/students/ni_supp/employ_law/hist_of_employ_law.pdf
9 Freeman JB (2018) *Behemoth: A History of the Factory and the Making of the Modern World*, W.W. Norton & Company, New York.
10 Blake W (1808) Second verse of a poem called "And Did Those Feet in Ancient Time," which appeared in the preface of his epic poem "Milton."
11 Freeman JB (2018) *Behemoth: A History of the Factory and the Making of the Modern World*, W.W. Norton & Company, New York.
12 Freeman JB (2018) *Behemoth: A History of the Factory and the Making of the Modern World*, W.W. Norton & Company, New York.
13 Freeman JB (2018) *Behemoth: A History of the Factory and the Making of the Modern World*, W.W. Norton & Company, New York.

14 Tolman WH (1901) *A "Trust" for Social Betterment: The World's Work*. Doubleday, New York.
15 Bartleby (2018) Working for a Purpose, *The Economist*, www.economist.com/business/2018/12/01/working-for-a-purpose
16 Freeman JB (2018) *Behemoth: A History of the Factory and the Making of the Modern World*, W.W. Norton & Company, New York.
17 Owen R (1813) *A New View of Society*.
18 Hazlitt W (1816) A New View of Society – Robert Owen: A William Hazlitt Essay, www.blupete.com/Literature/Essays/Hazlitt/Political/Owen.htm
19 Moore M (2012) 'Mass Suicide' Protest at Apple Manufacturer Foxconn Factory, *The Guardian*, www.telegraph.co.uk/news/worldnews/asia/china/9006988/Mass-suicide-protest-at-Apple-manufacturer-Foxconn-factory.html
20 D'Onfro J and England L (2015) An Inside Look at Google's Best Employee, Perks Inc, www.inc.com/business-insider/best-google-benefits.html
21 Freeman JB (2018) *Behemoth: A History of the Factory and the Making of the Modern World*, W.W. Norton & Company, New York.
22 Jones SE (2013) *Against Technology: From the Luddites to Neo-Luddism*, Routledge, London.

2 HR 2.0

The Power wave (1890–1945)

Harry Bennett liked to talk and act "tough."

Bennett was a powerful, intimidating man who allegedly kept lions as pets. Head of the services department at Ford, he used to sit in his office at the mighty River Rouge factory with his feet up on the desk, firing a .45 at a target at the other end of the room. It was Bennett who "managed" industrial relations for Ford, deploying "HR practice" very different from the accepted norms today. In fact, Bennett was so successful and so influential that it was rumoured he was in line to succeed Henry Ford.[1] This was incredibly unusual given that he was effectively head of the function that would now be known as HR.

At the peak of his authority in the early 1930s, at the start of the Great Depression, Bennett's activities represented the apex of the "Power era of HR." Viewed by many as a thug – and we'll explain why shortly – he was also a very senior, very effective leader, and his special brand of "HR practice" has not completely died, even today.

HR at this time was characterised by power, and we mean this literally and metaphorically, first because society was literally about power production. As technological innovation ushered in the age of steam and later electrical power, the factory system switched from creating textiles to manufacturing iron and steel. Factories expanded in size and scope, which led to social power. At its peak, for example, Ford's River Rouge plant employed over 100,000 people. Such huge operations were owned by single entrepreneurs, families, or small groups of investors, thus putting a huge amount of power and wealth into the hands of a few. And those same huge operations required correspondingly large workforces, who increasingly sought to congregate and push for better working conditions. The result: an intense power battle between owners and workers.

The first glimmers of Power

The tug of war between the power of the workforce and the power of business owners had been going on since the early years of the factory system, each side winning ground and then losing it depending on the prevailing political, economic, or social conditions at the time. Sometimes the demand for workers was high and supply was limited. Under such conditions, mill owners experimented with Paternalism to attract and keep staff. When demand for workers was high but there was a ready supply of labour, then Paternalistic measures were often phased out, increasing downward pressure on wages.

Periods when workers enjoyed some power can be seen as far back as the mid nineteenth century, when puddlers, essential in the making of iron and steel, enjoyed a high level of unionisation. This forced manufacturers into effective partnerships. The puddlers regulated all aspects of their work, including how much iron to produce and their hours of work. There were even examples of sliding pay scales linking puddlers' pay to their output and the selling price of iron. This meant that puddlers could gain financially based on their productivity – perhaps the very first instances of performance-related pay. But this type of power in the hands of individual workers was very rare.

The real strength was more often present in the sheer numbers of workers in the various mills. However, intermittent shows of strength by the workforce were normally squashed by the government and mill owners working together to prevent effective unionisation. Many politicians owned mills themselves, so most of the time the odds were very much stacked against the workforce.

Generally speaking, during the early years of the factory system, and certainly up until the late 1920s, most workers had no rights whatsoever. Many workers couldn't even vote for their own government. In the UK, it wasn't until the Representation of the People Act of 1918 that more of the working class were given a vote. Up until this Act, only men over 21 who owned property could vote. Even when subsequent reforms allowed more men to vote, they still excluded all women and the vast majority of working-class factory workers. The Act of 1918 removed practically all property ownership requirements for men over 21, giving all male workers the right to vote. Women over 30 were allowed to vote for the first time, although they still had to own property, which still denied female factory workers the vote. It wouldn't be until 1928 that women would have equal voting rights to men in the UK. In the US, white men, regardless of property ownership, were allowed to vote by 1856, non-white men and freed slaves could vote from 1870, although not in all parts of the US, and it would be 1920 before women would be allowed to vote.

Workers with no power to influence government often met fierce resistance when they sought to organise themselves in the workplace. In 1834, the Tolpuddle Martyrs, six UK agricultural workers from Dorset, were sentenced to penal transportation to Australia just for seeking to set up a "friendly society," or early trade union.

But by the beginning of the twentieth century, the tide was turning.

In the US, mill owners were having people problems and strikes were common. In 1912, 14,000 workers in Lawrence walked out for two months. Socialist Congressman Victor Berger called the strike over a pay cut "a rebellion of the wage-working class against unbearable conditions."[2] What made it special and perhaps especially troubling for mill owners was that it involved men and woman. It involved people from 40 ethnic groups who spoke many different languages, and a multilingual committee was set up to direct the struggle.

Many mill owners took the view that the working class didn't have the intelligence or organisational skills to muster themselves into an organised effort. The Lawrence strike must have badly shaken that belief and represented a real wake-up call.

Nevertheless, mill owners and government officials were determined to crush the strike and set an example. Martial law was declared, there was a ban on public meetings, strike leaders were arrested on false charges, the National Guard was mobilised, and strikers and supporters were physically attacked. But they overplayed their hand. Running out of food, many of the strikers began to send their children to live with supporters outside Lawrence. Police, ordered by mill owners and government officials, tried to stop them – clubbing adults and children as they sought to board trains. The public were outraged. In the end, the workers won, securing a substantial pay rise.

Although the organisation behind the strike, the Industrial Workers of the World (IWW), failed to consolidate their power after the strike at Lawrence, it was an important turning point towards a more stable unionisation dynamic within the workforce during this Power wave.

Workers began to realise that there was *real* power in organising themselves into trade unions. As the songwriter Joe Hill wrote in his song "There Is Power in a Union" in 1913:

There is power, there is power in a band of workingmen
When they stand hand in hand
That's a power, that's a power
That must rule in every land[3]

Other forces were also at work consolidating the Power wave during the time of the first "capitalist" depressions and recessions. In 1873, there was a fall in economic activity in the US of around 30 per cent, heralding what was called the Long Depression. Recessions followed regularly (1882, 1887, 1890, 1893, 1896, 1899, etc.).

When businesses and markets did eventually grow again, the pursuit of scale gradually and inevitably led to increasing consolidation of industry. Not all the power of scale sat with the workforce; sometimes it empowered the owners. The so-called "robber barons" emerged. Originally, the term "robber baron" was used to describe the business practices of one individual, Cornelius Vanderbilt. It was later adopted to describe many wealthy industrialists, such as Andrew Carnegie and John D. Rockefeller, who would regularly put smaller rivals out of business – often by market and price manipulation. Historian T.J. Stiles wrote that the metaphor "conjures up visions of titanic monopolists who crushed competitors, rigged markets, and corrupted government. In their greed and power, legend has it, they held sway over a helpless democracy."[4] In many businesses, the pressure for cost reduction became intense. To this day, the drive to remain competitive still results in layoffs, reduced wages, or the deterioration in working conditions as people still make up the bulk of variable business costs.

By the early 1900s, the "boom and bust" cycles of early capitalist economies were also starting to be better understood. The "business cycle," which is also still much talked about today, came to illustrate how boom could turn into bust as destocking took place. In some ways, such economic fluctuation is a natural cycle of consumer demand. Sometimes these cycles are driven by availability of credit and the ability of the banking system to retain trust and solvency. In the boom years, it was the owners who prospered. If they were lucky, the workers might enjoy more favourable working conditions during the good times. But when markets contracted, it was the workers who suffered as owners sought to change working conditions to preserve profits.

Immigration and a steady supply of migrant workers to take low-paying jobs amplified the suffering and allowed mill owners to drive costs even lower. In the US and the UK, for example, Irish migrants, keen to escape the bone-crushing poverty caused by the potato famine of the mid-1800s, held down wages and inhibited protests. The first economic downturn of 1873 and the rise of international competition further turned the mill owners' thoughts away from Paternalism, towards cost-cutting, imposed by Power.

In many ways, the Paternalistic policies described in HR 1.0 were the initial people practice response to the challenges of their day. Mill owners needed to attract a large workforce and ensure control over that workforce to prosper. As a result, they experimented with Paternalistic interventions such as building model villages or boarding houses to house their workers. Such an approach proved popular and effective. The Lowell mills were considered a "commercial utopia," but the influx of migrant labour desperate for work lessened the need for such Paternalistic interventions because they created an oversupply of labour.

To keep up dividends in the face of growing competition and falling prices, even the Paternalistic visionaries sought to cut costs.[5]

Following the economic fallout of the Great Depression in the 1930s, companies eliminated many of their Paternalistic welfare programmes all together. Wage cuts, machinery speed-ups, and layoffs became the norm. Never mind Paternalism; workers were lucky to have any job at all, and their wealthy, powerful employers knew it.

One of the most famous battlegrounds during the Power wave was the Ford Motor Company. As a cost-cutting measure in 1920, Ford downsized his sociological department until it effectively disappeared, replacing it with the "service department" – effectively a Power-based "spy system" to ensure control and stop any unionisation effort. And that's where Harry Bennett came in. Bennett, a former boxer, apparently hired by Ford for his street-fighting abilities, organised a system of spies who would keep him informed about what was happening on the factory floor. Together, they would regularly use brute force to maintain discipline and effort. These "HR practices" made up for in drama what they lacked in sophistication.

It was Bennett who led Ford's opposition to the Ford Hunger March, also known as the Ford Massacre, on 7 March 1932. The 1920s were booming;

Detroit was booming. In 1929, the US auto industry produced 5,337,000 cars. Many of Ford's own workers had bought their first car. Then the stock market crashed on 29 October 1929. Vehicle production plummeted and unemployment soared. The average annual wage for an auto worker dropped from $1,639 before the crash to $757 after the crash. A welfare allowance of 15 cents per person per day didn't go far. To make matters worse, a wave of bank closures also wiped out life savings for many of the unemployed or retired. Despair swept through the city.

The Detroit Unemployed Council and the Auto, Aircraft and Vehicle Workers of America called the march from Detroit to Dearborn, ending at Ford's River Rouge complex. The marchers intended to present 14 demands to Henry Ford, including the demand to rehire the unemployed, provide funds for healthcare, end racial discrimination in hiring and promotions, provide winter fuel for the unemployed, abolish the use of company spies and private police against workers, and give workers the right to organise unions. Up to 5,000 people attended the march on a bitterly cold day, but they never made it to River Rouge.

The Dearborn police tried to stop the march at the city limits by hitting marchers with batons. The unarmed crowd scattered into nearby fields and started picking up stones and throwing them at the police. Two fire engines arrived and sprayed cold water onto the marchers from an overpass. The police were then joined by Ford security guards and began shooting into the crowd. Just as the leaders decided to call off the march and began an orderly retreat, Harry Bennett drove up in his car, opened a window, and fired his pistol into the crowd. Immediately, the car was pelted with rocks. He got out of the car and continued firing at the retreating marchers. Dearborn police and Ford security men followed his lead and opened fire with machine guns. Four marchers were shot dead, 60 more were injured, and Bennett was hospitalised after being hit by a rock, although it's a miracle there were not more casualties.[6]

Franklin D. Roosevelt's New Deal and the National Labor Relations Act of 1935 began to tip the balance back towards the workers in the 1930s. The New Deal focused on what historians have since referred to as the "three Rs": deliver *Relief* to the victims of the Depression, kick-start an economic *Recovery*, and institute banking constraints and *Regulation* to prevent a repeat performance. In addition, the National Labor Relations Act (also known as the Wagner Act) guaranteed basic rights of private sector employees. It made trade unions legal, allowing collective bargaining, and permitted industrial action, including strikes.

General Motors (GM) was one of the first carmakers to find itself at the mercy of the new law. GM provided jobs for many of the men of Flint, Michigan, but conditions and pay were notoriously poor, making it a prime target for union organisation following the Wagner Act. The Flint sit-down strike of 1936–1937 changed American history because it changed the United Automobile Workers (UAW) from a collection of isolated individuals to a major union.

Encouraged by the new legal protection, GM employees started a "sit-in" on 30 December 1936 across the GM plants in Flint and refused to work or leave the premises. GM sought to break the strike by cutting off the plant's heat and electricity and preventing food deliveries, but the strikers remained disciplined and resolute, with the strike leaders establishing committees for cleaning, exercise, security, entertainment, and defence. Despite violent clashes between strikers, police, and GM's own versions of Harry Bennett, GM reached an agreement with the UAW after 44 days. The Flint sit-down strike entered labour history, and ultimately led to the unionisation of the US automobile industry.

Ford followed suit, although union recognition was delayed until the 1940s. It would be 1949 before Ford established its first industrial relations department. But in the end, even Ford succumbed to the rise of trade union power. In April 1941, there was a full-scale strike organised at the River Rouge complex. It soon spread to all Ford plants. In a reversal of fortune, Bennett and his men found themselves the subject of beatings. The vast majority of Ford employees voted in favour of unionisation, and Ford agreed to what historians describe as one of the most generous contracts any union had yet achieved, including a provision that required all new employees to join the union and the disbanding of the service department.

In the UK, power battles between owners and workers were also in full swing, with mixed results. While the General Strike of the 1920s represented the distance the trade unions had travelled over the previous 50 years, it wasn't the tipping point many hoped it would be. Called by the Trades Union Congress (TUC) in an attempt to force the UK government to stop coal mine owners from reducing miners' pay and extending their hours of work, the General Strike saw 1.7 million workers from other professions go out on strike in support of the miners. It was a demonstration of unprecedented solidarity among the working class, from road transport, bus, rail, docks, printing, gas, electricity, building, iron, steel, chemicals, and coal miners. However, the British trade union movement did not cast itself as a revolutionary force and the miners ended up accepting the terms.

That said, by this point, trade union power was well and truly established in the US and Europe. The romantic stories of this period are often about trade union leaders. "Big Jim Larkin," one of the founders of the Irish Labour Party, Sacco and Vanzetti, the Italian-born American working-class anarchists who inspired a Woody Guthrie song ("Two Good Men"), or the Bryant & May matchgirls – those willing to stand up to authority for the collective good – became the subject of songs and novels, tales of heroism and struggle.

There are, to the best of our knowledge, no songs about Harry Bennett.

Power-based leadership

The Power wave is the first time we really see what is commonly termed "strong leadership." Power-based leaders often see themselves as different and special by dint of their intelligence or often simply their wealth.

Andrew Carnegie is a classic example of an early Power leader. He was ruthless in the pursuit of what he believed was the right course of action, and heaven help those that stood in his way. Carnegie used force, often hiring the Pinkerton National Detective Agency to enforce factory lockouts and deliver take-it-or-leave-it work condition ultimatums to his workforce while he was out of the country.

A Power leader has their place, even today. They are very skilled at getting things done, launching a product, or opening up a new territory. As such, they are still incredibly common in the upper echelons of many modern businesses, from small and medium-sized enterprises (SMEs) to global multinationals. Often energetic, charismatic, "larger-than-life" individuals with a good sense of humour, they like to move fast and keep it simple. They create a sense of urgency, often deliberately provoking a crisis to achieve that end.

The Power-based leader is relentless and resilient. They learn by doing and seek to dominate. Their ultimate goal is, unsurprisingly, power. Their actions are still driven from a perspective of "I know best," but unlike the Paternalistic leader, who is making decisions for the collective good of the family, the Power leader is focused on self-interest, and it is personal ego and hubris that are often calling the shots. They believe that if they can just control the workforce, their position and influence in the world will increase. Remember, each evolutionary stage oscillates between focus on the collective and focus on the individual. The Paternalistic leader is focused on the collective "family," whereas the Power leader is focused on themselves. They tend to be egocentric – it's all about them and what they want. The Power leader wants to "go for it," take charge, and they believe in "work hard, play hard."

There are significant benefits derived from the emergence of the Power leader. All the tension that's created between the tribal factions of Paternalism starts to subside. The Power leader gives a very clear steer and establishes a common enemy – a competitor to be beaten, a new market to conquer, or a heroic corporate turnaround. As a result, the business becomes focused on one or two external "enemies" that are engaging enough to rally the troops behind. A great deal of the internal squabbles and toing and froing that go on at Paternalism disappear, and employees experience, initially at least, that things are a lot better. Workers become clearer about what is wanted from them and why. They no longer need to constantly watch their back because everyone is focused externally on crushing the competition or entering the new market, rather than internal competition between factions. All the cliques and subtribes of Paternalism start to align and move forward in a specific direction, which creates real business acceleration for the first time. One of the big benefits of Power leadership is that the business picks up speed significantly. As a result, the business grows and starts to benefit from that speed, clarity, and strong direction.

There is greater certainty because the Power leader, coming from his own egocentricity, believes in himself, and that filters down to others, who have no reason to doubt him (yet). Power leaders have no doubt, and that can be incredibly comforting to a Paternalistic workforce, instilling confidence in them, which can help productivity.

The Power leader is sure they have all the answers because they often lack humility. Humility would make them thoughtful and slow them down. There is often a lot of passion, intensity, and desire to "get on with it." This can be quite exciting for the workforce. At Paternalism, there is often caution, dithering, and internal bickering, but now there is certainty and clarity, and the Power leader quickly becomes the new, upgraded version of that father figure and people start to believe in him. (We are using "him" because leaders are still predominantly male, and Power leaders are almost always male.)

More often than not, the business flourishes under a Power leader, certainly in the early days. Things start working, improvements are evident, and the workers are often 100 per cent behind the leader because the early benefits seem to be a solution to the problems of the previous P-wave, so much so that he is often put on a pedestal, which further fuels his sense of omnipotence and lack of humility. This adoration, or even adulation, sows the pathological seeds of the Power leader's eventual demise. His clarity, determination, and certainty can also create a passivity in the workers, especially in other senior executives. The Power leader is so dominant and so controlling that other executives start to believe the myth that he and he alone has all the answers. Or even if they think they have something to contribute, he overrules them anyway, so they stop offering any of their own ideas. They start to step back from their own roles. This creates what Roger Martin refers to as the "responsibility virus" – where the dominant leader takes over and dominates across the board, micromanages, and becomes a bottleneck.[7] But he's so confident and controlling that others around him stop delivering on their responsibilities and allow him to take over.

The Power leader, initially at least, often creates followership among Paternalistic workers. They believe the Power leader has led them out of the tribal wilderness and so they trust him and do what he says. But eventually, as more and more decisions and more power are gathered in by the Power leader, and more and more workers step back to cede complete control to him, the more the leader believes he is invincible. There is often an unspoken complicity between the boss and the other executives. The leader wants the power and the executives are happy to cede that power, safe in the knowledge they will still be paid and can't or won't be sacked. Of course, this is naive as the Power leader is likely to sack them at a moment's notice for not delivering.

Such a dynamic is clearly unsustainable. No individual, however certain or gifted, can run a company alone. As the cracks start to appear and the early warning bells of the inevitable fall from grace begin to sound, workers begin to recognise that the Power leader is not infallible. But they still extend a huge amount of latitude to that leader because they want to believe.

The Power leader, in turn, usually still believes, despite the mounting evidence to the contrary, that they can do no wrong. Any mishaps or missteps will be blamed on someone else or something else. As a leader, he starts to test the boundaries to see just how much he can get away with, and this is when the wheels start to come off.

When thwarted, the Power leader will become even more aggressive, and often even more sure of his own invincibility, which leads to poor, impulsive, and ill-informed choices. The speed that was once his friend becomes his enemy, and things start to go wrong. As Lord Acton once said, "Power corrupts, and absolute power corrupts absolutely."[8]

Where a Paternalistic leader believes the business is his because he is the head of the family, a Power leader thinks the business is his personal property because he has heroically made it all happen. He alone is responsible for almost all of the success. There is little self-awareness of his own hubris.[9] This outlook is still common in businesses (and politics) today. In recent history, Dennis Kozlowski, CEO of Tyco, was convicted of grand larceny, conspiracy, and fraud for using the business as his own personal piggy bank. During his tenure, he would regularly speak on the need for ethics in business while using company funds to purchase everything from a $6,000 shower curtain, to lavish homes, to parties, to millions of dollars of art.[10]

The Power leader tends to steamroll others. Such a leader often deliberately instils fear, takes pleasure in being quite intimidating, and uses their strong will to rule or get their way. In an escalating and complex world, their "black or white" unsophisticated approach will eventually implode, as it fails to understand the size and the scale of the challenges at play. Such simplistic thinking rarely sustains and often just stores up more problems in the future. The workers often recognise that something is not right well before the Power leader even privately admits some things are not working.

But stopping a Power leader can be very difficult. The other senior leaders who need to stop him have often become very passive in the course of that journey from Paternalism to Power, or they have been intimidated, or they lack the courage to confront the problem head-on. Worse still, the workers don't feel they have any power to change the situation either. So, when change finally happens, it is often ugly and unpleasant and creates many causalities. The process of that change is never straightforward. It almost always starts with other executives or the workers putting up a "stalking horse" – their version of a Power bully to take on the incumbent Power leader. This is when we see the power battles between a strong "bully boy" union leader taking on a strong "bully boy" factory owner, each winning one battle only to lose the next, although the incumbent will often maintain the upper hand, especially when they have a network of spies and tactics in place to maintain the status quo. Such battles can be as epic as Caesar and Brutus, and the longer they go on, the more the company and its customers suffer from the distraction.

Eventually, factory owners and workers realise that fighting fire with fire, Power-based factory owners versus Power-based union leaders, doesn't work. If the coup works and the unions triumph, often it just replaces one bully with another. Sometimes the board try to circumvent the power battle between a CEO and the unions, and remove one of the leaders, usually the CEO, once they realise he has lost critical executive support. Very occasionally, the market, in the form of a clique of shareholders, investors, or banks move to remove the CEO. But regardless of who delivers the fatal blow, the board often make matters worse by importing another heroic figure cut from the same cloth as the previous Power leader. Their mistake only becomes apparent after the new leader's "honeymoon" is over and the same problems start to reoccur.

The only way to avoid wasting time and making the same error over and over is to realise that what is required is evolution. Preferably, everyone – leaders, the workforce, and the board – need to evolve up the values spiral and develop to the next level, from Paternalism, to Power, to Process, to Profit, to People, to Paradox, to Planet.

It is worth pointing out at this junction that the evolutionary process from Paternalism to Planet is not linear. It is more staggered, like a foxtrot – two steps forward, one to the side, and one step back. This is why evolution between P-waves is usually a long process, often taking a generation. Once each level starts to fail, the first attempts to correct the problem usually involve doubling down on the tactics of the P-wave that is failing. In the Power wave, this means ramping up the Power. But dogged "eye for an eye" narratives just blind everyone. When organisations realise that such simplistic approaches can't deliver, the next tactic is often to regress, to reach back into history to reintroduce tactics that worked before. During the Power wave, we see this with both Henry Ford and Andrew Carnegie, both fully fledged Power leaders of their day. Ford instituted a Paternalistic move to increase wages and Carnegie built Paternalistic housing for his employees at Homestead, offering low-interest loans repayed through small deductions from their wages. Such manoeuvres could easily be viewed as an attempt to re-energise the Power wave, which was starting to falter.

The problem with such backward-looking moves, while understandable, is that the world has moved on. Even if those tactics used to work, they worked in a different time, and seeking to retrofit them to a new business (or political) environment never works in the long term. We still see such ill-conceived "back to basics" calls in many areas of life even today. Unfortunately, significant suffering results from such regressive approaches. Evolutionary problems cannot be solved by regression. The future cannot be solved by going back to the past. But sometimes we must endure such pain until enough people realise that the tactics of doubling down or regression (more Power or Paternalistic interventions) can't work. When the pain becomes significant enough, the stage is set for the required evolutionary leap forward to the next P-wave. As we said in the Preface, genuine progress can only come from positive forward evolution. As Churchill allegedly said, "If you are going through hell, keep going."[11]

Teams at HR 2.0: battling experts

Teams at HR 2.0 are essentially a collection of talented individuals who now share a common goal, which has often been made clear by the Power leader who "grabbed the reins" and gave direction. While a single agreed goal creates a degree of peace within a leadership team, there is often still a fair amount of "storming" and "norming" required. The storming occurs because there is a battle for control of the agenda and the team must sort out its "pecking order."

Teams operating at HR 2.0 are either obviously or subtly dysfunctional. When subtle, the dysfunction is often concealed by a thin veneer of polite professionalism, surface civility, or false bonhomie. Underneath this veneer, factions form and break as the power struggle ebbs and flows far from sight in corridors and sidebar meetings. Individual team members subtly brief against each other and will often network outside the team to gain support for their own agenda in a series of divisive or passive-aggressive manoeuvrings. Teams operating at this level are extremely common in most organisations, particularly when the team leader is newly appointed or promoted. It can be particularly tricky if the new leader was previously a peer of the other team members.

Most team meetings at this level consist of animated passionate debates that can become intense as people try to force capitulation, win the argument, or coerce others to get their way. At times, debates can descend into open conflict, but this is unusual, unless encouraged by a poor leader who mistakenly believes internal competitiveness improves team performance or because he personally enjoys the conflict. Often a couple of team members dominate the airtime. These types of teams are characterised by very low levels of trust. Ironically, trust is often spoken of as absent or required, but the implication is that it is someone else's responsibility to build it.

There is little understanding of each other and little effort is made to understand each other's motives or experience. Although team members work for the same business, they see each other as the enemy. If there wasn't an operational or financial reason to stick together, the "team" would probably fragment. Teams of battling experts are characterised by a high turnover rate. The ongoing employee churn common in this P-wave may keep the team stuck at this level of team development, and "new arrivals" are often heralded as the answer to the team's dysfunction. Unfortunately, the new arrival usually gets drawn into the same dysfunction and the turbulence continues.

Ultimately, a team's dysfunction reflects badly on the leader. If they can't bring some semblance of order and raise the team's performance, the leader often becomes the casualty of the battling experts.

Emerging HR and people practices

The key HR dilemma of the Power wave was how to push costs down. Unsurprisingly, workers resisted the resulting restructuring and wage determination policies, which in turn led to the need for labour relations practices.

However, up until the 1870s, most strikes took the form of protests, with little organisation. From the 1870s, starting in the UK, we saw the rise of "new unionism," where, focusing on the skilled workers, the trade union movement gained momentum. Indeed, legislative changes in the UK between 1871 and 1875 established the right to collective bargaining for the first time. Trade union membership in the UK accelerated from 750,000 in 1888 to 4.1 million by 1914.[12]

The HR practice was initially to resist trade unionisation. Management would often make it a condition of employment that workers did not join trade unions. Where workers did anyway, the lockout would feature as a management practice, simply closing the factory and denying work, unless and until the workers agreed to management's terms. In 1888, Andrew Carnegie used a four-month lockout and guards from Pinkerton National Detective Agency to crush the union at his Edgar Thomas mill and implement a change in the shift system.[13] Carnegie, as mentioned earlier, was an archetypal Power leader. He wanted complete freedom to drive down labour costs, freedom to set wages and working conditions, without interference. He was the boss; he was right and he alone had the answers.

In the US, one of the greatest challenges to Power-based leadership came in 1919 when workers across the country mounted numerous strikes. In the UK, strike action peaked slightly earlier, in 1912.[14] Although the power battles between owners and workers were interrupted by the First World War, they resumed after the war and continued right up until the Second World War.

During the Power wave, the organisation of "HR" changed fundamentally. Workers now had a voice and it had to be "managed." The welfare departments established towards the end of Paternalism began to be replaced by industrial relations units. In the UK, the Institute of Industrial Welfare Workers became the Institute of Labour Management.

The organisation of the workplace also changed. During the age of Paternalism, the founders themselves often took a direct role in the management of the workers, assisted only by overseers or supervisors. In the age of Power, management hierarchies began, based on more impersonal rules and defined standards and tasks. The machines and production lines dictated the pace of work, and professional or managerial functions began to form to ensure effective administration, although this would only really take off in the age of Process, which we cover in the next chapter.

The main development in HR practice was the new field of industrial relations. In 1920, John R. Commons established the first academic industrial relations programme at the University of Wisconsin. Sidney and Beatrice Webb are commonly cited as the founders of industrial relations study in the UK, and were instrumental in helping to move the remit of HR – or industrial relations at that time – from a narrow focus on unions and collective bargaining to a broader consideration of the entire employment relationship.[15] G.D.H. Cole also made a significant contribution to the field in the interwar years. Cole was responsible for the establishment of a lectureship in industrial relations at Nuffield College, Oxford. Where the Webbs and Cole differed was that the Webbs believed with the right politicians at the top, and an enlightened class of administrators, the economy and society could be reformed. Cole didn't. He was a socialist at heart and believed in self-government for working people, through local units of control and accountability, with different centres of power.[16]

The practices of the Power wave were clear. Industrial relations managers learned how to manage strikes and lockouts and began to develop the skills to write procedural and substantive agreements. Industrial relations officers managed grievances and sought to resolve shop floor conflicts.

However, the age of Power is far from being a historical nicety.

HR 2.0 Power today

While the skills of managing lockouts and writing agreements are less apparent today, in the US, union avoidance is still the primary approach to trade unions. Many legal and consultancy firms advise companies on how to hold so-called "captive meetings" to resist any organising campaigns. In the US, it is considered "career death" for an HR manager to allow a successful unionisation campaign, and the skills and legalities of union avoidance are still front and centre for HR practitioners.

The rise in subcontracting means that many factories and shops have more agency workers than direct employees. Knowingly or not, this penchant for subcontracting mirrors the organisation of the mills before the advent of trade unions, where a skilled craftsman or an experienced worker would operate as a small entrepreneur and make a profit out of the difference between the price of his contract and the wages paid to the workers. The actual production was under the control of one or more subcontractors who hired workers, paid them their wages, supervised the work process, and received a rate from the factory owner for the finished goods.[17] This was useful because it inhibited the ability of workers to come together to bargain with the factory owner. The same is true in modern business. Mostly used as a cost management intervention to allow more dynamic staffing, widespread use of labour-only service providers also significantly reduces a trade union's ability to organise because the people working in the business don't work for that business directly.

Lockouts are still common practice in South Asia, where the age of Power is still the norm in many companies. Management hostage-taking by powerful trade unions is still more common than we might think in the West. Such interventions are still found in Europe, particularly in France. In 2009, the CEO of Caterpillar France and several other senior executives were taken hostage after negotiations over the restructuring of Caterpillar's operations in France broke down. They were only released when the French President at the time, Nicolas Sarkozy, promised to meet the union members and "save the site" in a radio interview.[18] In 2014, Goodyear Tire factory workers in northern France kidnapped the production manager and HR director after negotiations broke down over the closing of the plant.[19]

In India, such Power manoeuvres often have tragic consequences, including serious injury or death. For example, in 2011, following the suspension of 25 workers at a steel factory in India, the deputy general manager was burnt to death in his car by workers. Three years earlier, the Indian head of an Italian auto parts company in Delhi was beaten to death by a group of workers who had been dismissed after demanding a pay rise.[20] Labour activists in Bangladesh have been killed and others fear for their lives as they fight to secure better conditions for workers.[21] Violence of one form or another is still common in industrial disputes in Latin America, Bangladesh, and Turkey. The use of thugs to beat people up, sometimes resulting in death, is sadly not unusual. Even in the UK, which often likes to pride itself on its modern work practices, bonded labour is still much more common than most people realise.[22]

In addition, in some public-sector areas, where there is a monopoly supply situation and high levels of trade union solidarity, it is arguable that those trade unions exert their power to the full, perhaps at the expense of techno-logical progress and consumer service. Some have pointed to the London Underground as an example of this.[23]

The HR and trade union practices of the Power wave, put in this context, sound negative. However, the drive and action orientation, whether by the owner asserting his "right to manage" or the trade unionist demanding "a voice," are fundamental realities that will always require management. Some-times that drive and risk-taking has proved, in the longer term, to be of value. The best practitioners of the Power approach are able to take the action orientation required to respond quickly to changing events, integrate this with the realities of employee voice, and reframe people practices to retain the best of Paternalism, even as progress and agility is assured.

They acknowledge and work with the reality that under any system, there are winners and losers, there will be conflict, and there will be balances and imbalances of power. They explicitly accept that there is a need to manage power relationships. They know it is not and can never be about ego.

Historically, the most successful industrial relations practitioners, regardless of the economic climate, managed to ensure healthy "human relationships." As well as focusing on the immediate "doing" issues, such as salary, they also ensured that "relating" and "being" issues were in harmony. Healthy personal relationships were always maintained between company and employee represen-tatives, particularly where regional and national representative structures oversaw local discussions. National trade union officers and the heads of industrial rela-tions would normally ensure a backchannel when things got really tough.

This was evident as far back as the 1870s when trade unions and managers worked together to improve working conditions and efficiencies. Such col-laboration can still be found today between power brokers on both sides. The best HR practitioners in the field, when strikes occurred, were able to quickly ensure that working relationships could be re-established by avoiding personal insults and operating with high levels of emotional maturity and integrity, even during very tough times. Both authors have significant experience diffusing such organisational power battles.

A veteran – ex-miner – industrial relations manager once told one of the authors (ND) how he "framed" the emotion into something simple and practical: "Industrial relations and pay negotiations are easy, you have either got enough money or you haven't." In other words, it wasn't about him.

Evolution from HR 2.0 to HR 3.0

Power gets stuff done, and the Power wave was no exception. Once steam, iron, and steel came on the scene, productivity exploded. Technological improvements and advances in transportation and distribution, such as roads and rail, opened up new markets and allowed the workforce to move more freely. Workers had more options, which changed the nature of the working relationship. The tug of war between the power of the workers and the power of the owners went on for most of the nineteenth century.

More often it was the wealthy industrialist, supported by government, that won the power struggle. But the intoxicating nature of power can fuel a sense of omnipotence in the Power leader, which invariably starts to drive a wide range of unhelpful behaviours, and ultimately egomania. There is a tendency to "go too far," as evidenced by many of the actions and overreactions to strike action imposed by powerful owners and their zealots. The thirst for power can lead to narcissism and even solipsism. This type of self-obsession and abuse of power is often the evolutionary trigger for change.

When leaders on both sides of the struggle – owners and workers – slowly arrive at the realisation that they could transcend the worst outcomes of a powerful leader or powerful collective and include the best of both worlds, a breakthrough is imminent. Together, they can combine the welfare focus of Paternalism with the progress of Power to reach the Process wave of HR 3.0. The workers realise that rules and procedures can check the worst excesses of the Power leader, and the owners realise that rules and procedures can also improve performance and consistency of output. The arm-wrestling can stop. Nobody is defeated. Everyone gets to save face and both sides can claim a victory.

Once employee voices are accepted by employers, and owners stop seeing their company as an extension of themselves and their own personal property, evolution triumphs and the principle-based Process wave emerges. The street-fighting Harry Bennetts of the world become the nameless, albeit rule-observing, personnel managers.

Notes

1 Wilson A (2003) The Rise and Fall of Harry Bennett, *Automotive News*, www.auto news.com/article/20030602/SUB/306020843/the-rise-and-fall-of-harry-bennett

2   Freeman JB (2018) *Behemoth: A History of the Factory and the Making of the Modern World*, W.W. Norton & Company, New York.
3   Hill J (1913) There Is Power in a Union, *Wikipedia*, https://en.wikipedia.org/wiki/There_Is_Power_in_a_Union
4   Stiles TJ (2009) *The First Tycoon: The Epic Life of Cornelius Vanderbilt*, Knopf, New York.
5   Freeman JB (2018) *Behemoth: A History of the Factory and the Making of the Modern World*, W.W. Norton & Company, New York.
6   Sugar M (1980) *The Ford Hunger*, March, Berkeley, CA.
7   Martin R (2003) *The Responsibility Virus: How Control Freaks, Shrinking Violets – and the Rest of Us – Can Harness the Power of True Partnership*, Basic Books, New York.
8   Ratcliffe S (Ed) (1994) *The Little Oxford Dictionary of Quotations*, Oxford Univeristy Press, Oxford.
9   Freeman JB (2018) *Behemoth: A History of the Factory and the Making of the Modern World*, W.W. Norton & Company, New York.
10 de la Merced MJ (2013) Kozlowski Is Granted Parole, *New York Times*, https://dealbook.nytimes.com/2013/12/03/kozlowski-is-granted-parole/
11 Loftus G (2012) If You're Going through Hell, Keep Going – Winston Churchill, *Forbes*, www.forbes.com/sites/geoffloftus/2012/05/09/if-youre-going-through-hell-keep-going-winston-churchill/#39f16991d549
12 Wrigley CJ (1982) *A History of British Industrial Relations 1875–1914*, University of Massachusetts Press, Amherst, MA.
13 Freeman JB (2018) *Behemoth: A History of the Factory and the Making of the Modern World*, W.W. Norton & Company, New York.
14 Wrigley CJ (1982) *A History of British Industrial Relations 1875–1914*, University of Massachusetts Press, Amherst, MA.
15 Kaufman BE (2014) History of the British Industrial Relations Field Reconsidered: Getting from the Webbs to the New Employment Relations Paradigm, *British Journal of Industrial Relations*, 52(1): 1–31.
16 Richards P (2010) GDH Cole: The Socialist Who Invented the Real "Big Society" Labour List, https://labourlist.org/2010/10/gdh-cole-the-socialist-who-invented-the-real-big-society/
17 Wrigley CJ (1982) *A History of British Industrial Relations 1875–1914*, University of Massachusetts Press, Amherst, MA.
18 Jolly D (2009) Angry French Workers Take Their Bosses Hostage, *New York Times*, www.nytimes.com/2009/04/03/business/global/03iht-labor.html
19 Willsher K (2014) French Workers at Goodyear Tire Plant Take Bosses Captive, *The Guardian*, www.theguardian.com/world/2014/jan/06/french-workers-bosses-hostage-goodyear-amiens
20 BBC News (2011) India Manager "Killed by Workers," www.bbc.co.uk/news/world-south-asia-12644076
21 Young R (2018) Fashion to Die For, www.businessoffashion.com/articles/people/fashion-to-die-for
22 Foroudi L (2018) Forced Labour in the UK: "I Tried to Escape … They Cut My Finger Off," *Financial Times*, www.ft.com/content/f7ae5cf8-8f94-11e8-b639-7680cedcc421
23 Darlington RR (2001) *Union Militancy and Leftwing Leadership on London Underground*, http://usir.salford.ac.uk/id/eprint/10106/3/IRJ_London_Underground.pdf

3   HR 3.0

The Process wave (1935–1985)

Frederick Winslow Taylor *is* Mr Process.

While he died before the Process wave really gathered momentum, he was the first rule-maker and the first to professionalise management.

Although coming from a prominent Philadelphia family, Taylor skipped college and became an apprentice machinist and pattern-maker before moving into factory management. His route to management, however, gave him a unique insight because he understood the actual work employees did, as well as the management of the work. Working at Midvale Steel Works, near Philadelphia, and later at Andrew Carnegie's Bethlehem Steel, in Pennsylvania, Taylor was fascinated by the mechanics of steel production and metalworking. At the time, steel manufacture was chaotic, loud, hot, ad hoc, and dangerous. But he had an engineer's mind, ordered and systematic, and he began to apply that mind to the manufacturing process, leading to innovations in cost accounting, inventory control, tool standardisation, and shop floor layout. Taylor also knew, because of his time as an apprentice, that machinists would often set their own work rate or maximum output. The manager was often oblivious to this practice because they didn't have first-hand experience of doing the work, and therefore didn't really understand the task or appreciate what was possible. Taylor believed that if a task was observed and measured, quality and productivity could be systematically improved. His approach, "scientific management," split planning from execution for the first time. Workers were given detailed instructions on how best to carry out each task based on detailed observation and testing. Pay would be calculated by a piecework system that rewarded higher productivity for those that met agreed production norms.[1]

When he wrote *The Principles of Scientific Management* in 1911, he probably never imagined that 90 years later, it would be voted by the Fellows of the Academy of Management as the most influential book of the twentieth century.[2]

After his death, in March 1915, his name became famous way beyond his Philadelphia birthplace. Not only across continental USA and Europe, but everywhere else, there were factories, including Soviet Russia and Mao's China. Taylorism, as his system became known, gave us work study, the "men in white coats with a clipboard" who identified the most efficient way to get tasks done in factories and warehouses, set the standards of work, and optimised the factory system.

Initially, his approach led to fierce conflict during the Power wave. Machinists disliked the loss of autonomy and viewed the instruction cards as an attack on their craft and skill. Taylor himself believed that it would be good for workers and owners alike because it would lead to greater profit and higher wages. At least in theory, Taylorism eased the struggle between workers and owners and provided a path where both could prosper.

However, it would be long after Taylor's death and the devastation of the Second World War before his approach was really embraced and the industrial system settled down to a standardised way of doing things. The world had witnessed the violent destruction made possible when too many people dutifully followed a despotic Power leader. Globally, there was a collective recognition that there needed to be some order, structure, and process in every system to break the dependency on one or two powerful leaders and their inner circle or cabal of "yes-men." A view emerged that a more collective approach with appropriate checks and balances could help to stop a repeat performance. Rules became sacrosanct: rules of working, rules for conduct, rules for training, rules for health and safety, and rules for conducting labour relations and "doing the right thing" became increasingly important. Principles and ethics emerged. The Process era had begun.

The first glimmers of Process

The world of the early capitalist was one of open borders, international competition, boom, bust, and industry consolidation. Governments still largely adopted a "laissez-faire" approach to business. In other words, they deliberately chose an economic system where transactions between private parties were free from government intervention such as regulation, privileges, tariffs, and subsidies. The first glimmers of a change came as early as the days of Bismarck in Prussia/Germany, when he introduced early forms of National Insurance. Further glimmers were evident with the election of the interventionist Liberal government in the UK in 1905, and in the US when Theodore (Teddy) Roosevelt took on the "robber barons" and directly intervened to settle the 1905 miners' strike.[3]

However, the idea that rules and principles might be beneficial for business and society started to really take hold following the Great Depression of the 1930s and the ascension to the US presidency of Teddy's fifth cousin. Some argue that Franklin D. Roosevelt's New Deal, with its more active government role, ended the economic crisis that the early capitalist system had created. Others suggest that it was the Second World War that ended the Great Depression. Regardless of the catalyst, the post-war world was radically different from the world that existed before.

There were now rules. Economies were regulated. Welfare states and the "Great Society" were created. Like Roosevelt's New Deal, Lyndon B. Johnson launched a set of "Great Society" programmes to eliminate poverty and racial injustice that went even further, seeking to address education, medical care, urban problems, rural poverty, and transportation.

More importantly, "walls" had gone up, and not just in West Berlin; industry no longer had to contend with the free-for-all of international trade and volatile exchange rates. The Bretton Woods system provided fixed rates of exchange, offering some levels of certainty. Recognising that there was a great deal of rebuilding to do once the war finally ended, 730 delegates from all the 44 Allied nations gathered at a hotel in Bretton Woods, New Hampshire. Deliberating for three weeks, the group signed the Bretton Woods Agreement on the final day, which set up a system of rules, institutions, and procedures to regulate the international monetary system. These accords established the International Monetary Fund (IMF) and the International Bank for Reconstruction and Development (IBRD), which are still part of the World Bank Group today.

Governments introduced labour legislation dealing with concepts such as unfair dismissal and health and safety at work, immigration was controlled, and the communist world closed itself off. From 1945 until 1989, there were very real fears that the communist system might triumph. To ensure that it didn't, it was accepted that governments, businesses, and workers needed to work together to establish "social contracts" to ensure that all could benefit from the West's capitalist democratic alternative.

With wages and incomes policies, as well as nationalisation, accepted across the political spectrum, *The Economist* referred to this era as "Butskellism" in the UK. Combining the surname of Rad Butler, Chancellor of the Exchequer of the Conservative Party, and Hugh Gaitskell, leader of the Labour Party, the slightly satirical term sought to reflect the unusual situation where both parties had come to accept a "corporatist" approach.

There were now clear ways of doing things. Keynesianism, named after its originator John Maynard Keynes, had diagnosed the cause of the Great Depression – insufficient demand. As a result, governments sought to prevent future economic recessions and depressions by attempting to manage aggregate demand. There was also an appreciation that the sacrifice of ordinary people made during the war needed to be acknowledged and repaid through the government provision of a robust welfare system and educational bursaries.

In the US, the Servicemen's Readjustment Act of 1944, more commonly known as the GI Bill, was created to help veterans of the Second World War. It established hospitals, made low-interest mortgages available, and helped to pay tuition and expenses for veterans attending college or trade schools. From 1944 onwards, millions of US veterans received financial support in one form or another. The Readjustment Benefits Act of 1966 extended these benefits to all veterans of the armed forces, including those who had served during peacetime.

The community ethos generated in the victor countries, and the sheer horror of war and displacement experienced by the people in the defeated states, meant that it was no longer acceptable for a business owner to declare, "This company is my personal property." The social dimensions of work could no longer be ignored. People now felt they had the right to a say and needed to have a voice. This era saw a peak in trade union membership. In the UK, trade union membership peaked at 13 million in 1979, but it wasn't driven by the same Power urge of the previous era. People wanted to compromise and work together. They had seen enough of the horrors of Power-based conflict and dogma.

Business prospered. On the back of the Marshall Plan, initiated in 1948, the Western world was rebuilt, restoring cities, industry, and social systems. Officially called the European Recovery Program, the Marshall Plan was a US initiative to help Western Europe rebuild war-torn regions, remove trade barriers, modernise industry, improve European prosperity (which would in turn improve US prosperity), and prevent the spread of communism. The US underwrote an economic expansion to ensure that all workers had "a stake in the system." Interstate barriers were reduced, regulations were scaled back, and business was encouraged to increase productivity and trade union membership, as well as adopt modern business procedures and processes.

The largest recipient of Marshall Plan money was the UK, followed by France and West Germany. Eighteen European countries received financial assistance from the US. Perhaps unsurprisingly, considering the goal of preventing communism, the Soviet Union refused offered benefits, despite being an ally during the war. Russia also blocked proposed benefits to Eastern bloc communist countries at the time such as Hungary and Poland.

The Process era was, in many ways, the golden era of the working man. Able to live in the suburbs and own his own home, he could hold down a unionised job with healthcare provisions and a pension. For the first time ever, the working man was living the American Dream. In the UK, mimicking the line of the US Democratic Party, Prime Minister Harold Macmillan, addressing his fellow Conservatives during a speech in Bedford in 1957, said, "Let us be frank about it: most of our people have never had it so good."[4] He went on to celebrate the success of Britain's post-war economy, while at the same time urging wage restraint and warning against inflation. Industry, certainly in the West, sought to put the Power era in the past. The ways of doing business, "the rules," began to be codified.

Process-based leadership

The Process leader swings the focus back onto the collective. Usually, they have experienced the dithering futility of Paternalism and its corresponding inconsistent progress while also witnessing the autocratic bullying of a Power leader.

John Lewis's son John Spedan Lewis is a good example of Process-based leadership. After decades of owning only one, albeit successful, store, his father bought Peter Jones in Sloane Square, London. Having two stores nudged his father towards more Power-based leadership practice, where he had absolute autonomy and sought to push costs – mainly wages – down so that he could continue to provide value for his customers. Spedan went to work at Peter Jones and soon discovered that along with his brother, who also worked in the family business, and his father, the three of them made more money than the wage bill for the entire workforce. This bothered him, and while convalescing after a riding accident, an idea took hold. Spedan believed that if his father had put as much effort into his staff as he did his customers, then the business would be even more successful.

Peter Jones was failing at the time, and after a spat with his father, Spedan withdrew from the Oxford Street store in exchange for full control of Peter Jones. Spedan thought that the reason the business was failing was because staff had no incentive to do a good day's work. He shortened their working day, instituted a system of commission for each department, and held regular meetings where staff could air any grievances directly with him. He made improvements in staff conditions, including granting a third week's paid holiday each year, and published a fortnightly newspaper telling staff how the business was faring. The business flourished. Within five years, he and his staff had converted an annual deficit of £8,000 to a profit of £20,000.[5]

Spedan was determined to create a different sort of company where the profits generated by business were not just paid to shareholders as a reward for their capital, but also distributed to the people who did the work to make that profit in the first place. Spedan believed in the principle of "fairer shares." He went on to make peace with his father and cooperation between the stores resumed. He was left the business following his father's death and created the John Lewis Partnership that still exists today.

The Process leader has moved beyond the personal glory and hedonism of the Power wave and woken up to the idea that there are forces beyond them that matter. Meaning emerges for the first time. They recognise that there is a "higher authority" – for some, this is God; for others, it is government. Either way, Process leaders are motivated to do the right thing in the right way. Their ultimate goal is salvation, driven as they are by the principles of that higher authority. Process leaders have moved from the "I know best because I'm the father figure" of Paternalism or the "I know best because I'm in charge and I say so" of the Power leader. Process leaders seek to follow the rules of their higher power for the benefit of themselves, their family, or their "tribe."

John Spedan Lewis thought it was unfair that three people could make the same money as an entire 300-strong workforce who actually did the work to generate that profit. He also believed that if staff were well treated, they would work harder anyway, so acknowledging and rewarding this would be a better way to work in everyone's interest.

As mentioned earlier, the Second World War was a huge accelerator for the Process wave and the emergence of Process based leadership because the world had seen the devastation that could be wrought by an autocratic

Power leader (Hitler and Mussolini). Following the war, the United Nations was formed to institute some collective rules to prevent another conflict.

Interestingly, Process, like all the collectively focused stages, is more female. Women are, by nature, more inclusive and collaborative and less self-focused. As men went off to war, it was the women who filled the factories as they were repurposed for food or munitions. A lack of male Power leaders meant they had to figure it out themselves and create processes and procedures to get the work done. Although women were pushed out of the factories when the men came back from the war, their approach left a legacy of greater collaboration, process, and order, and that Process leadership reaped significant benefit as societies rebuilt. Process leadership is accurate, precise, crisp, and keen to deliver to a high-quality standard. Process leadership plans carefully and sticks with that plan in accordance with strong principles.

The EU, as originally conceived, is a great example of a group that started with a set of strong principles, not only as a peacekeeping initiative for Europe, but as a collective market that could rival the US. When it started, as with the early years of many P-waves, the benefits flowed. But when those principles burgeoned into a set of rules upon rules upon rules, it moved the EU from helpful initiative to a dogmatic, unyielding set of compliance procedures. The EU became as much about a debate on whether a Jaffa cake is a biscuit or a cake than it did about how to create a platform for growth and security across Europe. As the world sped up, rules for rules' sake became part of the reason behind widespread disillusionment across the eurozone. The drift from a set of fine principles, to forced national compliance, to a vast series of rigid rules made by bureaucrats, miles away from where such rules bite, was a key factor that drove the UK's vote for Brexit.

After the benefits of Process leadership start to subside, various Process pathologies begin to emerge. For example, workers often retreat into tightly defined roles, unwilling to flex or step outside their remit. They would become blind to changing business realities, often choosing to cut off their nose to spite their face in pay negotiations. In the 1970s, for example, workers would demand a huge pay increase even though it could bankrupt the business. Such short-sightedness suggested that the self-interest which would characterise the Profit wave was beginning to take root. Bosses would tell staff they couldn't afford the pay demands and workers would replay, "We don't believe that market conditions have changed. The company is making a profit, so you must honour the pay rise you agreed last year."

If the Process pathology that companies experienced wasn't rigidity in pay negotiations, then it was the over-reliance on Process to fix all HR 2.0 ills. Remember, when each P-wave starts to fail, the tendency is to ramp up whatever worked in that wave – in this case, rules and regulations. If addiction to Process fails, then there is often a deliberate reach back into history to break the deadlock – in this case, the desire to revert to "the good old days" and call a Power leader back in to fix the mess. Neither work.

Teams at HR 3.0: dependent experts

In this P-wave, where process and rules trump personal opinion, there's a greater recognition of the importance of team cohesion. The dysfunction of battling experts seen at HR 2.0 tends to subside, and a more mature team of "dependent experts" develops. At this level, there is an acceptance that obedience to the team leader is necessary for the team to make progress. Such acceptance reveals a preparedness to agree some social rules and norms for the sake of the collective. The Process leader starts to drive greater efficiency and effectiveness through social conformity. In so doing, the Process leader draws on the best of his Power leader qualities by "taking the reins," not in the "carte blanche" way of the autocrat, but rather in a more diplomatic way and in service of the team. If the Process leader clarifies the rules for such dependency, the collective will accept the process as a necessary stepping stone to the next level of team performance. In team meetings, mutual respect starts to emerge. Team members respect the authority of the leader and the team leader respects that team members need their voices to be heard. This lays the foundations for the rules, ways of working, and stability that all emerge at HR 3.0.

When the team leader is more prepared to listen to the views of team members, the pathological passivity of HR 2.0 diminishes. People still "report in" to the team, but do so as a matter of process and with the intention of informing each other rather than just defending their turf. Dependent expert teams often consider themselves as high-performing, but that is simply because most team members have probably never experienced what high performance really is and have never been part of a leadership team that functions at a more sophisticated level of capability. The truth is a dependent expert team is still a long way short of high performance. That is not to say they can't turn a profit or drive the required level of earnings before interest, tax, depreciation, and amortisation (EBITDA), but simply that they are not delivering what they are really capable of and are far from optimal team performance.

The greater levels of respect that exist in the Process wave also means there is often a higher degree of trust among dependent expert teams, but the team agenda is still set top-down by the Process leader and team members are still quite reliant on the "boss" to decide what happens and when. Team members often start to unconsciously match the behaviour modelled by the boss in an attempt to fit in, conform to the norms, and succeed.

Since the conflict seen in battling expert teams of HR 2.0 has subsided, there is often more friendliness and sense of connection in teams of dependent experts prevalent in HR 3.0. Team members may even enjoy each other's company and most issues are resolved in the room, but there is still a significant amount of untapped potential yet to be released. The team is still not that much more than a collection of individuals doing their job held together by the leader in charge (hence dependent). At this level, individual team members will often keep their own agenda hidden for self-protection purposes and only reveal the views that fit with the views of the team leader.

Dependant expert teams will engage in detailed debate (experts love details), but usually each individual passionately advocates their own perspective to impress the boss, assert their expertise, or establish their place in the "pecking order." Individuals rarely, if ever, build a shared concept across the team. The debate often feels like "popcorn," with each person just making their points and largely ignoring other people's views. Rarely does anyone take responsibility to integrate the different ideas that have emerged. Often what happens is the debate becomes repetitive, with little forward progress. As passion increases, usually because on some level people sense they are failing to impose their expert view, the debate descends into a "circular stampede": directionless, animated, forceful, but ultimately pointless.

Learning is slow in this type of team, despite surface goodwill, not least because experts live with the belief that they already know what all the answers are, hence the joke, "You can always tell an expert, you just can't tell them much." As a result, individual team members will often not trust the commercial judgement of other team members, although this is never made explicit or spoken about directly. Full disclosure rarely happens, and "offline" "positioning" conversations in the corridor after the meetings are still common. At battling experts, in HR 2.0, there is little psychological safety in a team. At dependent experts, in HR 3.0, there is a sufficient safety for team members to be able to draw attention to the fact that there is insufficient psychological safety. For some HR practitioners, the presence or absence of psychological safety can become an obsession.

The behaviour of HR 3.0 teams is based on compliance to a set of – often implicit – "team rules" that are largely about reverence or reference to the leader and maintaining the hierarchy. Although these teams may deliver results, they are typically not very reflective, which means there is often a significant bias for action. They find it difficult to hold concepts and defer decisions to allow learning and development to take place. Before making any decisions, there is often a reference to an external higher authority. Team members can become overly passive because they believe, usually from experience, that the boss will eventually overrule their decisions or impose his or her point of view, or because these are the rules of the team and the unspoken dynamics and hierarchy must be respected.

Emerging HR and people practices

Along with Frederick Winslow Taylor, arguably the first management consultant, the Process wave saw many more significant contributions.

In 1943, Edward N. Hay began his first compensation project with General Foods, establishing E.N. Hay & Associates – later becoming the Hay Group, which is still operational today. Alfred Chandler, a professor of business history at Harvard University, began analysing the workings of large-scale organisations in the 1960s. His book *Strategy and Structure* summarised the workings of DuPont, Standard Oil Company, General Motors, and Sears Roebuck.[6] Chandler was the first to make links between organisational strategy and business strategy. Peter Drucker codified the practice of management, publishing his first management book in 1939 and his last in 2008 (posthumous). Henry Mintzberg, professor of management studies at McGill University in Canada, outlined the nature of managerial work in a book of the same name in 1973.[7] *The Structuring of Organizations* was published in 1979, synthesising the research on organisation development and design.[8] He continues to analyse and comment on management practice to this day (2020). During this P-wave, business writers were mainly academics, not businessmen. The purpose of their writing was to seek to understand and record the rules of the game, generate knowledge, and search for the best ways of working that business could then use to improve results.

However, one businessman, Alfred Pritchard Sloan, president, chairman, and CEO of General Motors, did write about his experiences.[9] His book outlined his vision of the modern professional organisation, and, unlike many of the "celebrity CEO" books of today, is still viewed as a seminal text.

Sloan was the quintessential engineer, and as a result he created a very Process-oriented company that put huge store in policies, systems, and structures. Among other things, Sloan codified the rules on financial controls, the divisional structure, and functional approaches to organisation design. He described how professional "modern" businesses should operate. Even then, however, his approach attracted criticism as not paying sufficient attention to the people executing those processes. While he had admirably identified all the intricacies and contingencies of a foolproof system, that system often left out employees and society.[10] It's also interesting to note that Sloan only wrote the book as a belated response to Peter Drucker's book *Concept of the Corporation*.[11] Sloan believed his legacy would be better sustained if an outsider analysed and documented what they had created at GM, and Peter Drucker was chosen for the role. Drucker shadowed Sloan for two years and wrote a detailed and largely flattering book, but Sloan and his colleagues did not like the *Concept of Corporation* manuscript. Drucker's book was, however, well received elsewhere, and catapulted him to the position of sought-after management guru.[12]

In businesses across the country, agreements were being reached with trade unions, and any conflict became managed via a process. Companies codified "procedural agreements" with trade unions, defining how grievances and negotiations would be managed and processed. These institutionalised conflicts and reduced the "wildcat strikes" that had been at one time endemic. Substantive agreements were reached documenting the terms and conditions of employment and associated rules of the workplace. Such agreements became bibles in the factories, referenced back to almost as sacred texts, which gave both managers and employee representatives the reason why something had to happen, or could not happen, depending on the situation. What happened inside business became less about the whim and hubris of a Power leader and more about a collective "best way" identified by workers *and* management.

The countries who made the greatest success of the Process wave, and are still doing so today, were the countries that lost the war (Germany and Japan). The almost complete destruction and devastation of their industrial base meant that business in both countries needed to start from scratch. Considered catastrophic at the time, this blank slate did, however, deliver significant – albeit surprising – advantage. There was no going back to the way things were, no existing industry or business to become the role model – they could start again. And while extremely challenging, it allowed Germany and Japan to take the best thinking at the time and create an improved, collectively beneficial, and efficient system.

Germany fully embraced the new norms of the Process wave. Works councils and supervisory boards, with employee representation, were established in West Germany, based on the Weimar Republic model. Through the works councils, represented at plant and national level, members of the supervisory board were elected. Many would argue that the system of industrial relations in Germany at that time was fundamental to the German economic miracle.

The works councils have co-determination rights for specific issues under German law. They also exist in the Netherlands and other so-called "Rhineland" models of industrial relations. The processes of consultation were clearly laid down and enforceable by law. Since 1945, German industrial relations have been marked by the harmonious relationships between managers and workers. Unlike the Anglo-Saxon or French trade union model, works council members have an equal responsibility for the health of the company as well as the prosperity of the employees. Although the role of trade unions in Germany remains to negotiate the "price" of employees, the work of developing ways of working and agreeing change is primarily with the works councils.

In Japan, they did not have Germanic-type works councils, but instead a system of work that relied heavily on active worker engagement, security, and empowerment. W. Edwards Deming, an American engineer, statistician, and management consultant, went to Japan and taught the Japanese the next upgrade on Taylorism, total quality management (TQM).

In 1950, Deming delivered a speech to the leaders of Japanese industry in Tokyo called "Statistical Product Quality Administration,"[13] and he is widely credited as instrumental in what is known as the Japanese post-war economic miracle.

While the Germans, Dutch, Scandinavians, and Japanese embraced Process wave techniques and systems wholeheartedly, Anglo-Saxon and French businesses were never really that sure.

The collective rule and standard-setting became the norm for governments, businesses, and society. But somehow, many American, British, and French companies couldn't quite get the hang of it. Whether this was due to nationalistic cynicism, excessive self-confidence, or some other culturally embedded blindness is an interesting debate. Either way, in the Allied countries that "won" the war, the legacy of the Process age remains much more alive.

This may partly explain why, in the UK, industrial relations became bogged down in the limbo between Power and a partially adopted Process wave, with the significant benefits of the Process wave being reaped elsewhere. For example, the industrial relations travails of the British car industry are well documented. In 1968, in what would be a landmark labour relations dispute, the women sewing machinists who made the seat covers at Ford Motor Company in Dagenham, London, walked out, demanding equal pay. Machinists at Ford's Halewood Body & Assembly plant followed suit. The strike received a lot of attention around the world as women, post-war, had moved back into more traditional family roles. A thousand women attended an equal pay demonstration in Trafalgar Square in 1969, and the resulting movement was instrumental in the Equal Pay Act of 1970 – the film *Made in Dagenham* tells the story. In addition, "Red Robbo," Derek Robinson, was rarely off the news. Considered a working-class hero by many and a "notorious agitator"[14] by others, Robinson was largely vilified by a right-leaning press who viewed him as standing in the way of progress and corporate profit. At the time of his death in 2017, age 90, the BBC described Robinson as "the man behind 523 car factory strikes,"[15] as he had personally led 523 walkouts at the British Leyland Birmingham car plant in a 30-month period. While other countries were putting the benefits of Process to good use and making serious gains in productivity as a result, the UK was still largely locked in the old Power battles.

Remnants of the Power era were stubborn to shift, especially in countries that were *not* forced to rethink their approach as a result of losing the war. That said, the Process age was when HR, or personnel management as it was called then, really took off.

In 1945, the UK Institute of Labour Management changed its name to the Institute of Personnel Management (IPM), reflecting the increased focus not only on industrial relations, but also on training. The professionalisation stepped up in 1955, when a national curriculum was introduced and was run by colleges, with entry into the IPM being dependent on successfully passing the relevant exams. In the US, the American Society for Personnel Administration was created in 1948, reflecting the process orientation of early personnel management. In 1989, the organisation changed its name to the Society for Human Resources, as it is known today – a nod to the incoming Profit age, where people were viewed as resources like any other non-human assets. In the business world, Unilever established its first personnel department in 1947 at their international head office.

From the end of the second world war, the term "personnel" soon became the standard descriptor for the function that managed the people processes in an organisation. Personnel officers or personnel managers would today be described as "generalist." Although specialist roles, such as management development and compensation and benefits were emerging, most personnel officers looked after every aspect of the employment relationship.

Key to the success of the role was effective personnel administration. Employee record-keeping, ensuring payroll operated efficiently, and administering job changes, recruitment, and employee exits of one kind or another took up most of the personnel officer's time.

Industrial relations (IR) remained prominent. Personnel managers had to be effective IR managers to garner credibility with line management colleagues. Managing conflict, grievances, and pay negotiations were the bread and butter of the role.

Organisational development and design also emerged as a critical dimension to the way that personnel managers thought about the role. With GM's Alfred P. Sloan, the concept of functional and divisional organisation structures was established. This led to the codification of thinking on organisation structures, as mentioned earlier. E.N. Hay further codified how jobs could be designed; he developed the famous Hay Job Evaluation system, which identified job values based on three key factors – know-how, problem-solving, and accountability.

This led to an accepted wisdom on how organisations should look. Organisational charts started to become widespread in companies. Although a Scottish-American engineer, Daniel McCallum, is credited with developing the first modern organisational chart in 1854, the term "organogram" did not become common until the 1960s. Amazing to think they existed before PowerPoint!

Rules were established during the Process wave on what constituted a well-designed organisation. Clear hierarchies were established. Each business gave primacy to either the division, the geography, or a technology as the point of integration in the delivery of their product or service to their customer base. Some companies chose a divisional structure, some a geographic model, and some organised themselves around specific technologies or categories of service. On their main "executive leadership boards," companies would have either functional representatives or geographic "heads" or divisional leaders, depending on the corporate strategy. Spans of control, or the numbers of direct reports a manager could have, were documented, with anything between 5 and 12 deemed acceptable. Remember, even Jesus only had 12 apostles. However, if an organisation was built to be creative, different rules could apply. Mintzberg brilliantly captured these insights when he identified five different approaches for organisational design:

1.   the entrepreneurial organisation;
2.   the machine organisation;
3.   the professional organisation;
4.   the divisional (diversified) organisation; and
5.   the innovative organisation ("adhocracy").[16]

Personnel managers would apply this thinking and ensure "structure followed strategy." Thus, a business would decide on its growth plan and then choose a structural model that best suited that plan.

Canadian psychoanalyst, social scientist, and management consultant Elliott Jaques proposed work levels, arguing that a large business should have no more than five levels of hierarchy (work levels) based on an analysis of the time span of decisions.[17] This had a huge influence on the organisational design of large companies such as Unilever and Tesco. This was the genesis of a pyramid being used to visually represent the hierarchy of a business, with the CEO at the top.

During the Process wave, a skilled personnel practitioner, steeped in the thinking of Drucker, Mintzberg, Jaques, and others, could diagnose organisational issues from a desktop analysis of spans (i.e. the number of direct reports any particular manager had) and structures (i.e. the operating model the business adhered to). These pseudo-scientific approaches to organisational design lent themselves to highly structured and very hierarchical reward systems.

Using the Hay point system or other "objective" criteria, the job evaluation process would determine the rate for the job. In some places, including the Scandinavian countries, there were even national schemes identifying job families. This approach still happens today in the National Health Service (NHS) in the UK, for example.

In very large companies, job evaluation specialists emerged within the personnel function to manage "job evaluation claims" made by managers or workers. Variable pay for managers or workers doing the same role was unusual during the height of the Process wave. Piece rates had been replaced by "job-evaluated rates for the role," and managers paid according to their place in the hierarchy. Although well intentioned, this job ranking itself has become a source of significant bureaucratic slowdown.

The most significant performance management innovation of the process era was "management by objectives" (MBO),[18] also known as "management by results." In essence a process of target alignment, MBO was a means of defining objectives for the organisation, and then through its managers, ultimately to all employees. For the first time, MBO measured the actual performance against the objectives that were set, usually annually. Hewlett-Packard were among the early enthusiastic adopters.

Because fixed pay was the main element of compensation arrangements during the Process era, the MBO approach did not yet significantly impact salary, bonuses, or other variable pay. The tax systems (and wages and incomes policies) with higher levels of marginal tax rates deterred variable approaches, with management perks such as the company car being more usually favoured as a means of supplementing basic salaries. Because of this, the range of earnings differential between the top earners and the shop floor was modest during the Process wave. As the Process wave drew to a close, the average CEO earned 42.1 times the salary of the average employee. In the Profit wave, which we will explore in Chapter 4, this differential reached 325,[19] and in many cases vastly exceeded even that.

Government-established "wages boards" also existed, detailing the national or regional rates for blue-collar jobs. While trade unions and management generally persisted with unit-level "free collective bargaining" in the UK and the US, Germany and other European countries introduced sectoral or regional bargaining, applying a common "going rate," which in turn managed wage competition between companies for the wider societal benefit. Cutting wages to get a competitive advantage was almost impossible, and common industry or regional pay increases assisted the national management of inflation through effective application of incomes policies.

The big boom area for personnel in this wave was in the emerging field of "human relations." As far back as the late 1920s and early 1930s, psychologist, industrial researcher, and organisational theorist Elton Mayo had conducted experiments at the Western Electric factory at Hawthorne, a suburb of Chicago. The aim of the research was to establish whether changes to working environment and conditions influenced productivity. Environmental working conditions such as lighting and humidity were tested, as were the effect of changes in employment arrangements such as the number and length of breaks, working hours, and managerial leadership. Not only were the Hawthorne experiments the first attempt to study working conditions; they also appeared to produce remarkable evidence that conditions affected productivity.

Since the original study was published, the data has now largely been discredited.[20] But the facts have not stood in the way of a good story. In a lovely early example of "fake news," many people still believe the "Hawthorne effect" to be real. Certainly, the idea that working conditions are critical to productivity has become deeply entrenched in HR practice and still drives much thinking today, particularly in areas such as well-being. Despite the fake nature of the results, the Hawthorne claim changed the way owners and managers viewed their workforce. The Hawthorne experiments effectively gave birth to the "human relations" school of management. Despite the lack of scientific validity to these studies, two critical ideas still emerged: first, the basic belief that environmental conditions mattered to productivity; and second, when employees are watched, or someone is paying active attention to them, productivity improves.

This technocratic approach to management development, reward, organisational design, and recruitment reflected the stability of the times. The Western world was rebuilding anew. As the then leader of the UK Labour Party, and future prime minister, Harold Wilson, declared in 1963, "The Britain that is going to be forged in the white heat of this revolution will be no place for restrictive practices or outdated methods on either side of industry."[21]

Unfortunately, in the UK, the "outdated methods" turned out to be unhelpfully stubborn. While Japan, Germany, and the Scandinavian countries moved forwards, the UK and the US clung firmly to the past. The Germanic approach to the Process wave incorporated the collective focus of works council and worker co-determination needs as much as what needed to be achieved. The Anglo-Saxon version focused solely on the productivity (specifically falling productivity), with each side of course blaming a different cause – lack of investment for the trade unionists versus restrictive practices for the managers or owners.

HR 3.0 Process today

Although the heyday of the Process wave was between 1935 and 1985, it is still evident, healthy, and strong in most industrialised countries, including Germany and Scandinavia, although the Japanese bubble burst in 1992. Its enduring strength lies in a disciplined attention to the basics.

Deming's influence in this regard can still be seen in manufacturing around the world, where the focus is on:

- better design of products to improve service;
- higher level of uniform product quality;
- improvement of product testing in the workplace and in research centres; and
- greater sales through global markets.

Much of Deming's thinking became incorporated in the total quality management (TQM) movement. Essentially, TQM consists of the management of initiatives and procedures that are aimed at achieving the delivery of quality products and services. There are a number of key principles that define TQM, including:

- *TQM comes from the top*: The senior leadership of the business should act as the main driver for TQM and create an environment that ensures its success.
- *TQM is made possible by training*: Employees should receive regular training on the methods and concepts of quality.
- *TQM must focus on the customer*: Improvements in quality should improve customer satisfaction.
- *TQM should improve decision-making*: Quality decisions should be made based on results, feedback, data, and measurements.
- *TQM applies methodology and tools*: The use of appropriate methodology and tools ensures that non-conformance incidents are identified, measured, and responded to consistently.
- *TQM means continuous improvement*: Companies should continuously work towards improving manufacturing and quality procedures.
- *TQM should seep into the culture*: The culture of the company should aim at developing employees' ability to work together to improve quality.
- *TQM needs employee engagement*: Employees should be encouraged to be proactive in identifying and addressing quality-related problems.[22]

Following the Japanese success, TQM enjoyed widespread attention during the late 1980s and early 1990s alongside standards such as ISO 9000, lean manufacturing, and Six Sigma, all of which are still being used today. Processes, rules, standards, preferably international standards, and ways to do things "properly" are respected in this wave.

Most businesses today recognise the value of some form of systematic, objective analysis of work to identify and encourage best practice. Every business must go through the Process wave in order to build the stability of their operation and the efficiency of their production line before they can really step-change productivity and grow to scale. For example, most large retailers today have incredibly sophisticated process-based supply chain and logistics systems in place to deliver what the customer wants with minimal waste or costly storage time. Trading standards, national and international regulations, and tariffs are much more carefully constructed when organisations and countries reach the Process level of development. Corruption is easier to weed out because the process determines action and outcome rather than personal opinion or influence, which is the dominant driver in the Power wave.

Training people properly, recruiting people professionally, administering people well, attending to people's needs, and listening to people's views are all part and parcel of the Process wave.

The "human relations" ideas and the importance of environment moved management thinking beyond Taylorism and the focus on the task, to start to address the person doing the task and employee motivation. First, personnel departments sought to apply the best practices of the Paternalistic age through the provision of desirable employee facilities such as the works canteens and subsidised food – still present today in parts of the world. Such initiatives expanded over time to become the so-called "quality of working life" (QWL) initiatives. Academics identified the importance of "psychological growth needs" in the workplace. Job characteristics theory emerged to provide "a set of implementing principles for enriching jobs in organisational settings."[23]

What started as a network of like-minded academics in the 1970s, the QWL movement grew into an international initiative made up of trade unions, personnel managers, and social scientists. Training events and conferences proliferated as personnel managers sought to ensure employees' motivational needs could be addressed. The QWL philosophy sat well with the TQM approaches, organising employees into teams and empowering people to manage themselves. Beginning in the Process wave, teamworking as an aspiration became a widespread practice and is still a focus for many businesses today. Personnel managers are still at the forefront of devising change and training programmes accordingly.

This technocratic and respectful approach to workplace relations is still very evident in the working cultures in Japan, Germany, Switzerland, and Northern Europe in particular.

The Process wave is also responsible for the professionalisation of recruitment that we still see around the world. Graduate recruitment became a "thing" soon after the Second World War. Many multinationals ran selection boards, often supported by consultants such as the Tavistock Institute, a not-for-profit organisation set up in 1947 to apply social science to contemporary issues and problems. Using tests and methodologies originally designed to identify wartime army or air force officers, the selection boards now sought to identify future senior leaders for graduate schemes. The spatial awareness and intelligence test, used on selection boards in London as late as the mid-1980s, had originally been designed to test for potential RAF pilots in the Second World War. A whole suite of process-based profiling and testing methodologies are still employed in business.

The first Association of Executive Search Consultants was set up in 1960, having migrated from the US to Europe in the 1950s. Management development focused on training functional skills and ensuring training at key career transition times, such as when an employee was to be promoted to a supervisor. In 1954, Unilever purchased a site in Kingston upon Thames, Surrey, to set up its first corporate university. General Electric (GE) famously established its Crontonville training campus north of New York City two years later. Motorola and Deloitte also have their own university facilities. Training was systemised, with training manuals and curricula clearly identified. Some roles and functions, such as engineering and accountants, required external accreditation; others were based on internal company standards. Today, many multinational companies run such facilities, and they are often even called "universities." Many believe that corporate universities (CUs) could and should supplant traditional business education because in-house training and development is better suited than academia to deliver the targeted, strategy-focused programmes needed by executives.[24]

Process wave cultures are still very common within government departments, bureaucracies, and public-sector partnerships, where order, rank, and rules are imposed and adhered to. This is largely because the purpose of these organisations is to provide services or deliver benefit to a wider community rather than to make money for shareholders.

As business evolves, the smart companies transcend and include the best of the previous age, taking forward the best practices of the past and evolving a more agile way of operating into the future. Certainly, success in the modern world is virtually impossible without rigorous process, policy, and procedures that optimise and standardise successful operation. Without process, results are often too chaotic and unpredictable. A leader who constantly flies by the seat of their pants will eventually crash and burn.

Evolution from HR 3.0 to HR 4.0

In the Power wave, whoever had the most power won. The trouble with this, whether a forceful business leader or charismatic union leader, was that a single person or very small group of people made all the decisions, and those decisions were therefore at the mercy of the vagaries of human inconsistency, hubris, pride, ego, and bias. Decisions in the Power wave were not made as a result of analysis or adherence to a set of principles; they were largely driven by personal opinion, and likely to be wrong, at least some of the time. Decisions can also be made deliberately for the wrong reason to achieve personal gain. Needless to say, performance, productivity, quality of output, and efficiency were chaotic and inconsistent in the Power wave.

The Process wave changed all that and led to far greater consistency of output, and the benefits were significant. Pre-agreed rules and regulations about how a business would work created a more cooperative environment where both owners and employees worked more closely together for the good of the business. It was less about control and discipline, and more about the mutual following of rules – less dependent on individual whim or personal opinion. Many of these rules and regulations also standardised the best way of working at that time, which led to greater efficiency and higher-quality production and output.

However, its contradictions became evident too. Change is often slow due to extended consultation timelines to ensure due process. Creativity was often choked off. The control and disciple moved from the people doing the task to the process of that task. Yet too much process discipline, with its corresponding bureaucratic demands, can put the brakes on entrepreneurial progress. Some commentators believe this is why Europe has not developed a tech giant such as Google, Apple, or Facebook.[25] Too much process inhibited the type of liberated entrepreneurship seen in the US.

Each wave tends to go too far, and the Process wave was no exception. Issues of demarcation, where roles were tightly defined and a worker's role was given strict boundaries, created inflexibility in production or delivery. A form of industrial action known as "work to rule," where workers could cause major disruption by sticking to the rules, summed up the contradictions. In other words, workers would refuse to flex to what was needed to get the job done, instead uttering the famously infuriating words, "It's not my job." There is even a term for these types of workers (still evident in modern business) – "jobsworths" – people who delight in using their process-based job description to be deliberately uncooperative, obstructive, and unhelpful.

Unhealthy dominator hierarchies emerged as the 1970s ended and the 1980s began. These arose in pockets where bullies from the Power wave had managed to enshrine their power base, demanding obedience and imposing a set of rules in the Process wave that maintained absolute loyalty, normally from a weak executive around them. Most executives have experienced dominator hierarchies at some point, and such experiences sowed the seeds in many for a general dislike of hierarchies, which will erupt later in HR 5.0 People. But for most, the Process wave's inflexibility and the constraint of too many rules was now preventing progress. A need for greater individual freedom and self-determination emerged, leading to a more sensible view on rules and regulations. The view is that rules have their place, but they are no longer the be-all and end-all. There is a recognition that a more objective assessment of their merit delivers better outcomes. As a result, the pragmatic and competitive Profit wave emerges.

Ironically, the leap forward into HR 4.0 Profit emerged most powerfully in the countries that had never really fully embraced the Process era anyway, and had therefore never fully experienced the extent of its considerable benefit. Many American and British businesses moved into the age of Profit and reignited individualism and embraced entrepreneurialism. Many of these leaders swaggered with a new confidence, pointing to books such as *First Break All the Rules*[26] as validity of their anti-Process "manifesto." And with it, the horrible term "human resources management" arrived.

Notes

1 Freeman JB (2018) *Behemoth: A History of the Factory and the Making of the Modern World*, W.W. Norton & Company, New York.
2 Taylor FW (1911) *The Principles of Scientific Management*, Harper & Brothers, New York.
3 Kearns Goodwin D (2018) *Leadership in Turbulent Times*, Simon & Schuster, New York.
4 Macmillan H (1957) *Prime Minister's Speech at the Convervative Party Conference*, Bedford.
5 Information on the John Lewis Partnership from their corporate website, www. johnlewispartnership.co.uk/about/our-founder.html
6 Chandler A (1962) *Strategy and Structure: Chapters in the History of the American Industrial Enterprise*, MIT Press, Cambridge, MA.
7 Mintzberg H (1973) *The Nature of Managerial Work*, Harper & Row, New York.
8 Mintzberg H (1979) *The Structuring of Organizations*, Pearson, New York.
9 Sloan AP (1964) *My Years with General Motors*, Doubleday, New York.
10 Drucker PF (1946) *Concept of the Corporation*, John Day Company, New York.
11 Drucker PF (1946) *Concept of the Corporation*, John Day Company, New York.
12 Kay J (2019) The Concept of the Corporation, www.johnkay.com/2019/01/21/the-concept-of-the-corporation-2/
13 Deming WE (1950) *Statistical Product Quality Administration*, Tokyo.
14 Thatcher M (1995) *The Downing Street Years*, Harper, London.
15 Collins R (2017) Red Robbo: The Man behind 523 Car Factory Strikes, *BBC News*, www.bbc.co.uk/news/uk-england-birmingham-41834559
16 Mintzberg H (1979) *The Structuring of Organizations*, Pearson, New York.
17 Jaques E (1989) *Requisite Organization: A Total System for Effective Managerial Organization and Managerial Leadership for the Twenty-First Century*, Cason Hall & Co., Arlington, VA.
18 Drucker PF (1955) *The Practice of Management*, Butterworth-Heinemann, London.
19 Hampden-Turner C and Trompenaars F (2015) *Nine Versons of Capitalism*, Infinite Ideas, Oxford.
20 Levitt SD and List JA (2011) Was There Really a Hawthorne Effect at the Hawthorne Plant? An Analysis of the Original Illumination Experiments, *American Economic Journal: Applied Economics*, 3(1): 224–238.
21 Wilson H (1963) *Labour Party Conference*, Scarborough.
22 Murray M (2017) Total Quality Management (TQM) and Quality Improvement, www.thebalancesmb.com/total-quality-management-tqm-2221200
23 Hackman JR and Oldham GR (2005) How Job Characteristics Theory Happened. In: Smith KG and Hitt MA (Eds), *The Oxford Handbook of Management Theory: The Process of Theory Development*, Oxford University Press, Oxford, pp. 151–170.

24 Kessler B (2017) The Future of the Corporate University Insead, https://know
    ledge.insead.edu/leadership-organisations/the-future-of-the-corporate-university-
    5121
25 The Economist (2018) Europe's History Explains Why It Will Never Produce
    a Google, www.economist.com/europe/2018/10/13/europes-history-explains-
    why-it-will-never-produce-a-google
26 Buckingham M and Coffman C (2000) *First Break All the Rules: What the World's
    Greatest Managers Do Differently*, Simon & Schuster, New York.

4 HR 4.0

The Profit wave (1980–2010)

HR management is the economic love child of Margaret Thatcher and Ronald Reagan.

In the UK, the "Winter of Discontent" (1978–1979) saw widespread strikes by public-sector workers demanding higher pay and came to represent the end of the Process wave. The Labour government led by James Callaghan had sought to impose pay restraint as part of the government's wages and income policy to try to curb escalating inflation, which peaked at 24.2 per cent (1975).[1] In line with prevailing practices over the previous 30 years, they sought to apply rules to regulate the economy. But by the late 1970s, people had stopped believing that these "rules" worked. Stagflation (high unemployment *and* high inflation) had invalidated the economic models of the Keynesian era. Up until this point, the relationship between employment and inflation had been explained by economist William Phillips, and the "Phillips curve" suggested there was an inverse relationship between rates of unemployment and wage rises. In other words, with economic growth comes inflation, which in turn should lead to more jobs and less unemployment. But the stagflation of the 1970s proved the theory wrong, or at least incomplete. High inflation should have meant lower unemployment, but the opposite was true.

The UK trade unions broke ranks and demanded their right to "free collective bargaining" – to no longer be restrained by the rules and by the old processes. Ironic, considering this breaking of the rules and their subsequent demands meant they ended up suffering much more significantly under Margaret Thatcher.

Although the strikes were largely over by February 1979, following the coldest winter for 16 years, the stage was set for a change in government, and Margaret Thatcher came to power with promises of trade union reform, free markets, and a focus on the individual over the collective.

In the US, at the same time, Jimmy Carter had warned the American people, "We simply must balance our need for energy with our rapidly shrinking resources."[2] Carter suggested that sustainability, not rampant consumerism, was the key to long-term prosperity, but his message fell on deaf ears. The electorate's answer was to choose the Hollywood version of the truth as they made actor-turned-politician Ronald Reagan the 40th US president. Reagan too rolled back employee protections to allow business more freedom.

The first glimmers of Profit

Clearly, making money has been a central tenet of business since the beginning of time, but there were always other considerations influencing action. It was only once productivity slowed and profit dipped, blamed largely on excessive process, that a more determined focus on profit – and profit alone – emerged.

In the UK and the US, businesses found they could not compete with Japanese success and efficiency. Japan didn't have industrial disputes; they had W. Edwards Deming. In the space of a decade (1950–1960), Japan emerged from the devastation of war to become the second largest economy in the world through the application of process management techniques, influenced by Deming.

Japan flourished. In the late 1970s and early 1980s, the developed countries of North America and Western Europe (with the possible exception of West Germany) lagged behind. They simply couldn't compete with Japan's ability to produce high-quality goods at competitive prices.

In response, governments began to open markets, reduce regulation, and roll back employment protections. Wages and incomes policies were ditched in favour of floating exchange rates, control of the money supply, and a reduced role for government. The thinking of Milton Friedman replaced that of John Maynard Keynes.

Milton Friedman wrote his most famous article about business in 1970 – a good decade before HR 4.0 really took off, but it firmly planted the seeds for the Profit motive. His article "The Social Responsibility of Business Is to Increase Its Profits," which appeared in the New York Times, changed the very nature of business.[3] At the time, Friedman was the leader of the Chicago School of Economics; he would later win a Nobel Prize in Economics and was described by The Economist as "the most influential economist of the second half of the twentieth century ... possibly of all of it."[4] When such a luminary stated that the sole purpose of business was to make money for its shareholders, the business community took note. Friedman suggested any business executives who pursued a goal other than making money were, in his words, "unwitting puppets of the intellectual forces that have been undermining the basis of a free society these past decades." They were guilty of "analytical looseness and lack of rigor." They had even turned themselves into "unelected government officials" who were illegally taxing employers and customers.[5] Bold stuff, especially when viewed in the context of the previous era, when business believed it was being held back by bureaucracy and strong unions.

It was, however, finance professor Michael Jensen and dean William Meckling of the Simon School of Business at the University of Rochester who watered Friedman's seed and germinated an idea that is now so deeply intrenched in modern corporate culture that many struggle to imagine a different way. In 1976, Jensen and Meckling published a paper that effectively provided the action plan for Friedman's original ideas, and in so doing began the seismic corporate shift towards shareholder value maximisation that would sweep into business and facilitate the emergence of HR 4.0.[6]

What they did was identify a problem in business – the "principal–agent problem." Although they offered no real-world evidence that the problem even existed, they suggested that the shareholders (principals) were often disadvantaged by the firm's senior executives (agents) because they would naturally look after their own interests rather than the shareholders. For example, a senior executive might decide to travel first class to international business meetings, therefore creating an "agency cost" that would diminish shareholder returns. But the solution was easy – make the agents principles and you give senior executives a compelling reason to align with and maximise shareholder value. If the senior executives running the business are also shareholders, then the same previously feared self-interest would now operate for the benefit of all the shareholders!

Their paper became the single most frequently cited article in business academia and proved to be a watershed moment in business history. It provided senior executives and shareholders with a way to turn Friedman's earlier vision of what business should be all about into a commercial reality. In the 1970s, stock-based compensation packages accounted for less than 1 per cent of CEO remuneration. By the time HR 4.0 emerged on the scene (1985 onwards), executive compensation became increasingly stock-based.

As profit rose to the top of the corporate priority list, a number of very high-profile "downsizing" operations followed. Such interventions would never have been possible prior to the reboot of labour laws and workers' rights in North America and the UK.

Al "Chainsaw" Dunlap first rose to prominence in this Profit wave. Notorious for applying a myopic obsession with his companies' financials at the expense of absolutely everything else, Dunlap engineered a corporate restructure at Scott Paper that put 35 per cent of the workforce (11,000 people) out of a job. The share price simultaneously rose 225 per cent.[7] But this was only the start.

Workers may have suffered with massive layoffs and wage stagnation but shareholders were ecstatic. As a result, the business leaders who orchestrated these returns were treated like rock stars. Everyone wanted to listen to the emerging phenomena of the "celebrity CEO," people such as Jack Welch of GE or Lee Iacocca of Chrysler. It was a speech by Jack Welch at the Pierre Hotel in New York in 1981 that was said to have really kick-started the Profit wave.[8] With an often ruthless focus on profit, these leaders became superstars to shareholders, and everyone in business wanted to know their secrets. The celebrity CEOs obliged, and the era of the "business book" began. A spate of books extolling *their* way flooded the market, such as *Mean Business* by Al Dunlap and *Winning* by Jack Welch.[9] However, while providing an interesting insight into how large successful companies operated, these books were not describing *the* way to do business; they were describing *a* way. They epitomised and further mythologised the apparent merit of the "tough guy businessman."

The business guru also emerged during the Profit era – people such as Tom Peters and Robert Waterman, who wrote *In Search of Excellence.*[10] Sir John Harvey-Jones was another – working his way up ICI from junior training manager to chairman. Over the course of only 30 months in the top job, Jones cut the UK workforce by one-third, doubled the share price, and turned a loss into a £1 billion profit. The legend grew still further when he became the frontman in the BBC's *Troubleshooter* series, first broadcast in 1990, where Jones would travel around the UK solving company problems. While his influence did put the importance of business mentoring on the map, one of the most popular tools in the business turn-around toolkit was layoffs. It may be effective in improving profits but it's hardly groundbreaking! Of course a business is going to look in better shape if you remove a sizeable chunk of one of the biggest costs – people. The series, however, made Sir John Harvey-Jones a household name. Successful businessmen became more trusted in the eyes of the public than their elected politicians.

HR 4.0 marked a shift to the more individualistic approach to people management that gave us the concept of "human resources management," and this remains the predominant model for people management practice in the private sector and much of the Western world.

Today's "human resources" practitioners, whether they know it or not, are unconscious followers of the neoliberal economic world view that sits at its centre.

Neoliberalism has been defined as "the priority of the price mechanism, free enterprise, the system of competition, and a strong and impartial state."[11] Starting in the early 1980s in the UK and the US, it soon swept across the world to become the primary driver of open markets and globalisation.

And people management practices responded accordingly.

Profit-based leadership

The Profit-based leader shifts the focus back on the individual. Usually, they have experienced the autocratic bullying of the Power leader and realised its failings, but they have also witnessed the delays and ponderous productivity that comes from the failure of Process-based leadership. The Profit leader is the ideal person to lead businesses where the sole or primary emphasis is delivering shareholder value because they have the same values and view the world from the Profit-based narrative. They are also much more pragmatic and individualistic than Process leaders because they recognise that rules are useful but sometimes they need to be bent to achieve a better outcome.

The Profit leader learns by experimentation and is focused on delivering short-term performance to drive greater individual and corporate wealth.

They take a no-nonsense view of the world and are happy to do whatever it takes to achieve targets they set for themselves and the business. There is little sentiment in business for the Profit leader. The statement "It's not personal, it's just business" was almost certainly first uttered by a Profit leader. They see no grey area when it comes to making money. Everything is fair game. They are motivated by success and their ultimate goal is money – for the business and for them personally. The size of their bank balance is often the way they keep score. Profit leaders are driven to "make it work" and "figure it out." Although they may adapt based on feedback, they are ultimately focused on achieving targets and winning at any cost.

The distinction between the Profit leader and the last individually focused P-wave, the Power leader, is the ability to objectify and rationalise their own and other people's behaviour. At this level of development, the ability to really think about what they are doing in business comes online for the first time. There may be some rules and processes, and in all good business there should be, but the Profit leader is assessing whether those rules are delivering the desired result or not. If they are not, then there is analysis to investigate why not and genuine problem-solving kicks in for the first time, rather than just following a set of rules. They are prepared to "think the unthinkable,"[12] break the mould, or think "outside the box," all in pursuit of their goals. Such an attitude is widespread today, with various authors still advocating such a stance as a response to the plethora of wicked problem we are now facing. However, they offer no real solutions or genuine answers because they have little understanding that their "unthinkable thoughts" are largely just more Profit-based thoughts, only more extreme and less palatable ones than those that have already failed. They are wolves in sheep's clothing – HR 4.0 Profit manoeuvres dressed up as more inclusive, expansive HR 5.0 People manoeuvres (see Chapter 5).

The big driver of the shift from Process to Profit is self-interest. Profit-based leaders don't want to be told what to do by a set of outdated rules that are, in their mind, holding the business back. Profit restores self-interest at the heart of business, and although this may initially sound profoundly negative and potentially toxic, we would never have witnessed the economic booms of the 1980s and 1990s without the self-interest that was triggered by the policies of Thatcher in the UK and Reagan in the US. In parts of Europe, especially France, that boom never really happened, and as a result many businesses in France are still stuck in the Process wave.

Wealth worked as an operating model because it celebrated individual success and personal gain – traits particularly familiar to men, who make up the vast majority of leaders in global business. The Profit leader is able to rationalise anything because they can objectify what needs to happen and frame it in a way that makes financial sense. Profit leaders are constantly looking at the system to see how it can be improved, modified, or beaten, seeking to always stay one step ahead of a Process-based backlash and outsmart those seeking to rein them in. This ability to adapt in order to win and be successful can be an exceptionally positive trait, but taken too far it can also manifest as manipulation. Often their actions create huge unintended consequences – economic, political, and environmental – and we are still wrestling with many of them today.

When each P-wave starts to fail, the tendency is to ramp up whatever worked in that wave – in this case, the single-minded pursuit of profit. Such a response is still very common today. The basic assumption is often that business is a zero-sum game. Thus, for the Profit leader to win, someone else *must* lose. In fact, with the Profit leader, they may not believe they have won unless someone else loses.

But this approach now means that far too many people are losing, not to mention the other species that inhabit the world and the devastation such a mindset is having on the planet we live on. This consumptive, consumerist, self-serving approach has been the pathology that has accelerated the development of the People wave, with its suggested antidotes to the escalating inequality.

The failure of each P-wave is, however, a staged "foxtrot" phenomenon. The next "solution" is to deliberately reach back into history to break the deadlock – in this case, the desire for the "good old days" that more rules or a Process leader should facilitate. Even if additional rules are put in place, such as the Dodd–Frank Wall Street Reform and Consumer Protection Act signed into law by Obama in 2010 to prevent another financial crisis, or the efforts of the Financial Conduct Authority (FCA) and Banking Standards Board (BSB) in the UK, the Profit- or Power-focused lobby usually manage to roll them back or outmanoeuvre them. In 2018, this is exactly what happened when Trump signed into law a rollback of the Dodd–Frank legislation, potentially paving the way for another financial crash.

Teams at HR 4.0: independent and interdependent achievers

Most executive teams, even today, have yet to develop beyond the capability that first emerges in HR 3.0. In HR 3.0, teams use process to go beyond the norming and storming of HR 2.0 to become dependent experts. Their development stops at HR 3.0 for the simple reason that the team can now perform reasonably well and deliver results. But as we said in the previous chapter, delivery at HR 3.0 is dependent on the team leader for direction, adjudication when an impasse occurs, for the resolution of conflict, and for chairmanship of meetings. If the team complies with the "team rules" or the "law" laid down by the leader, results are delivered and the disagreements common in HR 2.0 become a thing of the past. Thus, HR 3.0 teams move from the norm/storm to the perform level of development.

But in HR 4.0, a team can move beyond effective functional performance, based on individual expertise, to achieve more with less (i.e. better outcomes with less time, less effort, and therefore less money spent). Few teams make this transition because in the early stages of the transition there is increased entropy, which is misinterpreted as regression. When the transition conflict arises, an immature leader often steps in to diffuse the tension rather than realising that this is an important developmental step and should be encouraged. What is actually happening is the team is starting to realise that process, team rules, or even compliance with the wishes of the leader is holding the team back.

At HR 4.0, individuals have to see themselves more as a leader of the company rather than as a silo expert. This means there needs to be a profound shift in the way they show up in the team. They must let go of their expertise, and stop thinking about "my role in this team" and start thinking about "this team's role in the business." Individual success is now about the team's ability to deliver their objectives.

HR 4.0 leaders can make this transition because they have developed the ability, as we discussed earlier, to objectify their own role and contribution. They can see, for the first time, the constraints of their own expertise. For example, if they conceive of themselves as purely an accountant (technical constraint) or a CFO (role constraint), this could prevent them from making the transition from manager to leader and reduce the possibility that they could one day become the CEO.

Team members start to connect much more effectively with each other and openly share their thoughts and feelings. They are less concerned about their differences, given the greater focus on team outcome. They reflect on the performance of the *whole* team, rather than focusing on their individual accountabilities. In fact, team members start to take a more constructive interest in areas beyond their own authority as they start to understand the interdependencies in the business.

HR 4.0 teams are also less dependent on their leader's authority for direction and start to push the leader out of the day-to-day operations so the leader can work at the level above. This move enables the team to self-organise to a much higher degree. This self-organising doesn't need the "permission" or sanction of the leader. At team meetings, the leader speaks much less, as the team's performance is much less dependent on the leader as it is in earlier P-waves.

This positive independence empowers the individuals in the team and the team itself. As the energy picks up and the team starts to achieve, individuals learn that working together is the route to success, so they start to look for further interdependencies as a route to achieving even more. Thus, the team moves from dependence (HR 3.0) to independence and interdependence (HR 4.0) in order to make things happen.

There is also a fundamental shift in how HR 4.0 teams see problems. Since they start to achieve more, they take a more constructive and pragmatic view of the problems they face. They realise that the resolution of a problem enables them to iron out any issues within the business and set the stage for even greater achievement. This sounds like a minor point, but within a team it can be transformational because it means issues are no longer hidden. Rather, they are brought openly to the table so they can be resolved, and they become a way of delivering even more. The second shift that occurs in the way that an HR 4.0 team handles issues is that problems cease to be "your problem" or "my problem." Rather, they are seen as "our problem," which "we" need to resolve in order to deliver our results.

Emerging HR and people practices

In addition to the step change that occurs in team performance, HR 4.0 heralded a change in employment relationships, with employees being viewed as individuals bringing unique strengths and weaknesses. In earlier waves, there were examples where management was not allowed to speak to employees without a trade union rep being present. No account could be taken of individual contribution – everyone in a specific role was paid the same, whether they were good in that role or not. Reducing differentials often saw routine roles being paid over "market rates" and more skilled roles being underpaid. In larger organisations, different unions represented different groups depending on their role or skill – including, ironically, management. Demarcation disputes were still common. The conventional wisdom in people management spheres echoed the political trend that in HR 3.0 Process, collectivism was holding people and business back.

The rolling back of trade union rights in Anglo-American business communities created a significant shift in the balance of power within business and a profound change in the focus of people management practitioners.

For some organisations trying to make the transition from HR 3.0 to HR 4.0, there was a return to the old-style Power relationship of HR 2.0. During chaos and change, there will always be those that regress to an earlier level rather than evolve to a new, better-operating model. In this case, with trade union and employee rights weakened, some employers saw this as an opportunity to exact revenge on decades of trade union power and reassert a fully unitary approach to their management of people. In the US, the first sign of this regression was the 1981 air traffic control dispute. In the UK, this regression was most famously seen during the coal miners' strike of 1984/85, which was then translated into the private sector by the Wapping print dispute of 1986.

On 3 August 1981, the Professional Air Traffic Controllers Organization (PATCO) declared a strike, seeking better working conditions, better pay, and a 32-hour workweek (four days at eight hours a day). By striking, PATCO violated US law, which prohibits strikes by federal government employees. Despite having supported PATCO's effort in his 1980 presidential campaign, Ronald Reagan declared the strike a "peril to national safety" and ordered them back to work. On 5 August, Reagan fired the 11,345 striking air traffic controllers who ignored the order and banned them from federal service for life. Considering it took three years to train an air traffic controller, it took almost a decade before overall staffing levels returned to normal, but Reagan dealt a game-changing blow to trade union power in the US.[13]

Six years later in the UK, Rupert Murdoch, owner of News International, was planning to move his newspaper production from Fleet Street to a new plant at Wapping. He sought a number of union assurances that were felt necessary to keep the new plant running successfully. However, they included a no-strike clause, flexible working, and the adoption of new technologies that would almost certainly have resulted in heavy job losses. Workers were angry, and representatives from two of the main unions at the time called a strike for 24 January 1986. Almost immediately, Murdoch fired everyone who walked out. In what many regarded as a pre-planned move, members of another union known for crossing picket lines were drafted in to keep the presses running. In addition, it quickly became clear that the government was on Murdoch's side. The Thatcher government had already been rolling back trade union power, and the police and Special Branch were involved. Every move on behalf of the striking workers and the unions was countered by Murdoch. Not a single day's newspaper production was disrupted.

Over a year after the strike began, walking the picket line surviving on minimal strike pay, the sacked print workers became desperate. Union funds were exhausted, and with little practical help from other unions, as well as active union participation on behalf of Murdoch running the plant and ensuring newspaper distribution, the strike came to an end. On 5 February 1987, the printers accepted a weak redundancy package and the power of the print unions was broken forever. Production was fully moved to the Wapping plant, and the new technology allowed print to be composed electronically and to be submitted directly by journalists. As suspected, the implementation of these changes led to thousands of additional forced redundancies in the printing industry. By now, the Conservative Party's anti-union legislation was making its mark on organised labour, and the Wapping dispute was one of the last major strikes of the 1980s, coming less than a year after the failure of the miners' strike. It is still widely considered that Margaret Thatcher broke the trade union movement in the UK.[14]

These changes not only shifted the balance of power on the shop floor; they also shifted the focus of HR. Newly named "human resources managers" (HRMs) became much more strategic. Their time was no longer taken up dealing with disputes; they could now focus on leadership development, strategic reward, and earning a place at the board table as all-round business leaders.

Under HR 3.0, all senior personnel leaders had earned their spurs in industrial relations. Under HR 4.0, industrial relations were considered passé.

Fundamentally, HRMs provided the intellectual frame for a shift of people management practice from the collective procedural focus of HR 3.0 to the more individual-centric approaches of HR 4.0, a move that also shifted the language from collective employee relations or personnel to HR business partner (HRBP).

Michael Armstrong had started this shift in mindset in the UK with his book *Human Resources Management*, but US author David Ulrich was the first to position HR as more than just a cost centre or the place someone went when they had a grievance.[15] He divided the functions of HR, and suggested that with the right mindset and practices, HR could and should have a seat at the board table because the function was instrumental in long-term business success and prosperity.

Ulrich, a professor of business at the Ross School of Business at the University of Michigan and co-founder of the RBL Group together with his colleagues, has written over 30 books that have shaped the HR profession, defined organisations as capabilities, and shown the impact of leadership on customers and investors. He is often referred to as the "father of HR," a moniker he acquired following the publication of his landmark text *HR Champions* in 1997.[16]

Ulrich's model swept away all before it. While the societal and business changes were predominantly Anglo-American trends of the developed world, the move towards adopting the Ulrich model of HR became truly global.

Large HR functions began to organise differently.

The personnel managers of HR 3.0 were generalists. They looked after all HR admin, grievances, disciplinary issues, and reward, managed absence, and oversaw training and development. In some areas, specialist roles existed, perhaps in leadership development or reward, but these were a minority activity.

Ulrich's HR model changed HR almost overnight (see Figure 4.1).

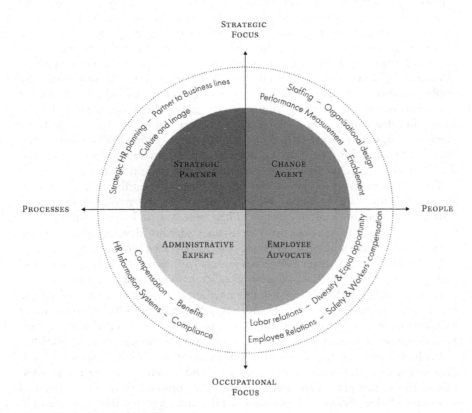

Figure 4.1 David Ulrich's HR model

HR Champions became the HR Bible, the zeitgeist of its time, because it changed the way people inside HR thought about themselves and it changed the way other people in the organisation viewed HR. Ulrich proposed that the HR function should be broken down into four clearly defined areas:

1. *Strategic partner:* Sits at the managerial table and contributes to the organisation's strategy and alignment of HR strategy. Communicates efficiently with line management. Understands the business environment and drives key business processes and activities.
2. *Change agent:* Supports, facilitates, and initiates change, acts as a stabilising force for employees in times of change.
3. *Employee advocate:* Acts to protect the interests and well-being of the employees and ensure they have a voice.
4. *Administrative expert:* Ensures policies and procedures are up to date, are legally compliant, and have the ability to deliver innovative HR practices in HR recruitment, employee development, and communication.

After Ulrich, the HR function specialised. HR business partners were the strategists focusing on business and individual development and performance. Roles often combined the HRBP and change agent descriptions championed by Ulrich.

Shared service organisations were set up to manage all admin and transactions. Shared services were often outsourced, opening up whole new business streams for major consultancy companies.

Interestingly, or perhaps ironically, the role of employee advocate, outlined by Ulrich, got largely forgotten!

HR 4.0 Profit today

Ulrich's contribution was profound. It changed the way the HR function worked and saw itself. The extent of the change Ulrich's ideas facilitated can be seen by looking at each of the HR practices in turn, and these interventions are still alive and well in most modern business.

HR practice really started to flourish at HR 4.0 Profit because the work of HR was objectified and scientifically deconstructed for the first time.

This is a key characteristic of HR 4.0 – the ability to objectify – and it is why it wasn't possible before this P-wave to pinpoint the various roles or areas of focus for HR. This P-wave is the first time we are able to break HR down into component parts such as "reward," "pay determination," "appraisal and performance management," etc. This more objective, pragmatic world view resulted in a more mechanistic approach to the various dimensions of HR.

As with earlier waves, these HR practices and interventions were, however, orchestrated and executed in pursuit of the dominant business world view at the time – in this case, Profit.

Reward

The job evaluation of HR 3.0 Process was increasingly seen as a symptom of demarcation and inflexibility. It was also too easy to "game" by employees in the early stages of the Profit wave. Increasingly, staff saw their job grade as a way of managing their career and securing a reward based on the grade they could negotiate or prove, rather than their real value to the company. Job evaluation therefore gave way to "paying for performance," not for just turning up and going through the motions, safe in the knowledge that a specific role paid a specific rate.

Pay became more linked to people's individual performance, and for senior leaders this became increasingly aligned with business performance and shareholder value. In the world of HR 4.0 Profit, people should be paid based on their effort, attitude, and value added, not just for their hours worked and skills.

In factories, this led to attempts to "appraise" factory workers and pay small bonuses based on the outcome. Painted as a developmental intervention, in many cases it was often about control and seeking to break down the collective norms in a factory. Factory productivity schemes were removed and replaced with more individualised bonuses.

Managers and senior leaders enjoyed a shift away from fixed pay to variable pay. More reward went into annual bonuses and share options or performance shares, where managers gained directly from increases in share price.

Final pension salary arrangements, common in Europe, began to be replaced by less lucrative and secure direct contribution schemes. This was often enabled by changes in legislation. The "portable pension" then enabled businesses to lower their future liabilities and increase shareholder value. Reward became more short-term and contingent on performance in the Profit wave. Of course, this reward mechanism went hand in hand with the quarter-by-quarter obsession with results and share price, because it amplified the "make your money and get out" modus operandi that emerged at this time in the C-suite. Thus, the loyalty that was often present in HR 3.0 was completely eroded. The new Darwinism of "every man or woman for themselves" was the new norm.

Pay determination

Pay determination also began to localise at HR 4.0. The era of "going rate" and national settlement died. Pay became contingent on local firm or even unit performance. The very notion of nationally determined rates for various job families became anathema.

In the UK and the US in particular, the role of trade unions began to decline. Led by the Electrical, Electronic, Telecommunications and Plumbing Union (EETPU), the notion of the "no-strike agreement" was born as the individual approach to industrial relations returned. Single-union agreements emerged; there were even experiments with something called "pendulum arbitration," whereby strikes became completely impossible. Pendulum arbitration is when each party puts their case to the arbitrator that outlines the furthest they are prepared to go to meet the other side. The arbitrator then considers each proposal and accepts the one considered most reasonable, which is then accepted – there is no negotiation or "splitting the difference."

The field of training and development also changed. Whereas the focus for most in HR 3.0 was on hard skills training, with apprenticeships and a trade being learned, under HR 4.0 we saw the first appearance of the concept of "competencies."

Although papers were written on the difference between competencies and competency, causing some confusion, the essence of the change lay in new attempts to measure employees' attitudes. Psychometrics became popular. Companies such as Saville & Holdsworth caught the zeitgeist as they provided organisations with psychometric assessments of their employees. Much gold was spent seeking to identify the "profile" of the ideal employee or leader, and then use this to recruit more of those types of people, and then appraise them against the profile.

This "descriptive" approach has become the dominant philosophy in leadership assessment. The assessment industry now largely relies on three basic types of description. The most common is typology. In this family, the Myers–Briggs Type Indicator (MBTI) is far and away the favourite, with well over 2 million tests done globally each year.[17] This is despite the fact that there is very little evidence that the MBTI can predict performance or is even valid.[18] If you have not been put into one of the 16 MBTI boxes, you may have been categorised as a certain type of team player by Belbin's team roles. If the assessment industry hasn't categorised your type, then they may have described your allegedly unique gifts with a "strengths finder." These instruments involve an almost random selection of "leadership strengths" that are claimed to be commercially important. Knowing such information is meant to make you a better leader, but again there is little evidence to support such an assertion.

If you haven't been caught in the typology or strengths net, then you will almost certainly have encountered personality profiling. These tests, such as the Hogan Assessment, are probably the most robust of all these descriptive assessments. They quantify where you are on the "big five" personality traits. In fairness, such descriptions can create curiosity and perhaps even some self-awareness, but they can't predict performance or success. There isn't one type of leader that always succeeds, there isn't one set of strengths that deliver results, and there is definitely not one specific personality that always wins. If anything, the entire leadership literature says the exact opposite. There is no "cookie-cutter" recipe for successful leadership, which is why, in recent years, the leadership literature has become obsessed with authenticity and its exhortation to just "be yourself."

It is ironic that companies spend so much money on descriptive assessments when such instruments can't identify how to improve performance.

Fortunately, a new methodology has emerged to solve this problem, and some of the more enlightened organisations and search firms have started to turn to "developmental" rather than "descriptive" assessments to enable talent breakthroughs. Developmental assessments identify an individual's level of sophistication or capability rather than just describing a set of features. One of the additional benefits of such an approach is that developmental assessments will automatically identify the next stage in a leader's developmental journey.

However, in the early days of talent assessment, the "good employee" was identified not as the person with initiative and creativity, but as the employee who did what the supervisor told them.

At a management level, the descriptive obsession resulted in every job being defined by a set of skills or competencies, and this competency approach even extended to management itself. These descriptions changed with each layer of seniority, but they still largely focused on observable technical skills or behaviours rather than a leader's inner abilities or interpersonal capabilities. Such skills, competencies, and behaviours then became the foundation for all annual appraisal and were often integrated with pay arrangements.

Appraisal and performance management

In HR 4.0, appraisal and performance management schemes often adopted a ranking scale. The annual appraisal discussion, so brilliantly lampooned by Ricky Gervais in the UK (and later US) sitcom *The Office*, became an institution.

Profit-based businesses still utilise some form of GE's "rank and yank" approach. Individual performance is ranked, and the bottom 10 per cent of performers are "yanked," or asked to leave the business, every year, while the top 10 per cent are paid additional bonuses – paid for by the removal of the bottom 10 per cent. Ranking systems lend themselves perfectly to payment for performance. However, such a brutal and simplistic approach to performance completely ignores the possibility that an individual's performance is sometimes dependent on the performance of the people around them or external macroeconomic conditions. But the ranking of performance within the annual appraisal emphasises the individualistic philosophy of HR 4.0.

Organisational theory

With the increased ability to objectify all dimensions of business, including business models, organisational theory began to develop in HR 4.0. The primary metaphor at this level of development is the notion of an organisation as a machine. The machine metaphor is now well established in the Profit wave. An effective machine is made up of many parts that can function independently. Each organisational division or function can therefore be managed similarly as an almost autonomous unit. To make such machinery work, the management of each unit is often delegated to power-broker in a throwback to HR 2.0. Such "command-and-control" managerial pyramids are often supported by a set of rules that have been developed in HR 3.0 to enable each manager to control their five to eight "direct reports." Any problems that are created with the machinery of business, known in commercial parlance as "trade-offs," are managed by the "committees" that proved successful at HR 3.0. The new idea that emerged at HR 4.0 was to re-engineer the bureaucracy of HR 3.0 and the autocracy of HR 2.0 by adopting the "manifesto for business revolution" outlined by Michael Hammer and James Champy in their seminal book.[19] Companies in the Profit wave organise around "end-to-end processes" – in other words, all the work that should be done to achieve the process goal and remove functional inefficiencies. Cross-functional teams also came into vogue.

Business also turns its attention to the customer in this wave. Customer service training using the new medium of video became big business in the early 1980s. Video Arts, founded by John Cleese, Sir Antony Jay, and a group of other television professionals, was the big name in this type of training, offering humorous and engaging soft skills training programmes to corporates. Hugely successful, Video Arts later expanded into e-learning courses and learning platforms, although they still use big-name comedians and actors to get the message across in a unique way. These initiatives, often coupled with various TQM programmes, gave birth to "matrix organisations," which began to replace functional or divisional structures. The Swiss-based company ABB was held up as the best practice in advanced organisational thinking, having apparently cracked the organisational "holy grail" of achieving both scale and responsiveness.

Matrix organisations promised an alternative organisational structure that facilitated greater horizontal flow of skills and information between departments. Most companies were functionally organised up to the early 1950s. However, the post-war boom led to burgeoning product lines and corporate complexity that struggled under the functional focus. Companies sought to regain control with product line rationality and a shift to the divisional focus seen in the late 1950s and 1960s. Broadly successful, the divisional structure was more coherent and meant that divisional managers could be held accountable for their operations. By the mid-1960s, longer-range, more elaborate capital investment projects called for partial recentralisation of decision-making, which meant that neither function nor division was responsible for performance. By the 1970s, divisional autonomy was put under additional pressure by requirements imposed by foreign governments regarding product specs.[20]

The matrix organisation was seen as the solution. Employees from different functional disciplines were assigned to various project teams for the purpose of delivering an objective without leaving their respective positions. In theory, the matrix organisation would combine functional autonomy with product autonomy to increase efficiency and output. High-profile success stories, such as the Polaris missile programme and NASA's moon-shot project, that employed this type of system probably inspired its continued embrace into business. Project teams sought to secure a coordinated functional, geographic, and divisional response to various current threats. However, the horizontal and vertical reporting necessary in a matrix organisation became hopelessly bogged down in practice. Bureaucracy exploded and corporate performance deteriorated.[21]

The Profit wave is all about productivity – how to increase productivity and get better results. And this means what the business does, as well as how they accomplished their objectives. For example, business frequently talked of "focus" or "sticking to your knitting" – in other words, sticking to what the business did best and perfecting that. As a result, HR 4.0 practitioners found themselves continually engaging in process engineering studies and perpetual reorganisations of the matrix. There was often much written about these re-engineering initiatives in the media and business press. If it worked, there was often a boost to the share price. If not, they became vulnerable to acquisition by "asset strippers," aiming to break them up, release inherent value, and ensure a focus on the core competence of a unit. This, in turn, put leaders under even more pressure to ensure a healthy share price. The Hollywood film *Wall Street*, where the main character Gordon Gekko declared, "Greed is good," captured the spirit and the early days of the Profit wave perfectly.

For the first time, HR 4.0 explicitly introduced the concept of managing culture, defined by MIT Sloan School of Management Professor Edgar Schein as a series of assumptions a person makes about the group in which they participate. Work on culture ignited activity to define the "mission" of the business or strategy and ensure that the strategy could then be converted into action. HR thought leaders such as Wayne Brockbank developed methodologies for identifying the key HR interventions needed to enable cultural change, such as reward, training, organisation, and job design.

Management by objectives (MBO) schemes, developed under HR 3.0, were adapted to ensure that they incorporated long-term as well as short-term objectives. Soft cultural targets as well as hard targets were sought, and social as well as business impacts were at least considered for the first time. Methodologies for ensuring a more rounded view included the balanced scorecard (BSC), which is still used today. Developed by Robert Kaplan and David Norton from Harvard Business School, the balanced scorecard sought to provide management and leadership with more information. They believed that while financial information was important, it related to the past and what had already occurred. In an increasingly fast-paced business environment, leaders need access to more and better information across the business in order to make better decisions and improve financial results. BSC therefore focuses around four "legs," which comprise four distinct business perspectives:

1. the customer leg;
2. the financial leg;
3. the internal business process leg; and
4. the knowledge, education, and growth leg.

Under HR 4.0, employee surveys became the primary vehicle for measuring culture and assessing the employee voice. HR practitioners soon found themselves accountable for the results of surveys, often having their pay linked to the outcomes. The new field of HR data analytics was born. Initially, HR analytics were used to measure the effectiveness of HR transactions and were often delivered via shared service organisations. Companies such as Saratoga would sell benchmarked data, outlining "average time to recruit," "average cost per recruit," "average cost of HR as a percentage of turnover," etc. Service-level agreements (SLAs) were developed between HR service organisations and the units they served, providing a whole new suite of "customer satisfaction" measures. At its most sophisticated, HR analytics began to look for links between HR processes and cultural outcomes: "If we change reward by 5 per cent, how will it impact attrition?" "If we introduce a gym, how will it impact well-being?" Employee surveys became a "thing." Leaders would spend hours locked in a room discussing a survey, in doing so missing the chance to get out of the room and simply speak to the people who completed the survey!

Leadership development

The biggest insight of HR 4.0 probably rests in the role and emphasis placed on leadership development. Many large companies had run "management development" activities for many years under HR 1.0, HR 2.0, and HR 3.0. Linking with the competency and culture needs, "leadership" as an upgrade on "management" became a key insight of HR 4.0. Managers "operate" and oversee the status quo; leaders, by contrast, change things, providing a mission, vision, and recipe for success for their followers. HR 4.0 promotes this leadership agenda as a fundamental article of faith.

It was during the Profit wave that the pursuit of "transformational leadership" began. To enable managers to become leaders, the more enlightened companies started to invest in their managers, who would be taken on "leadership journeys." Often this would involve a physical as well as metaphorical journey to a remote farmhouse. They would discuss mission, vision, the various "elephants in the room," and then be expected to "align." Building on the enthusiasm for T-groups, which had begun as early as the 1970s in the most thoughtful companies, companies began to wake up to the power of connection and interpersonal relationships.[22] Pioneered by Kurt Lewin, the founder of social psychology, T-groups, also known as sensitivity training, human relations training, or encounter groups, taught participants, through the use of feedback, problem-solving, and role play, to gain insights into themselves and the others in the group. Although promising as an indication of a more inclusive, diverse outlook, the individualistic underlying philosophy of HR 4.0 meant that the focus remained around individual stars, not on the power of the connected team or group. Leaders focused on their own development plans, although looking for the first time at their own personal development and the importance of relationships, their underlying belief remained, "It's all about me." The celebrity CEO evolved from the Power junkie to the Profit pilot.

Evolution from HR 4.0 to HR 5.0

HR 4.0 Profit is still the dominant approach in the bulk of modern business and their HR functions (2020). What's especially striking about this P-wave is that it is widely seen as the pinnacle of human development, even though it is far from it. Nevertheless, business has become the primary driving force for most societies' progress. As a result, the Profit wave, honed and polished in the corporate world, has significantly altered the political domain. Politicians have admitted as much in their "It's the economy, stupid" declarations. Modern politics in many developed countries is deeply impacted by political lobbying, where big business seeks to set the political agenda and dictate the political outcomes. So, it is little surprise that in 2016, a "businessman" with no political experience and, at the very least, questionable business experience was elected US president.

But the good news is that the tide has already turned, and the leading edge of thinking has already moved beyond profit.

Things started to really change on 9 August 2007. On this fateful date, BNP Paribas, France's most prominent bank, announced it was freezing three of its funds. On the surface, not a dramatic thing, but the reason they gave exposed the underlying dysfunction of the credit-fuelled nature of the Profit wave: "The complete evaporation of liquidity in certain market segments of the U.S. securitisation market has made it impossible to value certain assets fairly regardless of their quality or credit rating."[23]

The downsides of the Profit wave were now laid bare. The bubble had burst. The Ponzi scheme of credit built on exploiting the most vulnerable in society, whether people unable to get prime mortgages or the low-paid, came tumbling down.

Even as governments bailed out the banks and continued to underwrite the capitalist system through 2008 and 2009, it became evident that markets couldn't be trusted to self-regulate.

As we made the shift from stewardship to ownership in HR practice, we drove levels of inequality in the workplace to unprecedented levels. Management guru Peter Drucker suggested that the difference in pay between the CEO and the average worker should be no more than 20 to 1.[24] While the outgoing CEO of Grant Thornton, Sacha Romanovitch, chose to cap her salary at Drucker's suggested ratio, and then redistributed the difference with the rest of the staff, her actions are the exception, not the rule.[25] A 2018 executive pay study found that the mean pay ratio between FTSE 100 CEOs and the mean pay package of their employees was 145 to 1.[26] The study also illuminated some staggering exceptions, such as the CEO of Persimmon, who received a reward bundle worth £47 million – 1,130 times the average salary of a Persimmon employee.[27] In the US, Glassdoor Economic Research found that the mean differential between the S&P 500 CEO pay and the average worker way was 204 to 1. There were also similar exceptions, with the CEO of Discovery Communications earning 1,951 times the average salary of a Discovery Communications employee.[28]

The top 1 per cent may have prospered, but the majority of workers have struggled to make ends meet. As people struggle in low-paid roles, growth is stalling. In 2017, the levels of personal debt in the UK stood at £1,630.1 billion, up 7.3 per cent adjusted for inflation over the previous five years.[29] Payday lenders charging astronomical interest rates are on the increase. People now have to seek the cheapest product to buy, which in turn fuels price wars and leads to the need for firms to cut costs even further. This, in turn, leads to wages being cut further, even though we already know, courtesy of economist Richard Wolff, that prosperity is built on wage rises, not wage cuts. As mentioned in the Introduction, 100 years of unprecedented prosperity was caused by US labour shortage, which meant that employers had to pay good wages and keep increasing those wages every year. Today, such an approach is the very antithesis for global business as they push towards – or are forced to push towards – continuous cost-cutting, especially labour cost. Even the IMF has stated that the resulting inequality is damaging for economic growth.[30]

It's a vicious cycle. Lower wages mean people have to seek even cheaper products and services, which in turn puts further downward pressure on wages. The result: escalating misery and stalled growth. Certainly, in the consumer goods arena in the Western world, growth is stalling.

When business or a country such as China is in a growth phase or has a need for entrepreneurial energy, an HR 4.0 Profit focus remains an appropriate response. The singular focus on profit has also been extremely successful if you've inherited wealth, have saved enough to buy some rentable assets, or are employed in the C-suite of a large business. But when growth stalls and credit becomes difficult to obtain, everyone suffers.

As we move into the third decade of the twenty-first century, people are saying, "Enough is enough." People are also asking, "How much is enough?" especially in light of stark environmental challenges such as plastic pollution and the rise in extreme weather events.

Having been made to bail out the banks, the people are increasingly intolerant of "fat-cat" pay. People are getting angrier as they are made aware of the "tax planning" of stateless companies, which means they pay little or no tax at all. This while the working poor in the UK can face a marginal tax rate of up to 60 per cent when any benefits are accounted for.[31]

It is now clear to many that we urgently need to evolve to a more inclusive, equitable, and collaborative business model. Modern business is unsustainable not because of moral indignation or collective fury at the consequences of a world that values profit above all else, but because the very system of capitalism it's built on has become a victim of its own success.[32] We are already experiencing industry-wide disruption so profound and so far-reaching that the nature and purpose of business is being redefined in real time on an almost daily basis.

In addition, the mindset and world view of the workforce is also changing. According to the Deloitte Millennial Survey 2018, millennials overwhelmingly feel that business success should be measured in terms of more than financial performance – a view that Gen Z shares (83 per cent and 80 per cent, respectively). Considering that these cohorts alone will soon make up the vast majority of the workforce, business must adapt.[33]

There is nothing inherently wrong with wealth creation – far from it. Profit-focused leaders take a pragmatic, no-nonsense view of the world that has solved many significant problems. The Profit wave has transformed the lives of millions in the developing world, but to imagine that it doesn't also bring challenges is naive and irresponsible.

Business can be a phenomenal force for good, but an over-obsession with profit has led many off that path. The outcome has been increased wealth into the hands of the few. In many cases, that success has been polluted by excessive greed, which has in turn polluted the planet and created significant global problems, from escalating global warming to the global financial crisis and the governmental austerity that followed. The leading edge of HR 5.0 People started to emerge as an antidote to the excess of HR 4.0 Profit.

Notes

1 Historical UK inflation rates (CPI), www.whatsthecost.com/historic.cpi.aspx
2 Miller Center of Public Affairs, University of Virginia, Transcript of Jimmy Carter's Address to the Nation on Energy, 18 April 1977, https://millercenter. org/the-presidency/presidential-speeches/november-8-1977-address-nation-energy
3 Friedman M (1970) The Social Responsibility of Business is to Increase Its Profits, *New York Times*, 13 September.
4 Economist Special Report (2006) Milton Friedman: A Heavyweight Champ, at Five Foot Two, *The Economist*, www.economist.com/special-report/2006/11/23/ a-heavyweight-champ-at-five-foot-two
5 Friedman M (1970) The Social Responsibility of Business is to Increase Its Profits, *New York Times*, 13 September.
6 Jensen MC and Meckling WH (1976) Theory of the Firm: Managerial Behavior, Agency Costs and Ownership Structure, *Journal of Financial Economics*, 3(4): 305–360.
7 Fastenberg D (2010) Top 10 Worst Bosses, *Time*, http://content.time.com/time/ specials/packages/article/0,28804,2025898_2025900_2026107,00.html
8 Kay J (2019) The Concept of the Corporation, www.johnkay.com/2019/01/21/ the-concept-of-the-corporation-2/
9 Dunlap AJ (1996) *Mean Business: How I Save Bad Companies and Make Good Companies*, Great Times Books, New York. Welch J (2005) *Winning*, HarperCollins, New York.
10 Peters T and Waterman RH (1982) *In Search of Excellence*, Harper & Row, New York.
11 Mirowski P and Plehwe D (2009) *The Road from Mont Pèlerin: The Making of the Neoliberal Thought Collective*, Harvard University Press, Boston, MA.

12 Gowing N and Langdon C (2018) *Thinking the Unthinkable: A New Imperative for Leadership in the Digital Age*, John Catt Educational, Woodbridge.

13 McCartin JA (2011) The Strike That Busted Unions, *New York Times*, www.nytimes. com/2011/08/03/opinion/reagan-vs-patco-the-strike-that-busted-unions.html

14 Macintyre D (2016) Wapping Dispute 30 Years On: How Rupert Murdoch Changed Labour Relations – and Newspapers – Forever, *The Independent*, www. independent.co.uk/news/media/press/wapping-dispute-30-years-on-how-rupert-murdoch-changed-labour-relations-and-newspapers-forever-a6826316.html

15 Armstrong M (1992) *Human Resource Mangement*, Kogan Page, London.

16 Ulrich D (1997) *Human Resource Champions*, Harvard Business Review Press, Boston, MA.

17 Stromberg J and Caswell E (2015) Why the Myers-Briggs Test Is Totally Meaningless, *Vox*, www.vox.com/2014/7/15/5881947/myers-briggs-personality-test-meaningless

18 Winkie L (2017) The Myers-Briggs Personality Test Is Bullshit, *Vice*, www.vice. com/en_us/article/bjv8y5/the-myers-briggs-personality-test-bullshit

19 Hammer M and Champy J (1993) *Reengineer the Corporation: A Manifesto for Business Revolution*, HarperCollins, New York.

20 Peters T (1979) Beyond the Matrix Organization, *McKinsey Quarterly*, www. mckinsey.com/business-functions/organization/our-insights/beyond-the-matrix-organization

21 Peters T (1979) Beyond the Matrix Organization, *McKinsey Quarterly*, www. mckinsey.com/business-functions/organization/our-insights/beyond-the-matrix-organization

22 Kolbe DA (2014) *Experiential Learning Experience as the Source of Learning and Development*, Pearson, Englewood Cliffs, NJ.

23 Tooze A (2018) *Crashed: How a Decade of Financial Crises Changed the World*, Penguin, London.

24 Kiatpongsan S and Norton MI (2014) How Much (More) Should CEOs Make? A Universal Desire for More Equal Pay, *Perspectives on Psychological Science*, 9(6): 587–593.

25 Frei M (2018) Sacha Romanovitch, Grant Thornton CEO: "I Capped My Salary," *Chanel 4 News*, www.channel4.com/news/sacha-romanovitch-grant-thornton-ceo-i-capped-my-salary

26 High Pay Centre (2018) High Pay Centre/CIPD Executive Pay Survey 2018, http://highpaycentre.org/pubs/high-pay-centre-cipd-executive-pay-survey-2018

27 Howker E (2018) Executive Pay Rising Faster Than Rest of Workforce, *Channel 4 News*, www.channel4.com/news/executive-pay-rising-faster-than-rest-of-workforce

28 Glassdoor (2015) Here's How Much More CEOs Earn Than Their Employees, www.glassdoor.com/blog/heres-ceos-earn-employee/

29 Inman P and Barr C (2017) The UK's Debt Crisis – in Figures, *The Guardian*, www.theguardian.com/business/2017/sep/18/uk-debt-crisis-credit-cards-car-loans

30 Inman P (2014) IMF Study Finds Inequality Is Damaging to Economic Growth, *The Guardian*, www.theguardian.com/business/2014/feb/26/imf-inequality-economic-growth

31 Dyson R (2015) The Chart That Shows There Are 12 Rates of Income Tax, *The Telegraph*, www.telegraph.co.uk/finance/personalfinance/tax/11544301/The-chart-that-shows-there-are-12-rates-of-income-tax.html

32 Edgecliffe-Johnson A (2019) Beyond the Bottom Line: Should Business Put Purpose before Profit? *Financial Times*, www.ft.com/content/a84647f8-0d0b-11e9-a3aa-118c761d2745

33 Deloitte Global (2018) Deloitte Millennial Survey: Millennials Disappointed in Business, Unprepared for Industry 4.0, www2.deloitte.com/ro/en/pages/tax/articles/deloitte-millennial-survey-2018.html

5   HR 5.0

The People wave (2005–2025)

It happened suddenly: Jack Welch went out of fashion.

After the financial crisis of 2008, the penny finally dropped for a lot of businesspeople. A dawning realisation emerged that there was something seriously wrong with the mantra that companies exist solely to generate "shareholder value." Leadership commentator Steve Denning went as far as declaring Milton Friedman's advocation of shareholder value as "the world's dumbest idea."[1] This doctrine had effectively enslaved businesses and turned them into "money monsters."[2]

The corporate world started to acknowledge that some business leaders who they had previously dismissed as New Age evangelists, such as John Mackey of Whole Foods, Ben Cohen and Jerry Greenfield of Ben & Jerry's, and Anita Roddick of The Body Shop, may have been onto something.

Post-2008, the conversation suddenly changed. Established organisations started to talk of "triple bottom lines,"[3] "conscious capitalism,"[4] and "conscious business."[5] The academic community got involved, and we saw a rash of books exploring "post-capitalism,"[6] "full-spectrum economics,"[7] "sacred economics,"[8] "caring economics,"[9] and the "circular economy."[10] Some authors went further to describe what happens "when the money runs out"[11] and how this may exacerbate the current drift towards greater ethnocentricity in "every nation for itself."[12]

The basic realisation was that there are significant problems with the idea that business solely exists to generate profit and shareholder value. One particularly influential paper argued that profitability was not the only criterion of importance, and that shareholder welfare is affected by a broad range of factors, including social and environmental conditions.[13] Obsessive profit focus can too easily foster greed,[14] and the pursuit of money can lead to fiscal irresponsibility and massive debt. The US has been held up as the poster child for such short-termism and the corporate obsession with cash, to the exclusion of all else.[15]

In 2013, John Mackey was interviewed by Sarah Green for *Harvard Business Review*'s *IdeaCast*, and said:

> If you want to be competitive in the long term, your business needs to have discovered its higher purpose and it needs to adopt a stakeholder

philosophy. And it needs to alter its leadership and culture. I think we've [Whole Foods] tapped into what I think is going to be the dominant paradigm in business over the next 50 years because it simply works better.[16]

This type of grander, more expansive purpose is ultimately powered by people. The primary driver of this P-wave is a desire for inclusion, a recognition that in business people often get left behind. People count – that is why we call HR 5.0 the People wave. The purpose of the business in this P-wave goes beyond simply making money to "making a difference" for people.

In fact, the leading edge of business has embraced the idea that defining your organisational purpose matters. Purpose is the current hot trend, as we mentioned in the Preface. Many corporations now have grandiose mission statements that talk of changing the world. Established companies, noting the success of small founder-led insurgents, have woken up to the need for a company to have a larger purpose than just profit.

Bill George has suggested that not only do companies need to uncover their organisational purpose, but leaders themselves must find their "true north."[17] Chris Zook and James Allen of Bain & Company have stressed the importance of purpose in established businesses, suggesting that one approach is to rediscover their "founder's mentality" in order to compete effectively with new insurgents.[18]

Whether we see this as a cynical attempt to create an employee brand and attract increasingly informed and discerning customers or something sincerer, it is hard to deny that defining purpose is on most corporations' minds. Brands without purpose are quickly becoming commodities, and brands with purpose tend to be more sustainable.

The first glimmers of People

We first witnessed a greater emphasis on people and purpose in the 1960s. Some of the first advocates of a new type of business were the progressives of the counterculture of this era.

John Mackey co-founded his first health food store in Austin, Texas, in 1978, merging with another business two years later to create Whole Foods Market. It was an instant success, so much so that when the store was flooded and the business ruined, the local community, who had come to love the store, stepped in to help with the clean-up, investors put up more money, banks extended credit, and employees worked for free until the store was back up and running.[19] Since then, Mackey has built Whole Foods into a multinational organisation. Mackey became the face of conscious capitalism, and together with professor and Conscious Capitalism, Inc. co-founder Raj Sisodia, they wrote a book on the subject. The argument? That both business and capitalism are inherently good. When business is done properly – inclusive, ethical, and with an eye to sustainability – it can create value for all stakeholders, including customers, employees, suppliers, investors, society, and the environment.[20]

Childhood friends Ben Cohen and Jerry Greenfield were also early pioneers of HR 5.0 People and doing business differently. After taking a $5 course on ice cream making, they opened the first Ben & Jerry's in a converted Burlington gas station in 1978 (the same year Whole Foods started). The original scoop shop became a local favourite thanks to its warm welcome and creative flavours. Ben and Jerry made it their mission to connect with the people in the community, hosting a free film festival and giving away free scoops on the first anniversary of the store, a tradition that still continues today. The business grew, helped by new shops, making pints to sell to local grocers, and funky new flavours such as Cherry Garcia and New York Super Fudge Chunk. In 1985, the Ben & Jerry's Foundation was established with a gift from Ben and Jerry and 7.5 per cent of the company's annual pre-tax profits to fund community-oriented projects – a significant endowment considering that by 1987, sales reached $32 million. By the end of the following year, Ben & Jerry's was operating in 18 states and they had been awarded US Small Business Persons of the Year by President Ronald Reagan.[21] Not bad for two left-wing hippies!

Ben & Jerry's believed their purpose, apart from selling ice cream, centred around three missions. The *social mission* seeks to operate the business "in a way that actively recognizes the central role that business plays in society by initiating innovative ways to improve the quality of life locally, nationally, and internationally." The *product mission* is "to make, distribute and sell the finest quality ice cream and euphoric concoctions with a continued commitment to incorporating wholesome, natural ingredients and promoting business practices that respect the Earth and the Environment." And the *economic mission* is to operate the business "on a sustainable financial basis of profitable growth, increasing value for our stakeholders and expanding opportunities for development and career growth for our employees."[22]

The thinking behind these new types of business was emerging in academia around the same time as pioneers were trying it out in the wild.

In 1984, R. Edward Freeman, philosopher and professor of business administration at the University of Virginia, published *Strategic Management: A Stakeholder Approach.*[23] In it, Freeman explores stakeholder theory, which addresses the role of business ethics, morals, and values within business management. Freeman was one of the first people to identify business stakeholders and how business could give due attention to those various stakeholder groups. Prior to this, the traditional view was that the only stakeholder that mattered was the shareholder, and business had a binding duty to put their needs first. Freeman argued that other stakeholders, including governmental bodies, political groups, trade associations, trade unions, communities, financiers, suppliers, employees, and customers, were also important.

Concepts such as triple bottom line (TBL) were early glimmers of the People wave, having been around since 1994 – essentially an accounting framework that assesses performance across three areas: social (people), environmental (planet), and financial (profit). More recently, quadruple bottom line (QBL)[24] adds purpose to that mix.

As the People wave took hold, corporate social responsibility (CSR) became a "thing" in business. In 2011, just under 20 per cent of S&P 500 companies reported on their sustainability, CSR, environmental, social, and governance (ESG) performance, and related topics. In 2016, that number rose to 82 per cent, meaning that just 18 per cent of S&P 500 companies were not reporting in this way.[25] In 2015, even the mighty *Harvard Business Review* – the bible of shareholder value – shifted how it assesses its "100 best-performing CEOs." When assessment considered a variety of ESG metrics, the league table reordered significantly. Jeff Bezos fell from first place to 87th, and Netflix's CEO Reed Hasting was no longer on the list – all solid evidence that ideas such as TBL, CSR, and all the numerous iterations have finally entered the mainstream.[26]

We now also have things such as the Sustainable Development Goals (SDGs)[27] – a bold, ambitious, universal set of goals, targets, and indicators that UN member states are expected to use to frame their agendas and political policies over the next 15 years.

What makes the SDGs so impressive, apart from the fact that they simply would not have existed 20 years ago, is that they were developed in broad consultation between governments, businesses, and citizens. Their central premise is the often quoted statement by the United Nations Secretary-General at the time, Ban Ki-moon, "There can be no Plan B, because there is no Planet B."[28]

The emergence of the digital age

Digitisation and datafication have changed the business landscape once again and provided an accelerant for the People wave. The brakes are off in terms of how businesses can be structured and funded, how products can be designed, made, distributed, and marketed. Digitising each element of the value chain is transforming how business everywhere operates.

Thus, we saw, in the first decade of the twenty-first century, significant disruption in the world of publishing and music. Both markets imploded as "new-style" businesses – professing new people-centred values (Spotify, Skype, etc.) – established themselves as dominant forces in those markets. The same disruption is impacting TV and advertising as they seek to find new ways to speak to customers who are now able to skip past traditional TV advertising using their technology. It will hit transportation and logistics, the FMCG industry, and the energy sector very soon. Transportation and logistics are ripe for disruption; customers are demanding faster response times, the industry is fragmented, and there is little innovation within the incumbents. As mentioned in the Introduction, FMCG goods are facing severe disruption as voice technology potentially wipes out hard-won brand dominance. The energy sector is also facing new realities as costs plummet, making it possible that everyone will eventually create their own power from cheap panels on their roof, windmills, or even battery storage of energy taken from the grid at low usage times and sold back to the grid at high usage times.

Technology is evolving incredibly quickly, itself creating "weapons of mass disruption."

The first iPhone was released on 29 June 2007 and has proven a game-changer for many established industries. Today, new founders of companies seeking to realise their "purpose" do not have to invest in building factories, offices, hiring people on permanent contracts, paying social security, making expensive TV adverts, or investing in branding and marketing. They can utilise a suite of advanced technology to set up a platform, act as a middleman, use data analytics to target customers on Facebook, YouTube, etc., and then outsource production, logistics, and even administration to another supplier or platform – all from a smartphone, lightweight laptop, or tablet. These advances are levelling the playing field in business.

Now that the barriers to entry have all but evaporated, entrepreneurs with limited experience but huge followings can disrupt scale players. For example, German teenage beauty vlogger Bibi decided to develop her own beauty products and launched her brand bilou. Such was her reach and following, her shower mousses achieved a market share of 10 per cent in only 15, weeks making her leader of the category for 16–25-year-old consumers. This is astonishing disruption to established business.

Given this scenario, large established companies are now working hard to be the "hunter" rather than the "hunted." One of the many defences multinationals are employing against new insurgents is digital transformation in the hope that they have not left it too late and will be "Amazoned" out of existence. Scale is no longer the differentiator it once was, and it is increasingly difficult for scale players to use their muscle to dominate their markets.

With the loss of the normal advantages of scale in the People wave, the quality of the people – especially the executive talent pool – has become even more critical than ever. As Zenger and Folkman's study of 30,000 leaders pointed out, "good leaders create three times economic value than poor leaders and extraordinary leaders create significantly more economic value than all the rest."[29] This supported an earlier study by Hunter, Schmidt, and Judiesch across 59,000 jobs, which demonstrated that high performers deliver 48 per cent improved performance over the average performers in highly complex jobs.[30] Boston professor Bill Torbert agreed, suggesting, in a study of organisational change conducted over four years across ten companies, that the sophistication of a CEO's mind and that of their senior executives was "the single largest cause of whether or not the organisation transformed."[31] Such sentiments were echoed by Mark Zuckerberg when he commented, "Someone who is exceptional in their role is not just a little better than someone who is pretty good. They are 100 times better."[32]

In HR 5.0, people really have become the most important asset. And those people want to work for a company with a compelling purpose.

People-based leadership

The People leaders who are emerging in this new wave of organisational evolution are often very inclusive in style. They tend to be more emotionally intelligent than the leaders of the previous P-waves. They are driven by a genuine desire to understand and help others; they seek to embrace all views and avoid creating two-tier systems or hierarchies – they prefer a level playing field.

No one can get to this level of leadership development without going through the previous levels. At the earlier wave, leaders realised that blindly following the rules was too inflexible for a changing world. So, the Profit leader developed a willingness to review the rules and decide when they are helpful and when they are not. The primary benefit of the Profit wave was that leaders became more objective and more pragmatic. They started to assess their own leadership ability and think about how they could improve.

People leaders bring a new quality to the game. They start to realise that they don't have all the answers. This makes them more reflective. They learn by talking to others and they believe that all things are relative to an individual's unique vantage point. People leaders realise that there is a distinct commercial advantage to being inclusive and taking people with them on the journey.

As a result, they are much more likely to develop their listening skills and show greater sensitivity to their colleagues. And this is not the fake sensitivity often seen in the Profit leaders, who use such skill to secure an advantage. People leaders are genuinely interested, caring, and prefer to work collaboratively.

They are motivated by affiliation and sharing, and their ultimate goal is to build a community. Being liked is often more important than being right.

As they develop their ability to collaborate effectively with others, they start to notice that the smartest person in the room is not them or, frankly, anyone else. Rather, the smartest person in the room is everyone. They glimpse the power of collective wisdom for the first time. This reinforces People leaders' tendency to look to others for answers, allowing them to relinquish at least some of the "I'm right, you're wrong" thinking so common in earlier levels.

Having arrived at the People wave and transcended the Profit and Process waves, People leaders know that too much process or too much self-interest don't work because they either slow things down or fail to create the right motivation to sustain the results. People leaders start to realise that there has to be a better way. People leadership is therefore the attempt at that better way, where the principle of the Process wave and the pragmatism of the Profit wave are still present, but both are more nuanced.

In contrast to the Profit wave, which was more focused on the individual, People leadership is much more collectivist and more inclusive of different or diverse perspectives.

Where Process leadership often got stuck by feeling the need to follow the rules and constrained by structure or compliance, and Profit leadership also got stuck in a slightly larger but more self-serving profit narrative, People leadership opens up to everyone. This is a genuine game-changer for relationships.

This "opening up" started with a series of positive and healthy developments in the early 1960s: the civil rights movement, the environmental movement, feminism, anti-hate crime, and a heightened sensitivity to any and all forms of social oppression of minorities. The entire revolution of the sixties was driven primarily by this world view and stage of development. In 1959, 3 per cent of the population were at the People level of development; by 2020, it is much closer to 20 per cent of the population. This more people-centric world view changed everything, and its early manifestation is encapsulated by the Beatles song of the time, "All You Need Is Love."

Although the People-centric world view emerged from the 1960s onwards, it did not migrate into the business world to any great extent or become the leading edge until much later. However, early success stories, such as the ones mentioned, did help to legitimise this world view in a business context.

There was also a growing understanding of the crucial role of "context" in any knowledge claims. Those with this world view believe that if our experience is different, our belief is different, but equally valid. From here, it is a very small step to perceiving every view as legitimate where every view becomes "relative" to a person's experience. This tolerance and inclusion, when taken too far, is the central pathology that is currently causing the People wave to fail (more on that at the end of the chapter).

Once there is a degradation of the leading P-wave and its negative characteristics start to kick in, the next evolutionary dynamic tends to be a regression as evolution tries to retrace it steps to an earlier, less dysfunctional time. So, as our current People wave continues to fail, there is a reaching back into history for Profit or even Power wave solutions. We see this in business and politics.

In business, failed People leaders are replaced by more pragmatic Profit leaders who will return the focus to cash and stop "wasting time" on "purpose," or companies may install heroic Power leaders who claim they can bring clarity to the confusion and the stalled growth created by People leaders. Such a regressive step is reflected in the decisions and policies that flow from earlier P-wave leaders. For example, in the US, a renewed focus on coal, the withdrawing from the Paris climate agreement, and the election of Donald Trump, himself a card-carrying Power leader, is evidence of this backward-looking search for a solution. This same retrograde manoeuvre is being tried all over the world with the resurgence of far-right nationalistic and protectionist efforts (a Paternalistic move) and the emergence of strongman leaders, such as Duterte in the Philippines, Erdogan in Turkey, Putin in Russia, and the "Trump of the Tropics," Brazil's Jair Bolsonaro. These latest efforts won't solve the predicament, but ironically it may be the catastrophic failure of these "solutions" that will lead us to leap forward to HR 6.0 Paradox.

Teams at HR 5.0: diverse pluralists

Teams that made it to HR 4.0 first developed into *independent achievers* who no longer needed to follow the leader out of slavish loyalty or adherence to hierarchy, process, or structure. With their new-found abilities to objectify team performance, the better teams realised they could even go further and develop into *interdependent achievers*. As interdependent achievers, they understood that the fastest way to deliver their goals was to work together more effectively. This led to an appreciation of how everyone's individual contribution was dependent on other team members' efforts. As these interdependencies become clear, the sense of team becomes very palpable. Operating as interdependent achievers becomes very energising, and the focus is really on optimising performance of the team and the business.

For many, this is where the team development ends. They reach a plateau. Team meetings become the highlight of the quarter or month. Team members energise each other, and after the meeting each leader returns to the business with new vim and vigour.

But this is not the end of the journey for some teams. A small handful of teams have the potential to break through to a whole new level of performance that most teams at HR 4.0 don't think is possible. For earlier waves, such a breakthrough is nothing short of fantasy.

But a lucky few can reach the rarefied altitude of HR 5.0 diverse pluralists.

This level of team performance is extremely rare in organisations simply because most leadership teams don't consistently invest the time and effort required to become the best leadership team in their industry. If they did commit to such a goal, they would still need to find a coach who knows what it takes for them to reach such an altitude. Unfortunately, very few coaches know what it takes to guide a team to this level of exceptional capability. Even if they did understand the developmental practices, team dynamics, and changes required for the ascent, few coaches have had the opportunity to guide a team to this level of brilliance.

When the team makes the developmental leap from interdependent achievers to diverse pluralists, there is often a dramatic change in performance. This is down to six key shifts in the way the team functions, specifically:

1. *Commercial optimisation shifts to relationship leverage.* Interdependent achievers seek to optimise commercial performance by working more interdependently within the team. In contrast, diverse pluralists focus more on relationships within the team to leverage the different strengths available and create better answers. Such leverage enables the team to go further and faster and deliver more. An HR 5.0 team starts to experience genuine team learning rather than relying on individual reflection to drive progress. Shared team concepts emerge, and a real sense of a team spirit is palpable. At HR 3.0, any claims of "team" are normally lip service, spin, or aspiration. At HR4.0, we see a step change in energy during

team meetings as individuals challenge each other to succeed. At HR 5.0, there is a much more intimate appreciation that a stronger relationship more directly equates to commercial performance. This is why diverse pluralists become increasingly focused on each other.

2. *A 1D mindset shifts to 3D awareness.* There is a shift in focus from driving commercial results to leveraging relationships. An HR 4.0 team of interdependent achievers drives the results by increasing the interdependencies. An HR 5.0 team starts to understand more deeply that all three dimensions ("being," "doing," and "relating") are required to step-change team results. In addition, the leader of an HR 5.0 team is seen more as a team member with different responsibilities, rather than the source of all wisdom.

3. *Internal focus shifts to external focus.* A team operating at HR 4.0 interdependent achievers focus on how they collectively lead the business or division. In contrast, diverse pluralists broaden their horizons. HR 5.0 teams start looking to the group, the market sector, or the industry as their remit rather than simply just internally within the business. HR 4.0 teams seek to identify opportunities for cross-functional collaboration. Diverse pluralists have stopped seeing functions; they just see the business that the team is leading. At HR 5.0, team meetings often involve externally focused conversation about how to impact market dynamics and change the game. It is a given that if the team performs at this level, then they will lift company results and deliver on all other agendas of previous levels.

4. *Tension processing becomes agile.* At HR 4.0, the team stops hiding bad news and brings problems to the table. At HR 5.0, this capability develops further. There is a real honesty about silo underachievement. Failure is shared openly as team members focus on anything that is slowing progress. Rather than flipping into blame, judgement, or finger-pointing, the team welcomes news of underperformance. Such news provides an opportunity to accelerate. Each issue is seen as "our problem," and diverse pluralists work collectively to solve these problems together. The team interdependency that started at the previous level becomes the default, and the ideas generated are more sophisticated because they include all perspectives available in the team, and some beyond the team. But the real change at HR 5.0 is the speed with which the team can deal with tensions. This greater agility is based on much greater levels of trust, the increased strength of relationship bonds among diverse pluralists, and the ability to operate with higher levels of conceptual flexibility. The greater agility means teams operating at HR 5.0 resolve tensions and create better-quality answers much faster than HR 4.0 teams.

5. *High energy becomes a flow state in the team.* While a team of interdependent achievers are highly energised, the difference when they become diverse pluralists is that energy flows much more freely. Meetings are more frictionless and the team can experience moments of real "flow." This has to be experienced to be understood. If a leader is not sure

whether the team has ever experienced this, then it has not. The experience is palpable and not easily forgotten. In the People wave, team harmony and flow become recurring topics for discussion.

6. *Control shifts to downward delegation.* Because diverse pluralists increasingly trust others, recognise that results require much higher levels of engagement at all levels, and understand that the "wisdom of the crowd" requires decisions to be delegated to the people who are most affected by those decisions, they are much more comfortable with delegating authority. Effective empowerment of others, particularly lower work levels, becomes a big theme for the HR 5.0 team.

Emerging HR and people practices

Although the vast majority of businesses, certainly in the developed world, still operate from an HR 4.0 Profit perspective, HR 5.0, with a focus on purpose and people, is the leading edge (2020).

Seeded decades ago by the early People pioneers of the 1960s and 1970s, it was more widely embraced in business following the dot-com crash of 2000 and the global financial crisis, where the outcome of greed, hubris, and excess was laid bare. Starting around 2005, the leading edge of HR 5.0 focused on getting the best out of people and ensuring that the business had a meaningful purpose that all stakeholders could rally behind.

In the 1980s, during the Profit wave, companies frequently waxed lyrical about how "people are our greatest asset" when clearly this was just spin. Financial capital was the primary asset at that time. However, in the age of digital disruption, it turns out that people are not only the greatest asset; they may very well be a company's *only* real asset that can deliver sustainable value. In an age of minimal transactional friction and limited barriers to entry, financial capital and access to debt are no longer the obstacles to progress they once were. The ingenuity of people, the connections they make, the relationships they have, and the ability to create influence (i.e. social capital) is now the key to success.

As more people enter HR 5.0, the term "human resources" will gradually disappear. Increasingly, we are seeing the word "People" come back into job titles. The age of People, with its corresponding emphasis on purpose, will see the HR manager become the training and people development manager, or just people development manager and chief people officer. These roles can already be found on recruitment sites.

The people practices in HR 5.0 pivot towards a strategic focus on the concept of "purpose" for the company and for employees – a step up in diversity and inclusion interventions, a reframing of reward and performance management systems from the individualistic to a more collectivist perspective, and a profound focus on leadership and *human* development as a core for business success.

We unpack these themes below.

HR 5.0 People today

As we have said, purpose is central to HR 5.0 People, and there has been massive increased interest in the idea of purpose in organisations. Harvard and other major business schools now run programmes enabling executives and organisations to discover their purpose. It is certainly an idea whose time has come.

The very best companies have moved beyond the "corporate nursery rhymes" that used to be "mission statements" and now speak to fundamental truths. Often these are evident in the history of the company and seek to better reflect the founder's original thinking. For example, Lord Lever, the co-founder of Lever Brothers, which became part of Unilever, spoke of his goal of making "cleanliness commonplace" to help combat the scourge of disease in Victorian Britain. Unilever today outlines a "Unilever Sustainable Living Plan," with measured performance indicators aiming to reduce its environmental footprint (impact) and ensure a positive social impact (influence).[33] Like most companies, Unilever has been learning by doing in terms of embedding sustainability into its business, but the current business is committed and it's not greenwashing – it is in the DNA of the business.

Employees at many companies have the opportunity to explore their own purpose, to think through how this links to their development goals, how they spend their time each day, and how this could link to the company vision. When employees are able to see how their work facilitates them being able to live their own purpose and how that then links to the corporate purpose, they are much more likely to fully engage in their role and deliver high performance because they are intrinsically motivated. Considering that the Gallup *State of the Global Workplace Report 2017* reported that 85 per cent of employees worldwide are not engaged or are actively disengaged, tapping into personal purpose is viewed as essential for turning those statistics around.[34]

For senior leaders, connecting the dots between personal purpose and corporate purpose can game-change motivation and help facilitate the development of more mature leadership. If the personal and organisational purposes both belong to HR 5.0, they may translate into product innovations that directly seek to ensure positive social or environmental benefits. Such benefits may enable the connection to consumers' sustainability concerns, making products and services more likely to succeed in the marketplace.

There is growing evidence that companies with purpose who are seeking to deliver value to multiple stakeholder groups and solve problems are developing much greater levels of brand value and trust, and that trust is delivering a very real payback in financial returns and corporate growth.[35] Firms that pursue a CSR agenda, genuinely, enjoy higher returns, lower risks, and lower costs of capital.[36]

When companies get this right, it can deliver incredible commercial returns. For example, Unilever report that their sustainable living brands, ones that have a distinct social or environmental purpose, grew 46 per cent faster than other brands and delivered 70 per cent of company growth. In an EY and *Harvard Business Review* study, 87 per cent of respondents stated that "companies perform best over time if their purpose goes beyond profit," and over 80 per cent stated that a purpose created "greater employee satisfaction," "better customer advocacy," and "higher-quality products and services."[37]

That said, community connection goes way beyond just elevated financial return. Businesses are not only championing this work because it promotes human development. They are doing it because they increasingly realise that in the digital world, it will be the human connections that make the difference. They are doing it because they understand that eating up the world's resources at an unsustainable rate is not good long-term business. In Unilever, for example, the HR function, under the leadership of pioneering CHRO Leena Nair, is at the heart of this development.

Diversity and inclusion

When both the authors were younger men, it was quite normal, certainly in the UK, even in polite company, to hear casual racist, sexist, or homophobic remarks. Today, such discourse is considered completely unacceptable in the workplace – and rightly so. The 2017 #MeToo movement, born of the backlash against sexism and misogyny that has been deeply intrenched in patriarchal companies for centuries, is another indicator of a further shift in standards and expectations. There is also an increase in legislation that forces companies to publish their gender pay gap, although real diversity goes way beyond gender. With the rise in awareness of LGBTQ+, a lot of companies are now thinking much more comprehensively about diversity not just in terms of gender (even though they haven't managed to find a way to bring genuine equality to gender, never mind the fluidity of gender).

Diversity based on age, gender, ethnicity, religion, disability, sexual orientation, education, and national origin are often too blunt, and don't really address the issue of what someone is like on the inside. It's quite possible to have the appearance of a diverse senior management team, for example, that includes a broad mix of people who look or act differently from one another, but if they all operate from the same world view and are guided by the same value systems, then there is no *real* diversity at all. The mantra of business is therefore no longer focused on diversity, but diversity and inclusion (DNI).

In the People wave, both diversity and inclusion are considered business imperatives as getting this right is seen as a source of competitive advantage. Whereas diversity is about increasing the number of underrepresented groups in business and integrating those groups at all levels of the business, inclusion is about enabling everyone to contribute to that business as their authentic self. Inclusion is about ensuring that the people from the diverse groups feel as though they belong in the business, and are not just the token woman or the token Asian, but valued members of staff who have a different perspective that can deliver new insights and observations to the business.

There is also growing evidence of the financial benefit DNI can bring. Research conducted in 2014 by the New York-based Center for Talent Innovation (CTI), involving more than 40 case studies and 1,800 employee surveys, found that publicly traded companies with inherent diversity (gender, ethnicity, or sexual orientation) were 45 per cent more likely than those without to have expanded market share in the past year and 70 per cent more likely to have captured a new market.[38] A 2012 Deloitte report looking at 1,550 employees in three large Australian businesses identified an 80 per cent improvement in business performance when levels of diversity and inclusion were high.[39]

It is already clear that diversity and inclusion programmes, common in many companies, will become increasingly integrated into the business agenda and the leadership development process.

It is very likely that by the 2020s, it will be commercially unacceptable for organisations to have employees who are predominantly one gender or one ethnic group, as has been the norm in the past. This will be true of the entire employee base, including senior management and leadership teams. But this is not about political correctness gone mad; it's simply the commercial recognition that customers are diverse, and if a company is to communicate with those diverse customer groups more effectively, the external diversity needs to be matched internally with the staff and decision-makers. Decades ago, white men in suits decided how to sell products to everyone. With big budgets and burgeoning TV and print media, it worked. But that approach is not working anymore. Nuance and understanding are required to speak directly to different customer groups, and that can only be achieved authentically when the product development and presentation is inclusive of the types of people the product or service is targeting. And this has already been proven. The CTI study also found that when teams had one or more members who represented a target end user, the entire team was as much as 158 per cent more likely to understand that target end user and innovate accordingly.[40]

Consumers are increasingly rejecting the one-size-fits-all products and services and the old-school, generic shotgun marketing that used to promote them. They want personalisation. They want to be talked to directly, and the tailoring capabilities and power of social media are making that possible. Increasingly, HR departments, or people development departments, are being required to ensure that diversity and inclusion is a reality of day-to-day life, not just an initiative to add as a footnote in the annual report. Businesses and organisations that fail on the DNI agenda will lose trust, leak social capital, and increasingly struggle, until one day they "fall off a cliff." Leading an effective DNI agenda will not be easy and will definitely require the leadership capability upgrades we will discuss shortly.

Diagnostic tools such as the Leadership Values Profile (LVP) will become increasingly useful at HR 5.0 and beyond to facilitate the diversity and inclusion agenda.

The LVP is a proprietary online tool that allows the senior leadership team to understand their own and everyone else's dominant world view. It is based on the integration of the work of many investigators, including Clare Graves, who we mentioned in the Preface. It also takes into consideration multiple streams of research over the last 30 years to illuminate the way individuals adapt to their circumstances. The insights gained from the LVP can ensure genuine diversity and inclusion, and they also have profound implications for how team members work together to deliver on the business objective and how the team best communicates to get things done.

The LVP allows us to see who people are on the inside, or at least the way they see the world, which can ensure that there is a real cross-section of perspectives, regardless of what the people around the board table may look like on the outside.

When an individual knows their own value system and the strengths and weaknesses inherent in that world view, they understand themselves better and are better able to explain themselves to others and ensure they are understood. In a meeting, for example, an executive aware of their values system and which P-wave they operate from could say:

> Look, I tend to over-discuss ideas and strategy [if they operate from the Paradox wave]. You may be frustrated by that [because you operate from the Power wave]. I accept that you would prefer to just get on with something. So, can we agree on a 30-minute strategic discussion where I can share some big-picture thinking, and once we have settled on an idea you can inject some urgency to make this idea come alive? As a result, we can harness my contribution [ideas] and your contribution [pace], so together we make a perfect pair and utilise the best of both of us.

This approach can also take a lot of the heat and irritation out of discussions because each person recognises the other person's world view, acknowledges it, and honours the value it brings, without allowing the downside of each to manifest – in this case, the Paradox leader's propensity to endlessly dissect options and the Power leader's propensity to rush into a decision too quickly.

The LVP therefore provides a way of understanding the difference between our own and other people's perspective, which can enable executives to reconcile their differences, reduce any conflict, and improve the quality of their communication. This single intervention can dramatically transform relationships at work and at home as it allows us to harness the power of diversity while mitigating the roadblocks that difference can bring if not properly understood and managed.

Issues previously misdiagnosed as "personality clashes" are seen for what they really are – different values perspectives. Discussions and negotiations become much less personal. A better appreciation of difference can also give everyone more insight into how to communicate with the values diversity in the group to achieve better outcomes and harness the collective more productively.

Diverse teams deliver better results. All teams need a good blend of different people to function optimally. A team where everyone has the same world view will never deliver high performance. But relying on obvious, often "external" diversity, such as gender, sexual orientation, or ethnicity, is misleading and allows us to believe we've ticked the DNI box when we haven't. This is why there are still people in business who point enthusiastically to failed diversity initiatives as evidence that the whole agenda is flawed. It's not. It's just that what we consider as diversity is not the diversity that really matters. Diversity in values or world view is what really matters because it is a key driver of wisdom.[41]

Diversity and inclusion, along with escalating longevity, will also probably require a radical rethink of how work is organised, starting in the Western world. Lynda Gratton, professor of management practice at London Business School, and Andrew Scott, professor of economics at the same school, wrote about the "100-year life."[42] In their book, they describe how a child born in the mid-1990s is likely to live, on average, until they are 105 years old. This means they need to gear up to work for up to 80 years. The twentieth-century model – education, followed by work, followed by retirement – is done for. People can't be retired for 40 years (65–105), and society certainly can't afford it!

The future way of working will also require more diversity and inclusion in the way people approach and engage with work throughout their life. It may include education, exploration, full-time work, flex work, re-education or sabbatical followed by different full-time work and flex work, then retirement or scaling back to part-time.

Taking time out of the workplace will become the norm rather than viewed as a career-limiting move. This should mean that men and women are taking equivalent breaks to raise children or take a sabbatical. The current break women take for maternity leave will no longer represent a unique disadvantage to women as opposed to men. We are already seeing this in business, and that's going to be beneficial to everyone, including the children. Surely it is no coincidence that in the Scandinavian countries, where extensive paternity leave provision is the norm, meaning men and women often break for the same amount of time to raise children, female representation in the higher levels of management is higher than in countries where only women raise children.

As employment models adapt to address longer working lives, we may see the issue of gender diversity addressed once and for all.

Performance management

In HR 5.0, the annual performance appraisal is seen as outdated, a thing of the past, simply because the commercial world for many businesses is changing so quickly that it's unproductive and inefficient to wait 12 months to talk about performance. Performance management schemes are starting to reflect the approaches championed in high-tech or in smaller companies – more collective, quicker, and linked to people and purpose, not just the quarter-by-quarter profits.

While we are already seeing an increasing dissatisfaction with the quarterly reporting cycle demanded of stock-listed companies, ironically we will see a move within business to more regular "always-on" reviews. The performance management cycle time for teams and individuals is being reduced to quarterly instead of annually or is initiated on a project-by-project basis. Annual goals are also becoming subject to quarterly revision as the commercial environment moves underfoot. Companies such as Accenture, Deloitte, Adobe, Juniper Systems, Dell, Microsoft, and IBM have already moved to this approach.[43]

At the People wave, longer-term purpose-based objectives are included in corporate goals beyond the balanced scorecard. Some companies now include specific environmental and social targets into the long-term elements of their senior managers' remuneration packages and stated company goals.

This P-wave also sees the end, thankfully, of the "rank and yank" type of performance management practices, where the bottom 10 per cent are sacked and the top 10 per cent get an extra bonus. This overtly individualistic assessment is counterproductive in a world where end-to-end working, interdependence, and team building need cooperation and agility.

As the People wave unfolds further, we will see a much more collective assessment – teams being given performance management feedback and a greater use of 360-degree feedback mechanisms. Talent development processes will increasingly focus on team fit and developing duos of people, mimicking successful founders who often work in tight-knit teams or as pairs. Interventions such as organisational network analysis (see Chapter 6) will increasingly be used to assess performance across the whole business, showing which teams link well and which leaders are key influencers in the network, and it is these inclusive considerations that will drive performance judgements and corresponding reward.

Reward

In HR 5.0, the thinking on compensation and benefits also changes – large bonuses become both socially and academically discredited as a means of motivating employees.[44] In late 2018, the CEO of Persimmons was asked to step down because of the continued controversy over his £75 million bonus. In a statement, the company said, "The board believes that the distraction around his [Fairburn's] remuneration from the 2012 LTIP scheme continues to have a negative impact on the reputation of the business."[45]

In addition, the annual cycles of reward are proving too slow; new, innovative ways of rewarding and motivating people are being sought.

Reward management systems are certainly more collective in HR 5.0. This is largely due to the role performance-based pay played in the financial crash of 2007 and the mounting evidence that variable pay is a poor motivational tool for any roles requiring agility, problem-solving, and a longer-term perspective. This is likely to mean a shift back towards base pay so as to reduce the excesses of the past, where corporate bad behaviour was almost encouraged, so long as it delivered results and led to nice fat bonuses.

Share options and the granting of performance shares to senior leaders will also increasingly change in HR 5.0 and beyond. Performance shares are likely to require an investment by senior executives to qualify so they have "skin in the game," rather than a free ride. Increasingly using this principle, performance share investment opportunities will then be made more democratic and inclusive, with any employee, regardless of seniority, being able to participate.

There is already far more flexibility and choice around pay. Employees can already choose how their "total reward" is made up. What percentage of their package is variable, and therefore at greater risk, and what percentage is fixed, what investment in shares, what percentage in pension or perks? This change in reward philosophy will also reflect the changing needs of an extended working life. Employees will opt for different levels of security, fixed versus variable, in their total reward to suit where they are in their working life cycle.

CEO pay is also changing. We already see shareholder pressure being applied to many large corporates over the significant pay and bonuses paid to senior staff. There is also a backlash from consumers. This will continue as the excessive ratios between average workers and CEOs becomes increasingly unjustifiable, and potentially damaging to business reputation and turnover.

In the People wave, government intervention on pay – not seen since the Process wave – is highly likely, especially if there is another financial crash as predicted.[46] Governments will increasingly cap "golden hellos" and "golden goodbyes." This has already happened in the Netherlands, where redundancy payouts are capped at €100,000 – a far cry from the payouts of the past.

Leadership and human development

We are now in a full digitally facilitated age, and anyone with digital skills is "hot" in the marketplace, even though they often don't seek a traditional employment relationship. Since the "right" people are thin on the ground, organisations are once again declaring a "race for talent." Since many organisations can't find the people they need, they are prioritising people initiatives, such as talent development and succession planning, as strategic imperatives.

Leaders who feel the need to build and drive hierarchies around themselves will increasingly hold back the development of the business. Leaders unable to think systemically and who lack a connection with a deeper purpose are also likely to slow progress. Alternatively, leaders who live their life on purpose and inspire others to do the same will create followership. Leaders who are able to magnify the talents of the people around them, leaders who can build, not destroy, social capital, will be in increasingly high demand.

In HR 5.0, and to a lesser extent in HR 4.0, it is widely understood that management and leadership development must deliver an urgent upgrade if it is to provide organisations with the type of leaders required to address today and tomorrow's complex, multidimensional problems.

Prior to the People wave, employee development, including management and leadership, focused on:

- *skills development* – classic functional training;
- *general management skills* – ensuring people are prepared for management-level transitions (e.g. supervisor to departmental manager); and
- *transformational journeys* – programmes designed to transition a manager to a leader.

Programmes to cultivate skills, either functional or general, will always be needed. However, increasingly, they will be digitised, outsourced, and/or managed differently. There is already a lot of work focusing on "transformational leadership" because genuine transformational leadership enhances the core of the business while simultaneously developing new revenue streams, which often becomes the new core.[47] But, as we shall outline, much, much more is needed.

A radically new approach to leadership and human development is needed in the People wave and beyond.

Every P-wave that has so far graced the planet, from Paternalistic to People, shares one central fault line that causes each to collapse. They each believe that their view of the world is right and everyone else is wrong. Collectively, these first five P-waves are known as first-tier value systems, which create first-tier thinking. The People wave is the last evolutionary level of the first tier, and, according to Ken Wilber, it is the main obstacle for evolution and progress – in business, government, and beyond.[48] Very few business leaders make it past HR 5.0, and if they make it this far, they often remain stuck in the consensual swamp. Most are still firmly rooted in the earlier P-wave of HR 4.0 Profit or below. Less than 5 per cent of leaders make it to the second-tier value systems that could ignite major transformation and unlock our collective potential.

Let's consider the global financial crisis as an example. It caused worldwide devastation, and yet there is compelling evidence that it was caused by as few as 50 individuals.[49] Surely what they did was unforgivable. Their actions, greed, and hubris brought the global financial system to its knees, and millions of people around the world are still suffering as a result.

It would be easy to demonise those individuals and demand they are punished in some way. But the decisions they took, largely to line their own pockets, were because they were primarily driven by self-interest and greed, with scant regard for the care of or impact on others. They were operating from the dark side of the Profit wave. If you imagine each evolutionary level from Paternalism to Planet as a rung on a ladder, with each progressive developmental step upward, we can see further, appreciate more of the landscape before us, and consequently make better decisions. When development is arrested at any one of the first-tier P-waves, we only see the world from that vantage point on the ladder.

Those in the first tier are driven by the corresponding values and motives of that P-wave, and will often passionately believe that anyone who is driven from values and motives of a different P-wave is wrong, ill-informed, or just plain stupid. This limitation, bias, or blindness means that they can't easily step into other people's shoes and may not fully appreciate the complexity, depth, or breadth of the challenges they face. They only see part of the puzzle because they are viewing that puzzle through a particular world view. As a result, they make choices that often make matters worse or create new unintended problems. Needless to say, when those people are in positions of authority, power, or influence, then the consequences can be catastrophic – as evidenced by the global financial crisis. Whether these leaders solve or exacerbate the problems they face largely comes down to how "vertically developed" they are across the commercially relevant "lines of development" (more on this in Chapter 6).

Right now, too few of us, and certainly too few HR professionals and learning and development managers, leaders, and senior executives, understand the fundamental difference between horizontal learning and vertical development. This failure is, by far, the biggest hurdle facing business today. If we don't embrace this difference and switch our collective focus to vertical development, we will not make the leap to the next evolutionary P-wave in enough numbers to facilitate the new business paradigm that is so desperately needed.

Not only that; we are likely to continue to repeat the mistakes of the past. Since the global financial crisis, both the Banking Standards Board (BSB) and the Financial Conduct Authority (FCA) have been asked by industry and the government in the UK to address the problems within banking culture to see what needs to be done to avoid a repetition. It has become apparent that neither the BSB nor the FCA have sufficient understanding of how values and culture evolve to make the distinction between one P-wave, with its inherent pathology, and the next P-wave. In short, they don't yet appreciate the difference between horizontal and vertical development. If they don't understand why this distinction is absolutely critical, it is highly unlikely that they will be able to come up with any recommendations that will stop another financial meltdown in the future.

So, what is vertical development, and why is it so profoundly important?

Harvard professor Robert Kegan suggests that horizontal learning is about filling a glass with water while vertical development expands the glass itself.[50] Whereas horizontal learning focuses on the acquisition of skills knowledge and experience in the world of "doing," vertical development fundamentally changes the "being" or person doing the doing. If a person matures or "grows up" as an adult, then what they can do and how well they can do it also develops. In addition, a more mature person is more likely to improve how they relate to others.

Vertical development is a bit like unlocking several new levels on a computer game that allow the player to do things that they simply couldn't do at previous levels. With these new-found abilities, people are better able to create complex solutions because they have deeper, more nuanced perspectives that can transform results and unlock potential across multiple dimensions. Vertical development is critical in the pivot from first-tier to second-tier thinking, and allows us to include the benefits of each of the previous P-waves while transcending their limitations. Vertical development therefore unlocks our "superpowers," which can step-change performance. Where horizontal learning is the equivalent of adding more "apps," vertical development upgrades the operating system.

One of the easiest ways to appreciate the real-world difference between horizontal learning and vertical development is to consider algebra. If you were to ask a 7-year-old child, "If $4x = 16$, what does x equal?" they would understand the words you said, but they would not understand the question because their frontal cortex is not sufficiently developed. Seven-year-olds think in literal, concrete terms. They are not yet capable of understanding abstractions such as algebra. But if you ask a 14-year-old the same question, they will probably be able to tell you that $x = 4$. At 14, the frontal cortex has sped up massively, and is therefore capable of abstract thought. It's as though the child's ability to understand algebra has finally "come online." The older child has a level of capability and sophistication that simply doesn't exist in a 7-year-old. Vertical development offers that same type of quantum leap forward. If we remain open to the possibility that we are not fully developed, even though we may look like adults on the outside, we can tap into the real competitive advantage that lies not in what we know, but the way that we know it.[51]

Right now, almost without exception, all the learning and development initiatives facilitated by HR are focused on horizontal learning, not vertical development. That must change. This is the business emergency, and we must move to the emergent world view of HR 6.0 Paradox.

We need many more stakeholders, especially those in leadership and executive roles, to be vertically developed, operating at second-tier value systems so they can see further, appreciate more of the complexity, and bring more sophisticated thinking to the problems we face.

To drive home the urgency of this step change, consider the findings of a study on 43,060 transnational corporations. The study suggested that there were only 147 companies that determine global outcomes across the planet.[52] Due to their share ownership, these companies, many of which are banks or financial institutions, control what happens in most of the other companies. For example, a few pension funds, insurance companies, mutual funds, and sovereign wealth funds hold \$65 trillion, or 35 per cent of all the world's financial assets.[53] Within each of these 147 companies, there are probably three people who are calling the shots (the CEO, the CFO, and the COO). This means that in effect, less than 450 individuals run the planet. These 450 people pull the ownership strings of 147 companies that indirectly control the other 43,060 multinational companies, which in turn drive the global economy and determine the destiny of over 7 billion people.[54] Imagine what the world could be like if those 450 individuals were operating from second-tier thinking.

Imagine what could be achieved.

We believe it is the primary task of people development specialists in companies all over the world to embrace the transformational capabilities of vertical development, and ensure that everyone from the leadership down has access to interventions that will help them evolve to a more advanced world view.

The key HR intervention at HR 5.0 (and beyond) is therefore the vertical development journey of employees – especially leadership. If HR, or whatever it becomes known as in the future, focuses on vertical development and facilitates a world view shift among the workforce from first tier to second tier, then not only will that shift unlock vast reservoirs of capability, but it will help to resolve all the other issues HR currently wrestles with. Orchestrate vertical development of the people in the business and you automatically help resolve culture and purpose issues, diversity and inclusion issues, performance management issues, reward issues, and much more. Start at vertical development and the rest will follow.

Evolution from HR 5.0 to HR 6.0

Each evolutionary advance is a reaction to the worst of the excesses of the previous P-wave. Sadly, we still witness those excesses in companies that value profit above all else, as they seek to wring out all the money they can from outdated and often damaging business practices. They probably won't change until they are made to change through public opinion or legislation. The Profit focus delivered huge gains economically and allowed individuals in the system to flourish, but it went too far.

The People wave was the antidote, and initially it worked. People, all people, not just the high potentials or talented, were valued. It was also more widely recognised that for business to succeed, the employee demographic needs to reflect the customer demographic, especially in the upper echelons. Gender equality made some progress, as did all other forms of diversity. Unfortunately, the people advocating for greater inclusion and diversity were often portrayed as "bleeding-heart liberals" or "snowflakes," although such criticism is only ever levelled by those operating from an earlier world view.

Every P-wave must and will fail, and it is in the failure that business, society, and individuals find the motivation or momentum to evolve to the next level. Initially, more inclusion was a huge boon in the People wave, especially for those who had previously been ignored or marginalised.

The first glimmers of the decline of the People wave are already evident, Brexit and the election of President Trump being in many ways a reaction to a world where many started to believe that inclusion had gone too far and tipped into political correctness.

Bringing everyone with you is also extremely time-consuming, and businesses seeking to operate from this world view found themselves in the swamp of consensus where nothing is ever fully decided or actioned. And of course, the biggest scourge to emerge from this People wave is the narcissistic vacuum of the "post-truth" world.

The idea that all views are relative undermines the idea central to the Profit wave that there is an objective reality or, as the Process wave claimed, an absolute truth.

If there is no objective reality or objective truth and all perspectives are just relative, then it becomes very difficult to separate fact from opinion. Such context arguments have already started to decay into what is known as "rampant relativism" and set the stage for the nihilistic vacuum that has emerged. Claims to know the answers are seen as a desire to impose your relative view on others, and therefore such claims are invalidated. In the nihilistic confusion that has emerged, the conditions are now set for the emergence of extreme narcissism.

We can see the appearance of narcissists in politics and society at large. People leaders are in panic as the narcissists take control in the vacuum they created. It is obvious to those operating from the People wave that something is going terribly wrong. In their frustration that they are losing their influence, their mean side emerges. Ironically, their tolerance and inclusion cease as they try to exclude the narcissist and resist the regressive step that narcissists represent. Unfortunately, this only serves to make matters worse – think Hillary Clinton's "basket of deplorables" comment. People leaders are meant to embrace everyone, and here they were rejecting some.

This has created a very strong backlash as people experience the ultimate let-down. The very people who extolled inclusivity were now excluding people. This felt like a betrayal. In essence, the leading edge has stopped leading and is starting to fail. That failure is now (2020).

If all knowledge or truth is contextual, then facts become merely opinions, all of which are stated as fact or classed as "alternative fact." We stop listening to experts and the people who have dedicated their lives to understanding a topic area. We stop believing science and instead simply choose whatever facts we prefer or the ones that suit our narrative or point of view.

This means we are now in the middle of the utterly bizarre situation where US rapper Kanye West, a man who has never been to prison or knows much about the life that leads to prison, is in the Oval Office with the President of the United States discussing prison reform, gang violence, and manufacturing![55] Or when another of the Kardashians, Kylie Jenner, can tweet to her millions of followers that she doesn't like the new Snapchat interface and stock price plummets.[56] Or when teenage vloggers who know nothing about product safety or testing can launch products that grab a huge slice of the market share almost overnight. Where online platforms tell whatever version of the truth suits their purpose, or when movers and shakers at the World Economic Forum at Davos queue to listen to Goldie Hawn talk about meditation rather than perhaps a Nobel laureate discussing inequality.[57] When we include everyone and everyone can say whatever they want, we create the post-truth world we are in the middle of right now. No one needs any validity anymore. Those who are celebrated and followed don't need a degree or years of experience; they just need to say something controversial or something that other people like. If they are good-looking, it also helps, but beyond that they can say whatever they want, and people believe them because truth has become subjective.

In many ways, the People wave of HR practices reflects the era of postmodern "identity politics." We can point to great work on diversity, inclusion, ways of working, even concern for employee well-being and the need for everyone to have a purpose. Yet we all know that in reality, there is a significant disconnect between the words on an annual report and the experience of the people on the front line. The People wave may be leading edge, but we can see it is already failing.

Take Jeff Bezos, founder and CEO of Amazon, as an example. Bezos states, "The question really is, *are you improving the world*? And you can do that in many models. You can do that in government, you can do that in a non-profit, and you can do that in commercial enterprise."[58] Sounds great. And yet Amazon staff report having to urinate in bottles or rubbish bins because they fear that a bathroom break would take too long and would cause them to miss their strict targets.[59] Bezos is unlikely to be alone in facing such juxtaposition. All large companies embracing a Purpose agenda are likely to face the same paradoxes.

John Mackey, who we started this chapter with, is now himself at least a partial victim of the failure of this People world view, when, pressured by shareholders, he sold Whole Foods to Amazon – a company with a *very* different purpose and ethos. In the end, for all the noble aspirations of a different type of business, money – $13.7 billion to be exact – called the shots.[60]

This is in no way a criticism of Mackey. He found himself up against an ingrained ownership and governance structure that favoured the Profit motive, and he is not alone. Seeds of Change sold to Mars in 1997. Organic chocolate business Green & Black's sold to Cadbury Schweppes in 2005. The Body Shop sold to L'Oréal a year later. Countless companies have found themselves in a similar situation and have chosen – or been forced via shareholders – to relinquish their "different type of business."

Clearly, there are two very powerful forces at work in business: a deeply entrenched drive for profit, and an equally potent desire to do things differently and make the world a better place. These forces are not happy bedfellows. It's very hard to reconcile the "race to the bottom" we are already witnessing in many sectors with the corresponding protestations of the importance of people and purpose. The words say one thing and the actions say another. Which remit has the upper hand depends on the individual business, the prevailing economic conditions, and the leadership maturity within the company.

Increasingly, we are coming to appreciate that we need to change the *way* business is structured and organised, change ownership and governance, otherwise no real long-term inclusive sustainability agenda will be possible. Inspiring words on a corporate document or even the very best of intentions to run the business differently are simply not enough. As we evolve from HR 5.0 to HR 6.0, HR will need to take the leading role in highlighting and grappling with these contradictions. As Gorbachev said to Reagan in Reykjavik, "If not us, then who? If not now, when?"[61] There is no function in business that is better placed to do so. If we do not step up and take on this challenge, then a regression will be certain.

Notes

1 Denning S (2013) The Origin of "The World's Dumbest Idea": Milton Friedman, *Forbes*, www.forbes.com/sites/stevedenning/2013/06/26/the-origin-of-the-worlds-dumbest-idea-milton-friedman/

2 Mayer C (2018) *Prosperity: Better Business Makes the Greater Good*, Oxford University Press, Oxford.

3 Savitz AW (2014) *The Triple Bottom Line*, Jossey-Bass, London.

4 Mackey J and Sisodia R (2012) *Conscious Capitalism: Liberating the Heroic Spirit of Business*, Harvard Business Publishing, Boston, MA.

5 Kofman F (2014) *Conscious Business: How to Build Value through Value*, Sounds True, Boulder, CO.

6 Mason P (2016) *PostCapitalism: A Guide to Our Future*, Penguin, London.

7 Arnsperger C (2010) *Full-Spectrum Economics: Toward an Inclusive and Emancipatory Social Science*, Routledge, London.

8 Eisenstein C (2011) *Sacred Economics: Money, Gift, and Society in the Age of Transition*, Evolver Editions, Berkeley, CA.

9 Singer T and Ricard M (Eds) (2015) *Caring Economics: Conversations on Altruism and Compassion, between Scientists, Economists, and the Dalai Lama*, St. Martin's Press, New York.

10 Webster K and MacArthur E (2016) *The Circular Economy: The Wealth of Flows*, 2nd edition, Ellen MacArthur Foundation Publishing, Isle of Wight.

11 King SD (2018) *When the Money Runs Out: The End of Western Affluence*, Yale University Press, New Haven, CT and London.

12 Bremmer I (2013) *Every Nation for Itself: Winners and Losers in a G-Zero World Portfolio*, Penguin, London.

13 Hart O and Zingales L (2017) Serving Shareholders Doesn't Mean Putting Profit above All Else, *Harvard Business Review*, https://hbr.org/2017/10/serving-shareholders-doesnt-mean-putting-profit-above-all-else

14 Rowland W (2005) *Greed, Inc.: Why Corporations Rule Our World and How We Let It Happen*, Thomas Allen Publishers, Toronto, ON.

15 Wiggin A and Incontrera K (2008) *I.O.U.S.A.: One Nation. Under Stress. In Debt.* John Wiley & Sons, New York.

16 Green S (2013) Whole Foods' John Mackey on Capitalism's Moral Code Podcase, https://hbr.org/2013/01/whole-foods-john-mackey-on-cap

17 George B (2015) *Discover Your True North*, updated edition, John Wiley & Sons, New York.
18 Zook C and Allen J (2016) *The Founder's Mentality: How to Overcome the Predictable Crises of Growth*, Harvard Business Review Press, Boston, MA.
19 Clifford C (2018) Whole Foods Turns 38, *CNBC*, www.cnbc.com/2018/09/20/how-john-mackey-started-whole-foods-which-amazon-bought-for-billions.html
20 Mackey J and Sisodia R (2012) *Conscious Capitalism: Liberating the Heroic Spirit of Business*, Harvard Business Review Press, Boston, MA.
21 Richards D (2018) The Men Behind Ben & Jerry's Ice Cream, *The Balance Small Business*, www.thebalancesmb.com/ben-and-jerry-s-the-men-behind-the-ice-cream-1200942
22 Ben & Jerry's website, www.benjerry.com/values
23 Freeman RE (1984) *Strategic Management: A Stakeholder Approach*, Prentice Hall, London.
24 Sawaf A and Rowan G (2014) *Sacred Commerce: A Blueprint for a New Humanity*, EQ Enterprises, Ojai, CA.
25 G&A Institute (2017) 82 Per Cent of the S&P 500 Companies Published CSR Reports in 2016: A Four-Fold Increase from 2011, www.sustainability-reports.com/82-of-the-sp-500-companies-published-corporate-sustainability-reports-in-2016/
26 Schiller B (2016) It's Time for Exponential Thinking about Corporate Responsibility, *Fast Company*, www.fastcoexist.com/3064851/its-time-for-exponential-thinking-about-corporate-responsibility
27 United Nations Sustainable Development Goals Knowledge Platform, https://sustainabledevelopment.un.org/
28 Ki-moon B (2014) Speaking at the Opening of Climate Week, New York, *YouTube*, www.youtube.com/watch?v=ivuudknkewk
29 Zenger J, Folkman J, and Edinger SK (2010) How Extraordinary Leaders Double Profits: Decoding Leadership Trends to Discover the Patterns, www.inspiredmastery.com/Double-Profits.pdf
30 Hunter JE, Schmidt FL, and Judiesch MK (1990) Individual Differences in Output Variability as a Function of Job Complexity, *Journal of Applied Psychology*, 75: 28–42.
31 Torbert WR et al. (2013) Developing Transforming Leadership: The Case of Warren Buffett, presented at the Integral Theory Conference, San Francisco, CA, www.williamrtorbert.com/wp-content/uploads/2013/09/EKellyWRTBuffett.pdf
32 Taylor B (2011) Great People Are Overrated, *Harvard Business Review*, https://hbr.org/2011/06/great-people-are-overrated
33 Unilever website, www.unilever.com/about/who-we-are/our-history/
34 Gallup (2017) State of the Global Workplace, www.gallup.com/workplace/238079/state-global-workplace-2017.aspx
35 Kimmel B (2018) Return on Trust: The "State of Trust" 2018, https://trustacrossamerica.com/documents/index/Return-Methodology.pdf
36 Eccles RG, Ioannou I, and Serafeim G (2014 revised) The Impact of Corporate Sustainability on Organizational Processes and Performance, www.hbs.edu/faculty/Publication%20Files/SSRN-id1964011_6791edac-7daa-4603-a220-4a0c6c7a3f7a.pdf
37 EY and Harvard Business Review (2015) The Business Case for Purpose, www.ey.com/Publication/vwLUAssets/ey-the-business-case-for-purpose/$FILE/ey-the-business-case-for-purpose.pdf

38 Smedley T (2014) The Evidence Is Growing – There Really Is a Business Case for Diversity, *Financial Times*, www.ft.com/cms/s/0/4f4b3c8e-d521-11e3-9187-00144feabdc0.html#axzz3p0vNtogT

39 Deloitte (2012) Waiter, Is That Inclusion in My Soup? A New Recipe to Improve Business Performance, www2.deloitte.com/content/dam/Deloitte/au/Documents/human-capital/deloitte-au-waiter_is_that_inclusion-150615.pdf

40 Smedley T (2014) The Evidence Is Growing – There Really Is a Business Case for Diversity, *Financial Times*, www.ft.com/cms/s/0/4f4b3c8e-d521-11e3-9187-00144feabdc0.html#axzz3p0vNtogT

41 Watkins A and Stratenus I (2016) *Crowdocracy: The End of Politics*, Urbane Publications, Kent.

42 Gratton L and Scott A (2016) *The 100-Year Life: Living and Working in an Age of Longevity*, Bloomsbury, London.

43 Hougaard R and Carter J (2018) *The Mind of the Leader: How to Lead Yourself, Your People and Your Organisation for Extraordinary Results*, Harvard Business Review Press, Boston, MA.

44 Pink D (2009) *Drive: The Surprising Truth about What Motivates Us*, Penguin, New York.

45 Neate R and Monaghan A (2018) Persimmon Boss Asked to Leave Amid Outrage over Bonus, *The Guardian*, www.theguardian.com/business/2018/nov/07/persimmon-boss-asked-to-leave-amid-ongoing-outrage-over-bonus

46 ABC News (2018) Bill Gates Says Another Financial Crash "Is a Certainty" in Reddit AMA, www.abc.net.au/news/2018-03-01/bill-gates-says-financial-crash-certainty-reddit-ama/9500326

47 Anthony S and Schwartz EI (2017) What the Best Transformational Leaders Do, *Harvard Business Review*, https://hbr.org/2017/05/what-the-best-transformational-leaders-do

48 Wilber K (2003) *Boomeritis: A Novel That Will Set You Free*, Shambhala Productions, Boston, MA.

49 Lewis M (2011) *The Big Short: Inside the Doomsday Machine*, Penguin, New York.

50 Petrie N (2011) *A White Paper: Future Trends in Leadership Development*, Center for Creative Leadership, Greensborough, NC.

51 Watkins A (2015) *4D Leadership*, Kogan Page, London.

52 Vitali S, Glattfelder JB, and Battiston S (2011) The Network of Global Corporate Control, *PLoS One*, 6(10): e25995.

53 Barton D (2011) Capitalism for the Long Term, *Harvard Business Review*, March 2011.

54 Rothkopf D (2009) *Superclass: The Global Power Elite and the World They Are Making*, Farrar, Straus and Giroux, New York.

55 Riota C (2018) Trump Meets Kanye West: Prison Reform, Gang Violence and Manufacturing on the Agenda for White House Lunch, *The Independent*, www.independent.co.uk/news/world/americas/donald-trump-kanye-west-meet-lunch-kim-kardashian-white-house-prison-chicago-gangs-a8579231.html

56 Flynn K (2018) Did Kylie Jenner Really Screw over Snapchat? *Mashable*, https://mashable.com/2018/02/22/kylie-jenner-snapchat-comment-twitter-stock-price-snap/?europe=true#PWaT4vY_cOqu

57 Treanor J and Elliott H (2014) And Breathe ... Goldie Hawn and a Monk Bring Meditation to Davos, *The Guardian*, www.theguardian.com/business/2014/jan/23/davos-2014-meditation-goldie-hawn

58 Boyle A (2018) Jeff Bezos: "We Will Have to Leave This Planet ... and It's Going to Make This Planet Better," *GeekWire*, www.geekwire.com/2018/jeff-bezos-isdc-space-vision/

59 Ghosh S (2018) Peeing in Trash Cans, Constant Surveillance, and Asthma Attacks on the Job: Amazon Workers Tell Us Their Warehouse Horror Stories, *Business Insider UK*, http://uk.businessinsider.com/amazon-warehouse-workers-share-their-horror-stories-2018-4

60 Clifford C (2018) Whole Foods Turns 38, *CNBC*, www.cnbc.com/2018/09/20/how-john-mackey-started-whole-foods-which-amazon-bought-for-billions.html

61 Barrypopik (2010) Origin of "If Not Us, Who? If Not Now, When?" (Not RFK), *RedState*, www.redstate.com/diary/barrypopik/2010/04/26/origin-of-if-not-us-who-if-not-now-when-not-rfk/

6   HR 6.0

The Paradox wave (2020–2040)

What's not to like about the People wave?

The world was crying out for a more people-centric, less greedy way of running business, and the People wave appeared to deliver. Purpose-driven companies are now seeking to change the world. Purpose-driven brands allow people to feel good about themselves as they consume their daily staples. Inclusion and diversity has almost mainstreamed, not only because it's viewed as the right thing to do, but because it's proven to be good business practice, as the world of marketing veers towards social media and away from mainstream media. In addition, moving away from performance management and reward systems that promote short-termism and self-interest to more sustainable, collective, longer-term incentives increasingly makes sound commercial sense to more and more businesses and encourages more cooperative and less toxic workplaces.

And yet despite all the great gifts bestowed on the world by the People wave, it is failing. And it's failing because of the paradoxes that it creates. We need to start to surf the Paradox wave.

The Paradox wave is the simultaneous explosion of opposites.

Despite the widespread adoption of purpose, diversity, and inclusion into the business world, we are also seeing a rise in global ethnocentricity, particularly in the political arena, with many modern countries polarising (think Brazil, Italy, Turkey, Poland, Ukraine, France, the UK, and the US). The "Overton window" (the term used to describe what is acceptable to say and debate) has moved backward in the last few years. People are saying things now that were last considered "acceptable" 80-plus years ago.

Yet, at the same time, we are on the brink of a real breakthrough in human consciousness.

These and many other paradoxes reveal that we are simultaneously at a point of emergency and emergence.

The People wave gave birth to the first glimmers of emergent thinking. But the paradox is that despite there being a genuine desire to do business differently, our existing business models, forms of governance, and operating principles, with their emphasis on shareholder value, quarterly numbers, ever-increasing growth, and margins, are forcing businesses to maintain the status quo, despite the grand words.

Once a business goes public, it may gain access to capital reserves for expansion and further growth, but it also loses a huge amount of control over how it is run, and ultimately its own destiny. John Mackey found that out the hard way. Mackey is clearly a man of principle, with decades of expertise in doing business differently, but even if he wanted to, he couldn't stop his shareholders accepting a takeover bid from Amazon. Shareholders, by their nature, are looking for business opportunities that will deliver a financial return. Some may share the ideals of the founder; many won't. In a system where the only thing that matters is shareholder value, where profits and the payment of dividends nearly always trump purpose, it can be impossible to hold back the tide. Publicly, Mackey was positive about the deal, telling employees that it was a "historic moment," and how together they would make a "big difference to the food industry."[1] But the marriage of sense and soul, of Amazon and Whole Foods, has not been an easy one – such unions never are.[2] Access to greater funding and greater reach was always going to come at a cost, especially when the values and operating principles of both companies were so diametrically opposed.

Many of today's exciting idealistic start-ups will experience the same challenge and fate.

The same is true for many more established/traditional businesses. As we write this chapter, Marks & Spencer have announced store closures in the UK and another "revamp." They were heavily criticised in the media for their performance, and their share price dropped 3.2 per cent. This despite the fact that their pre-tax profits rose by 7.1 per cent to £126.7 million. Just stop and consider that for a moment. M&S increased their profits, yet this is still not enough for some commentators.[3] How can such a paradox make sense? Why is such an improvement still not enough? If we cling onto the Profit wave and declare that the only thing that matters is delivering on market expectations of financial performance, then we may be unhappy with a 7 per cent increase in profits. If we take a People wave stance and acknowledge that M&S is still a great business and has much to offer beyond just cash generation, then we run the risk of ignoring the markets.

So, how do we square that circle? Such difficulties are at the core of the Paradox wave, and only when we embrace the Paradox wave will we unlock the sophistication of models and minds to adequately resolve such contradictions. Only when we fully acknowledge the failure of the People wave, and come to recognise that real change will not be possible without corresponding changes to operating models, governance, and ultimately legislation, will a new type of business become the norm.

If we believe that the failure of the People wave proves that the profit-only model is correct, then we will regress. We will reverse progress and risk squandering all the wonderful gifts bestowed by the People wave. We will create harsher economic conditions for millions and set the stage for the kind of civil disobedience witnessed in Venezuela, where evolution is blocked.[4]

The Paradox wave offers the best of both worlds; it offers a resolution of the conflict between Profit and People – an *and*, not an *or*, solution to a divided world.

But to reach such a nirvana, we must start to establish *and* principles in the way we structure our nations, in the way we write our laws. For example, professor of management studies Colin Mayer suggests that once this principle really sinks in, the law should require firms to *demonstrate* that their governance, leadership and incentives are organised in accordance with the higher ideals of HR 5.0 People. They will have to prove that "doing well is doing good."[5] We agree. It can no longer just be about profit. It must be Profit *and* People.

The first glimmers of Paradox

As we mentioned in Chapter 5, business leaders have known for some time that "something has to give." The focus on people and purpose was an attempt to address the imbalance that had arisen from the Profit wave. But when the ideals and operating principles of Profit are still so deeply entrenched into the mindset of business, it's almost impossible to change that paradigm.

Over the years, we have seen courageous leaders try, including many we have mentioned already. Paul Polman, Unilever's ex-CEO, tried to shift the reporting cycle to the city by refusing to report profit quarterly. He believed that the quarterly obsession with results was distorting behaviour and facilitating short-term thinking. He also believed that the time taken preparing the reports to satisfy analysts would be better spent satisfying customers. Unfortunately, not enough leaders followed suit, and so business is still engaged in the quarter-by-quarter battle.[6] Analysts want sustainable growth, but their demand for information necessitates behaviour that distracts leaders from creating such growth. This is the paradox.

For a global company, Unilever is doing its bit for the planet and has a strong core purpose, but even that's not enough when a private equity or rival firm believes they can turn a 15 per cent return into 22 per cent. Again, such is the paradox. Why is 15 per cent not enough?

Inside the capitalist model, there is no time to even consider that question. Under attack, even leaders with the best intentions are called to park their admirable and often genuine visions of sustainability in favour of radical short-term countermeasures to prevent a hostile takeover.

And that's exactly what happened to Unilever. In early 2017, Kraft Heinz, backed by 3G Capital, a private equity firm driven by three Brazilian corporate raiders, made a $143 billion bid for Unilever. Seen by some as just another corporate battle, more enlightened commentators saw it as something much more – nothing short of a fight for the soul of global corporations.[7] Although a big business in its own right, Kraft Heinz was still one-third the size of Unilever. The bid was even supported by Warren Buffett. It was a bold and audacious move, and their unexpected approach shocked the markets.[8]

If a company the size of Unilever could be "taken out" by an aggressor, then no company was safe. Such a move would also have sent a clear signal to the markets and beyond that a regressive move to profit and power were valid and would continue to trump people and purpose. These particular raiders had honed their capabilities over ten years and had never lost a fight, creating $300 billion for their backers in the process. They offered to buy shares above the market price at the time and planned to fund their takeover by restructuring Unilever's own balance sheet.

In the end, 3G underestimated the depth of Unilever's attachment to its culture, its pursuit of long-term sustainable growth,[9] and how much its stance on purpose-driven sustainability was supported by its shareholders. The outright rejection of the 3G bid meant the takeover would have been hostile, and 3G and Buffett withdrew. In the thick of the battle, Unilever announced a strategic restructuring of its business, including an intention to sell off its spreads business, increase profit margins, and alter the way it is listed on the stock exchange and the way it reports to the markets.[10] Unilever was already planning to make the changes, but the unsuccessful takeover was widely perceived as the catalyst.

This battle for the corporate soul is a sign of the times in which we live. The 3G business model is to cut costs and merge separate businesses to create mega-companies and operational efficiency. Its strategy of "zero-based budgeting" requires managers to justify their expenses from scratch every year. After applying this strategy to one company, it buys another and fuses them. They are viewed as ruthless, largely because the approach always comes at the cost of thousands of workers.[11] 3G is pure Profit wave with a healthy dose of Power. Unilever is rooted in the People wave with glimpses of Paradox. The fact that Unilever saw off the 3G attack and the leadership has since doubled down on their commitment to the "Unilever Sustainable Living Plan" provides a further ray of hope.

Companies who can balance Profit demands and People wave pressure, as well as change their business models and ways of operating, can reap the benefits of the Paradox wave and set the stage for the next phase of evolution.[12]

Paradox-based leadership

As People-based leadership fails and progress stalls once more, Paradox leaders step forward and take personal responsibility for reigniting the dream of a better tomorrow. This means that the pendulum swings back to a focus on the individual. Paradox leaders recognise the swamp that People leaders have created, and while they value inclusion, they also recognise the complexity that trying to embrace so many different views can bring. The fresh thinking they bring step-changes innovation capability while offering a genuine ability to integrate multiple perspectives and provide real skill in managing this constructively.

A Paradox leader embodies F. Scott Fitzgerald's famous quote, "The test of a first-rate intelligence is the ability to hold two opposed ideas in mind at the same time and still retain the ability to function."[13] For a Paradox leader, nothing is binary. They recognise that we live in a highly complex, highly interdependent world, which means that there are no easy answers. They understand that no one is right or wrong all the time. Thus, they move beyond the need to be right all the time themselves, a problem that is so prevalent in the first-tier waves.

Paradox leaders are the first leaders to truly see value and merit in all the world views offered by their first-tier predecessors. Paradox leaders can construct smart complex solutions as a result. An intellectual appreciation for diversity and inclusion evolves into a deeper appreciation for everyone in the system. As the Paradox leader opens up second-tier thinking, they begin to understand some fundamental realities about adult human development, namely that development doesn't stop once they leave university or finish a training programme. It can, and *must*, continue if they and their business are to stand any chance of meeting and harnessing the rapidly escalating complexity of the world.

At this P-wave, leaders wake up completely to their own development and the journey they are on. As a result, they are much more open and receptive to their own development, how they could develop their team, and thinking the unthinkable in relation to their business. As a result, they are much more likely to embrace the multidimensional nature of business and life, as well as the multiple lines of development that contribute to their horizontal learning, and more importantly their vertical development.

It was integral philosopher Ken Wilber who first organised the entire human experience into "dimensions" when he set out to construct a "theory of everything."[14] What he found was that each major theory put forward to explain some aspect of life focused on just one quadrant. All the theories, whether relating to leadership, management practice, philosophy, psychology, spirituality, ecology, or any academic discipline, could be placed within his four-quadrant map of reality. This AQAL model (see Figure 6.1) separates the interior from the exterior landscape of human experience for both the individual and the collective. As such, it describes individuals and teams, as well as the interior and exterior reality of each.

Wilber's objective was to provide a framework that would allow us to understand the complexity of the modern world, and ultimately to create an integral theory that, more than any other single theory, is more inclusive and more accurately explains reality. He succeeded.

Working with leaders from multiple market sectors all over the world, one of us (AW) has adapted Wilber's model slightly by rotating it anticlockwise one quarter-turn, making it three-dimensional and putting the leader at the centre of the enlightened leadership model (see Figure 6.2).

For the first time, the Paradox leader sees that their performance and capability are more than just what they do in the "IT" and "ITS" quadrants, but who

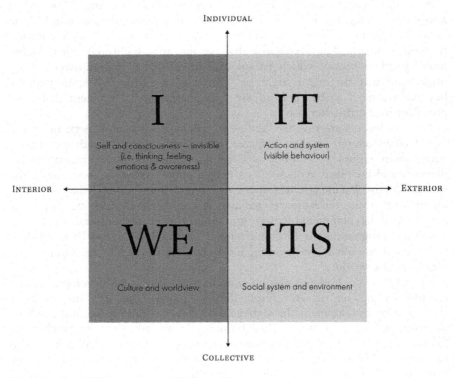

Figure 6.1 Ken Wilber's original AQAL model

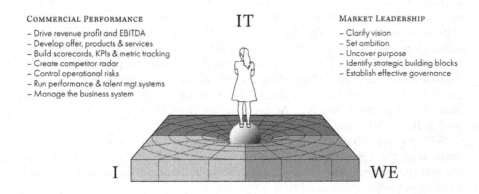

Figure 6.2 The enlightened leadership model

they are ("I") and how they interact and relate to others ("WE"). First-tier business leaders from the Paternalistic wave to the Profit wave are almost exclusively focused on "doing." Most have yet to realise that the source of their real competitive advantage and opportunity for exceptional performance and influence lies behind them in the dimensions of "I" and "WE." People leaders in HR 5.0 start to understand the value of focusing more on the "WE" dimension. As such, they begin to realise the crucial difference between horizontal learning and vertical development. But Paradox leaders go further and embrace both the "I" and "WE" dimensions more fully.

Up to the Profit wave, almost every training initiative or performance improvement intervention conceived of and executed in business through HR is focused on improving the "doing" – in other words, horizontal learning. HR professionals and business leaders have squeezed, squashed, poked, and prodded virtually every last ounce of benefit from the "doing" quadrant, whether through skills training, behavioural change initiatives, or systems and process improvements. There is often much less benefit to be extracted from these "doing" dimensions than targeted investment in the "I" and "WE" dimensions.

In all P-waves from Profit and below, employee well-being, which is really an "I" dimension phenomenon, was always subservient to wider business objectives. A more genuine consideration of the "I" dimension emerged in HR 5.0 People, but it only really starts to get seriously integrated into business through governance shifts in the Paradox wave.

The same is true of the "WE" dimension. Before HR 6.0, businesses did focus on relationships and how employees and owners interacted. But these relationships and "WE" dynamics were not deeply integrated with the "I" and "IT" dimensions. In HR 2.0 Power, relationships were often characterised by open battles in "us versus them" scuffles for control and power. Again, it was only at the emergence of HR 5.0, with its corresponding pursuits of people and purpose, that win/win solutions were sought. But "WE" quadrant considerations were still subservient to the wider business objectives – hence the contradictions that cause the People wave to fail. At HR 6.0, business understands that good intentions will almost always fly out the window when the shareholders are rattling the gates. As a result, HR 6.0 proactively moves to a new business model and governance approach to integrate and liberate the "WE" dimension.

Prior to HR 5.0, the "I" and the "WE" may have existed, but they were often in competition and conflict with the "IT" and "ITS" dimensions of "doing." Often "doing" initiatives such as bonuses and incentives were dressed up as "I" and "WE" manoeuvres, but they were still initiatives that were designed to change behaviour for the sake of delivering more revenue or profit. Incentives were not focused on how people related to each other. At HR 5.0, a recognition emerges that the tension between People and Profit is unsustainable, and ultimately not good business. The HR 5.0 realisation is that a new approach is required that can deliver both People *and*

Profit goals. When the leader evolves into the Paradox wave and the second tier, the sophistication of this new approach improves significantly. It is less of a balance or trade-off, and much more a deeper integration that facilitates lasting solutions.

It's almost as though these additional dimensions suddenly pop into focus like one of those "magic eye" puzzles. Those in the first tier could stare at the graphic for a year and only occasionally glimpse the secret image hidden within, but as soon as the Paradox world view comes online and second-tier thinking opens up, there it is as plain as day.

Having spent over 20 years working with leaders, teams, and organisations, it is clear to both authors that sustainable transformation in business can only ever occur if there is an equal commitment to development in the "being" dimension (the inner, subjective personal performance world of "I") and the "relating" dimension (the interpersonal people leadership world of "WE") as there is in the "doing" dimensions of "IT" and "ITS."

To some in the first tier, even talking about the "I" and "WE" dimensions can sound like New Age "mumbo jumbo" or touchy-feely nonsense. Results are all that matter, right? But by 2020, most business leaders, regardless of world view, now know that they perform better when they are passionate and determined as opposed to angry and frustrated. They know that bad news can upend their day and pollute more than just their commercial judgement. How we are "being," the speed and quality of our mind, our energy, and our emotional state all fundamentally change how well we can "do" anything, as well as what we choose to "do." Thus, the effectiveness of our "doing" is determined by the sophistication of our "being."

Similarly, when the business operates from within silos and cross-functional relationships are based on transactions rather than trust, then delivering productive outcomes becomes much harder. The quality of relationships between different divisions, or even between individuals within the same division, often determines our ability to get things done.

The stronger the bonds between leaders, the more productive the team. Yet when organisations try to improve team dynamics and performance of the business, they frequently invest their time and energy into changing structures, re-engineering processes, reworking strategy, and reordering their "to-do" list of priorities. Most companies do not forensically dissect the nature of human relationships and how they can step-change the quality of the connections with those around them, let alone try to work with a developmental frame to strengthen bonds within the company.

If we are to reap the competitive advantage inherent in the "I" and "WE" dimensions that become visible to the Paradox leader, we must appreciate that our efforts in the rational, objective world are actually built on the subjective, internal world of "I" (physiology, emotions, feelings, thoughts, etc.), and that the success of what we want to build requires strong relationships, a performance culture, great teams that trust each other, and high-quality connectivity with customers and staff in the interpersonal world of "WE."

This is ultimately what drives sustainable positive impact in the objective external world of "IT."

For the Paradox leader, it finally dawns on them that the *only* way out of the daunting complexity we face is an acceleration and expansion of the "I" and "WE" quadrants to create 4D leadership.

HR 6.0 and the emergence of 4D leadership

Most business leaders and C-suite executives are already very proficient in many of the tasks within the world of doing ("IT"/"ITS"), so much so that many have often lost touch with their "being" and have become addicted to "doing." For them, work can degrade into an endless series of activities, goals, gambits, and initiatives. Seasons can come and go without leaders noticing, and the pressure mounts day after day, quarter after quarter, until it seems unrelenting. No wonder there is a rising tide of mental health issues. With so much to do, many executives struggle to even make time for "relating," and many are on to their third marriage to prove it. Few leaders know how to bring all of themselves to work. Many end up living a partial, fragmented, one-dimensional life as opposed to a enjoying a fulfilling four-dimensional working experience.

But it's not just businesspeople who sell themselves short. Some people choose to turn their back on the world of "doing," disenfranchised with the greed, avarice, political manoeuvring, and manipulation commonplace in many organisations – not to mention the inequality in what they see as a money-grabbing capitalist world full of ego and self-serving behaviour. Instead, they pursue a more "noble" life of inner contemplation and spiritual development. They have effectively turned inward to the interior world of "I." Rejecting material possessions, they may be highly evolved with a dedicated commitment to spiritual practice, but such a mono-focused interior exploration is every bit as one-dimensional as the single-minded business leader who focuses exclusively on the external world of doing at the expense of his health, relationships, and environment.

Similarly, some people, often those in the caring professions, not-for-profit organisations, or the service industry, choose to immerse themselves in the interpersonal world of "WE" and dedicate their lives to service of one sort or another. These individuals often put others' needs before their own to such an extent that they become ill. They fail to sufficiently look after their own "being," sacrificing what they may need in the service of others – there for everyone else but not themselves.

Ironically, the single-minded business executive, the spiritual seeker, and the carer may look completely different, live very different lives, and yet they are all making the same fundamental error – they live their lives largely in one dimension.

In order for us to be fully functioning human beings, we need to bring "all of us" to our daily lives, not just "fragments of us." We need to be very capable in all four dimensions, "I," "WE," "IT," and "ITS." The recognition of this urgent need only fully comes online at HR 6.0 Paradox. But awareness is not enough; we need to develop our "altitude" across the key lines of development that span the four dimensions and facilitate vertical development.

Over the last 20-plus years, one of us (AW) has identified the eight most commercially relevant *lines of development* for most business leaders (see Figure 6.3). Drawing on very rich scientific literature on adult development, these separate but interconnected and cumulative lines of development facilitate much needed verticality across these two largely ignored dimensions to create 4D leadership.[15]

Multidimensional vertical development offers significant competitive advantage, but the biggest gains are from interventions that deliberately develop the dimensions of "being" ("I") and "relating" ("WE").[16] You can find much more detail on the techniques and interventions used to create vertical development across the various lines of development in *Coherence: The Secret Science of Brilliant Leadership.*[17]

Part of the excitement that comes online in the Paradox wave is the recognition that there *is* a clear way forward where a brick wall stood before. We don't have to suffer and struggle at an individual and collective level. There is potential for complete reinvigoration.

We need more of these types of leaders (4D or Paradox leaders) because they can, more than any leader in the P-waves before them, "change the game." And that's exactly what's required in business. Paradox leaders will

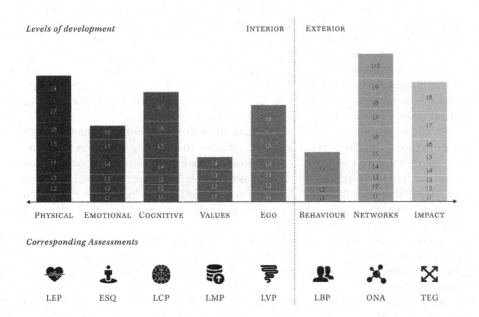

Figure 6.3 Lines of development

bring a new operating model, a new business paradigm that includes but genuinely goes beyond profit, regardless of the prevailing economic winds or internal and external threats. Paradox leaders set a new context. They are competitive because they are fast, flexible, and able to "hack" around older, less optimal structures. That is partly because they make more connections than most between a much greater variety of phenomena. They are exactly what's needed to usher in a new way of doing business that sticks, does not regress under pressure, and is robust enough and competitive enough to become the new normal.

Paradox leaders can see multiple perspectives and can more easily handle conflicts of interest. Drawn towards complex problems, these leaders want to make an impact beyond their company. Such a stance is timely as we face a smorgasbord of wicked problems desperate for a solution – problems that range from political instability, to economic inequality, to climate change.[18] It is the leaders and entrepreneurs from the Paradox wave who are coming up with game-changing technology or solutions to thorny issues such as how to remove plastics from the oceans.

Interestingly, Gen Y or the millennials born from 1981 to 2000 often operate from the Paradox wave. Gen Y workers are expected to make up roughly 75 per cent of the global workforce by 2025,[19] and are known as "Gen Why."[20] They are confused by what they see in the world and want to do something about it. We saw that first-hand following the school shooting at Parkland in 2018 – young people coming together to fight against gun violence. This generation is more technologically sophisticated than their parents, and are looking for purpose and fulfilment as well as a way to make a living. They don't necessarily feel loyalty to a company or brands, and are happy to job-hop to a position they feel suits them and their ideology. Considering how employment is changing, this new breed of worker is arriving in the workforce in the nick of time. It's going to take a special type of company and a special type of leader to attract these digital natives and harness the potential they bring. That leader is the Paradox leader.

It is the millennials and Gen Z behind them that will transform the workplace. These are individuals who have not known a world without tech or political and financial turmoil. They are, in many respects, much more comfortable with the reality that everything is getting better and worse at the same time. They are much more comfortable with paradox in all its forms.

There is little doubt that this new workforce and the product and service demands they make will bring innovation and insight to business, which will further accelerate our progress to a business model that goes beyond pure capitalism.

During the People wave, smart businesses realised that they need to have a compelling purpose if they are to attract and keep the right people. Corporate aspirations must embrace all stakeholders, not just shareholders. This means developing a strong employer brand, separate from the products or services that business may produce. This is much easier with a Paradox leader in charge, who is purposefully shaping a corporate identity that is authentic, credible, relevant, distinct, and inspirational.

Teams at HR 6.0: integrated pluralists

The jump from an HR 4.0 team of *interdependent achievers* to an HR 5.0 team of *diverse pluralists* is greater than the jump to an HR 6.0 team of *integrated pluralists*. Diverse pluralists start to experience states of flow. With integrated pluralists, frictionless performance and flow states become common in team meetings.[21] This is because the energy boost that kicks in at HR 4.0 and the flow state that emerges at HR 5.0 integrate to create entrainment. Entrainment is the well-described synchronisation that occurs in many natural groups such as the spectacular murmurings of starlings at dusk or the shoal of fish who change direction en masse as if they were one giant organism.[22] The physics of such harmony is now understood, but it is extremely rare to see this in an executive team until you reach HR 6.0 integrated pluralists.

As we suggested earlier, HR 5.0 diverse pluralists have developed the ability to work with multiple perspectives. Their evolution into HR 6.0 is marked by the speed with which the team can integrate these perspectives into a more unified whole. We may witness decision-making innovations such as Holacracy[23] at this level.

Holacracy itself is a term coined by the founders of HolacracyOne in the US. They describe it as a:

> comprehensive practice for structuring, governing, and running an organization. It replaces today's top-down predict-and-control paradigm [Power, Process, and Profit] with a new way of distributing power and achieving control. It is a new "operating system" which instills rapid evolution in the core processes of an organization.[24]

One of the primary characteristics of the Paradox wave is the acceptance and embrace of complexity and the corresponding ability to integrate multiple perspectives towards a genuinely collaborative solution – not one where some people have been outvoted by others, as seen in the Profit wave, and not some watered-down consensual fudge that often occurs in the People wave, but a genuine integration where all views are incorporated into a solution that everyone can get behind. At the Paradox wave, teams utilise a faster, more sophisticated decision-making process called "integrative decision-making" (IDM). The value of IDM is that it transcends the "democratic" process, which, in a group of ten people, aims to produce a 6 versus 4 vote. The goal of the IDM process is to create complete alignment within a team and generate a 10 versus 0 vote. This is achieved without getting stuck in the consensual hell of the People wave. Being able to rapidly reach a genuinely collective, mutually agreed upon 10 versus 0 decision within an executive board or work group saves a huge amount of time and energy. It is no longer necessary to neutralise the effects of the minority that are unhappy with the decision because no one has to "tow the party line," and therefore no one feels the need to plot against the outcome.

Holacracy is, however, more than just a decision-making process – it's a way of dealing with incredibly complex situations and decisions by facilitating a much greater level of inclusion, integration, and feedback within the system.[25] Without IDM and many more holocratic processes, business can easily regress to an earlier P-wave.

The downside of the Paradox wave is it can massively overcomplicate any situation and then struggle to explain its very nuanced world view. The role of HR is therefore to help better articulate the benefits of this second-tier vantage point, so people, teams, and organisations can better embrace its profound benefits.

A team of integrated pluralists also exhibits elevated agility; tension resolution is rapid and wisdom starts to emerge consistently across a whole range of topics. In fact, the consistency of the team's productivity becomes a focus point for the team.

The increased industry focus of the team that kicked in at HR 5.0 becomes more structured. External networks and market dynamics become a significant area of focus for integrated pluralists, supported by their increased systems thinking capability. When integrated pluralists meet, the conversation transcends many of the concerns that occupy teams operating at earlier P-waves. They are aware of the different levels of the system, and move up and down the levels, switching between the complex and the pragmatic as the need arises. The team focus also moves readily around "I," "WE," and "IT" agendas.

HR 6.0 teams construct multiple strategic options and leverage the different perspectives available to them from leaders at all levels of the organisation and integrate the team's views. There is a much greater involvement of the entire organisation and a desire to unlock the wisdom of the crowd because they have realised that there are useful insights sitting at all levels of the organisation that need to be mined.

These team members have also begun to understand that many of the problems faced in complex systems are not problems that can be solved, but polarities that must be managed.[26] For example, the team ceases to see short- and long-term or centralised and delegated authority as trade-offs, and starts to see them as dependent poles of the same polarity. Ultimately, the team is able to enhance individual and collective performance across the organisation to build a more inclusive and successful business.

Recalibration of "mental health"

As mentioned in the Introduction, Jeremy Rifkin talks about organisations designed around the "collaborative commons" – a sharing society where well-being is the primary economic goal.[27] We are still some way off well-being becoming an economic goal, but it is definitely on the corporate agenda.

In the Profit wave, few cared about well-being. Employees were expected to "man up" and just get on with it. Stress was almost a badge of honour. Lunch was for wimps. In the People wave, well-being became a major issue. It's now almost impossible to avoid information and adverts on "mental health" – what it is and what we should be doing about it.

Although the collective focus on mental health and well-being is giving this issue voice and bringing it to public awareness, the explanations and solutions put forward in the People wave, which the most progressive organisations are in now (2020), are largely ineffective.

For a start, not enough people understand the importance of addressing the challenge across the dimensions of "doing," "being," and "relating." One of us (AW) works extensively with organisations, and nearly all of them already have an employee assistance programme (EAP) of some sort. In one breakfast meeting on the topic, HR professionals from multiple organisations shared the 34 different well-being initiatives they were running in their companies. However, on closer inspection of these initiatives, which included things such as access to bowls of fruit and water, increased time for breaks, play-rooms, and playing relaxing music, all but one was a "doing" initiative.

Well-being and "mental health" is not a "doing" phenomenon – it's a "being" phenomenon. We will never solve a "being" problem with a "doing" solution. Useful mental and emotional health interventions must therefore consist of "being" solutions, and that means development of the "I" quadrant, as we discussed earlier.

The second problem is that the term "mental health" is misleading and allows too much to be lumped together under that term. This misdiagnosis is at least in part due to a lack of sophistication around the phenomena that are currently lumped together as mental health. For example, many of the issues highlighted as mental health issues, such as anxiety and panic attacks, are emotional health issues, not mental. They relate to our emotional intelligence and emotional flexibility and resilience, not some type of mental challenge. In most cases of anxiety and depression, "mentation" or cognitive processes are entirely normal.

The rise of mental and emotional health issues was in part due to the fact that middle-income earners in the US and Europe have fared much worse during the rampant globalisation driven during the Profit wave.[28] There has been much talk of a fairer society, but a lot of this has been spin and frankly deliberate manipulation characteristic of HR 4.0. In this wave, there was talk for the first time of "transformational leadership," and yet transformational leadership can be a fundamentally manipulative concept.[29] All that happened was existing Profit-focused initiatives were simply rebranded and dressed up in transformational language. Those locked in the Profit motive did the same when the People wave swept through via greenwashing – where Profit-driven businesses would simply rebrand or reframe initiatives to tap into the consumer desire to be more environmentally responsible and buy from businesses who could demonstrate that commitment.

The same is happening with "mental health" in the People wave. Right now (2020), mindfulness is driving the bandwagon.

What will happen as the Paradox wave becomes the leading edge is that we will come to recognise what some currently term as "mental health" is often really development.

Clearly, there are clinical issues, and the People wave has contributed greatly to removing the stigma applied in the past to these types of health issues. However, the mental health challenges that many people now relate to and buy into are opportunities for development, not something bad that must be accepted and managed. In the Paradox wave, HR will embrace them as a good thing to be embraced. As adult human beings, we are meant to be out of our comfort zone, we are meant to struggle occasionally as we find greater resilience and fortitude. Stress is a signal, not a lifestyle. Being uncertain and confused is a normal part of the learning and development process. They are invitations to change, to develop as an adult, and evolve to a higher level of consciousness.

Such a view is not well understood. Mental health has effectively been hijacked to sell more books and seminars. And one of the best ways to keep people stuck at that lucrative developmental crossroads is to apply a label that people then take on as their own. "I'm depressed" or "I'm stressed" or "I suffer from anxiety" becomes part of that person's identity.

What will increasingly happen in the Paradox wave, facilitated by HR professionals, is the individual will instead be encouraged to recognise their symptoms as an opportunity for development, and HR will provide support to make that transition to a healthier, more enlightened stance. As such, HR will be on the frontier of shifting perspectives and turning "mental health issues" into human development opportunities so individuals and companies can access greater well-being, expanded capability, and happiness.

Emerging HR and people practices

People practices in the Paradox wave will make a leap in terms of sophistication and business impact. The Paradox wave will be the "make or break" era for the function currently known as HR.

The paradox for HR at this level will be that while the wave calls for HR to make its world-changing contribution, this wave will see "HR," as we have known it for the last 100 years, all but disappear.

The Paradox wave will not just have a profound impact on HR; it will see the structuring of companies radically change, with traditional organisational design thinking and machine metaphors upended by the elimination of "functions" and the rise of network thinking and analysis.

It will see the rise of new models of employment, and the breaking down of the internal/external and permanent/temp distinctions fixed/flex, as organisations seek to "swarm," "flex," and "sprint" their ways of working.

It will see a true revolution in employee relations and engagement as businesses start to crowdsource and trade unions become brokers in a wider network.

However, most significantly of all, the signature change in the Paradox era will be in how companies are governed. The Paradox wave will bring to shore a whole new diverse set of business governance models, enabling a rebirth of entrepreneurship, a true realisation of purpose, as business, for the first time since the Industrial Revolution, becomes about *us*, not just money.

We will now unpack each of these emerging practices.

The disappearing "HR function"

The departmental responsibilities of the old HR function are likely to change significantly in the Paradox wave because of digitisation and other evolutionary dynamics.

For example, people working on day-to-day people issues, HR admin, transactions, and operations (including grievance-handling and even those managing negotiations with trade unions) will, over time, no longer be in a dedicated people department. We envisage that they will migrate to something like a "chief productivity officer's" office.

Some AI-driven healthcare companies, such as Babylon Healthcare, are already experimenting with such models.

A chief productivity office will be more of a hybrid in-house/outsourced function that will provide companies and organisations with all their "back office" activities.

These entities will be cross-functional, flexible, and manage a portfolio of critical partnerships, rather than suppliers, to deliver on the changing needs of a company. They will be more involved in basic commercial activity, such as automated "order to cash" processes and machine learning planning for production companies. They will provide data warehousing for reporting and ensure effective HR, marketing, and sales operations and financial transactions. They will be the "RPA" (robotic process automation) gurus, providing an infrastructure so that employees and customers will interact via bots (chatlines), telephone, and – in the best companies – through networks of care involving real people!

Organisations such as Capgemini, Accenture, and Genpact, originally the "business services unit" for GE (now a spin-off), are already gaining massive market traction by offering to "digitise" organisations quickly using their platforms and RPA expertise.

As we see this wave gather momentum, we may see – paradoxically – some reversal of the outsourcing and offshoring that happened in the Profit wave. Companies will be much more discerning about which core processes and tasks need to remain in-house or will be embedded if outsourced, to enable commercial speed and innovation agility.

If outsourced, they may find they work for a consortium of companies, not just one, but they will be embedded rather than remote, avoiding the mistakes of the outsourcing failures of the Profit wave.

Unlike the old outsourced service providers, new cross-functional service organisations, with the right leader, utilising the power of a network (see below), will seek to reconnect and work intimately with the people they serve. If such chief productivity offices continue to be led by Profit wave or Power wave leaders, they will fail badly. There will be no traditional service-level agreements (SLAs), indicating only a transactional relationship. These will be replaced by institutional and personal trust. This institutional trust will be one of the competitive advantages that such new service organisations will seek to market themselves on.

People administrators, operators, and industrial relations managers are all likely to find themselves no longer in the "people development department," but subsumed into the chief productivity office or a bespoke service organisation of some description.

With chief productivity-type organisational constructs, the link with the origins of HR, admin, welfare, and industrial relations, going back 105 years, will be broken. The generalist HR professional will have gone for good.

This is the existential threat that faces the HR function of today. The vast majority of activity undertaken by HR up to this point, including industrial relations, recruitment, administration, and training routines, will become digitised and part of the cross-functional "chief productivity" type organisation. Like other functions such as finance and operations, the old functional barriers will fall. New activity areas, driven by the digital revolution, will arise.

"HR" or people and team performance professionals will then have to prove they are worth keeping and will have to add exceptional levels of value or risk being pushed out the door.

The value creation opportunity is clear.

HR professionals/people and team performance specialists, whatever they end up being known as, will have to develop organisations that can operate at new levels of capability and work with agility, scale, and at higher levels of effectiveness. They will need to develop leaders who are the "Nelson Mandelas of the business world" – who energise, inspire, and grow those around them. They will need to enable organisations and the people within them to connect to a higher purpose – so ensuring that the profit versus everything else polarity is transcended once and for all – all while devising new models of employment that enable flex but bring security into an ever-more volatile world, and enable human development rather than increased exploitation and inequality in the workplace.

The organisational alchemy required, including making sense of the various paradoxes and polarities, can only be achieved by and through people. All of this requires a step up in leadership sophistication and subtlety, organisational design thinking, leadership development practice, employment models, and employee engagement. The agenda is very clear!

Organisational design and development: the networked org Mark I

The need to be "agile" and respond quickly to volatile markets is more critical than ever in the Paradox wave. The largest companies are seeking to identify the organisational design formula for what would be the "organisational holy grail," the ability to demonstrate both agility and scale. The search is likely to lead to the networked organisation.

We have already described that when faced with the need to cut costs and increase profits, most large companies instinctively centralise. In the Profit wave, this made sense. Shedding the weight that many companies gain in "middle age" enables them to become lean, more efficient, and fight on in the relentless pursuit of growth. Where there is excessive duplication and waste, this strategy still makes sense.

But centralisation as a mechanism for cost reduction is extremely fragile. Creating single centralised systems often brings enormous risk, slows responsiveness, and frequently alienates customers, as experienced by British Airways when their global IT system failed in 2017.

This is why new organisational design solutions will come on stream in the Paradox wave – solutions not born in machine thinking, but solutions owing more to biology. The network graph will replace the org chart.

HR professionals must add, and are already adding, significant value in this space by acting as architects for new organisational structures. For example, tech start-up Qubit, who are currently one of the world's best AI personalisation companies, have used network analysis to guide organisational restructuring as well as focus their leadership development efforts in what is a very fast-paced market sector, requiring companies to continually reshape themselves and do so at speed.

Being networked enables more "boundary-less" working, with minimal layers, fewer silos, and being "semipermeable" to insourced partners who work alongside the company's own employees, thereby allowing increased flex and responsiveness to market changes.

In their early book on the subject, authors including David Ulrich stated that there was a growing need to permeate boundaries across functions, geographies, and hierarchies, both internally and externally.[30] While the authors claimed a number of organisations are becoming "boundary-less" (e.g. GE Capital), practical examples still focused on process interventions such as the famous GE "Work-Out" techniques (a form of work organisation/meeting process). The initial suggestion of "boundary-lessness" have therefore not yet materialised, but the power of the original idea remains compelling.

The digital market and sector are actively beginning to explore networked models through the concepts of agile working, as they already recognise the need for communities or clusters of capability rather than rigid hierarchies or command-and-control empires.[31] The primary organisational challenge for HR to solve in the Paradox wave will be how to create such clusters of capability.

We believe that the upgraded organisational design thinking in the Paradox wave transcends the old centralisation versus decentralisation debates. It is built around the idea of integration and decentralisation.

Integration is not just centralisation by another name; it is how we connect people, systems, and processes to strategies and goals. It is the "whole" coming together, whereas centralisation looks at how we organise power, symbolised by where the boxes and lines go on an organisational chart.

The best organisations have always been more effectively integrated, but that integration was often localised or in service of a centralised hierarchy.[32] In the Paradox wave, integration moves to a whole new level. Integrated and networked organisations are emerging, and existing organisations are beginning to embrace such ideas. If they do, then they are much better placed to respond with agility to the digitised world. Their agile networks will be in the service of decentralised communities, not centralised hierarchies.

Integration ensures we scale where we must. Decentralisation will enable us to connect with who we serve more intimately by putting the power in the hands of the people closest to the customers so they can make better decisions. We can achieve both through *networks*, not hierarchy (see Figure 6.4).

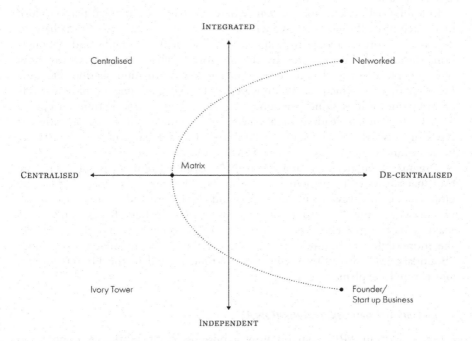

Figure 6.4 The decentralised, integrated sweet spot for organisational design

The "sweet spot" is represented in the top-right quadrant – the networked organisation – where the benefits of scale are retained through integration, but the magic of responsiveness is reawakened through decentralisation enabled by networks.

There are a maximum of three layers of hierarchy in a networked organisation. A digitally enabled business does not need any more than:

1.   a strategic layer;
2.   an integrating layer; and
3.   the front line.

To make a networked organisation function, the integrating layer is pivotal. Leaders in this layer work vertically across all dimensions of the business. The leaders in these roles are key to making the entire system work. They must manage the polarities that committees used to address, although the committee often saw such tensions as trade-offs rather than polarities. Silos disappear and functions wither away as people are increasingly organised in smaller end-to-end teams. These teams are likely to be no bigger than the magic number of 150, as identified by evolutionary biology.[33] Smaller teams share common platforms (services, specialists, productions units), enabling responsiveness and scale, and only the Paradox leaders can fill the integrated roles and orchestrate the networks.

In a fully networked organisation, where front-line operational players work in a much more fluid fashion, we will no longer look at "old-style" org charts to describe our organisations. Instead, we will use network graphs and organisational health will be measured by the network health – in other words, how often people connect, levels of trust, quality of information sharing, etc. (see Figure 6.5), all of which can be measured.[34] The network graph will be the reference point for how things get done, and who is key to making things happen.

HR professionals leading organisation development will focus on different types of networks.[35] The level of "linking" a leader has will be a key factor in determining and explaining performance outcomes.

Organisational network analysis (ONA) is an extremely useful diagnostic tool that allows us to recognise and map that "linking." As a result, it can be employed at this wave to better understand the nature and depth of the existing networks and how to facilitate constructive further change (and avoid making destructive change to those networks). The healthier the network, the more agile the business and the greater the ability to operate in a more "boundary-less" way. ONA will become fundamental in the HR6.0 toolkit, and is briefly explained below.

Organisational network analysis (ONA)

ONA is like an MRI scan on how a business really works, as opposed to how the organisational chart thinks it works. It allows a business to:

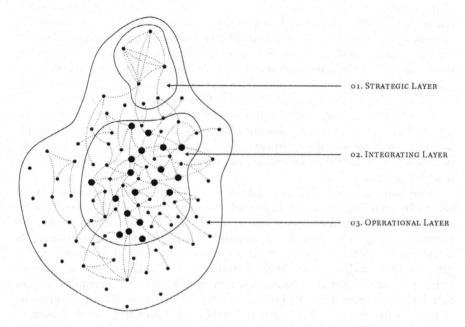

Figure 6.5 Graphic on network health

- identify their most influential executives and quantify their impact in relation to each other, operationally, culturally, and strategically;
- save money by targeting HR investment on people and initiatives that will transform the business;
- uncover the people at risk of exit or those who need more support before they start to underperform and impair operational delivery;
- clarify how well connected the critical divisions of their organisation are and whether those relationships are driven geographically, functionally, or by seniority;
- pinpoint the best people to bridge the gaps between different divisions and step-change the connectivity where the business really needs it to ensure optimal productivity and sustainable growth; and
- reveal how well each leadership team is performing and the capability gap between the leader and the rest of the team that must be addressed to accelerate each team's contribution.

The origins of ONA go back more than 50 years when sociologists in the 1960s started to use mathematics (graph theory) to understand critical workplace interactions. Since then, ONA has developed into a distinct field within the wider function of people analytics.

By asking any group, team, collective, cohort, whole organisation, or nation nine simple questions, Complete, the company founded by one of the authors (AW), can generate hundreds of thousands of data points that illuminate the informal and often invisible interactions between people in organisations *and* provide insights into the quality of those interactions. By applying big data analytics to these data points, it's possible to reveal invaluable actionable insights about three critical networks: functional, social, and strategic.

The resulting ONA charts and scatterplots provide precise data on the quality and pattern of the relationships between individuals that drive individual, team, and divisional performance. As a result, it provides the critical link between organisational development and people development, something that is so often missing.

ONA can reduce costs and deliver a significant return on investment (ROI) by enabling leaders to know where to best intervene to drive results, and what kind of interventions are required. For example, if improved sales are what is required, research has found that individuals who form networks across many different parts of an organisation (brokers) perform better, improve sales, and are more likely to innovate.[36] If collaboration and greater innovation are required, separate research has shown that Formula 1 teams that leveraged their network brokers performed better in World Championships than those teams that did not.[37] Efficiency issues have been shown to improve by encouraging knowledge-sharing between different teams.[38] And finally, the effectiveness of mergers and acquisitions has been shown to come down to the activity of the network.[39]

New forms of employment

Networked organisations will require different employment models. Companies will value flex – functional flex, working time flex, project focus flex. As agile ways of working become the norm in offices and factories, people will no longer have a fixed job description. Jobs as we know them today are likely to be permeable, described as discrete activity statements rather than responsibility and accountability checklists.

In the Paradox wave, we will see a desire for conceptual and operational flexibility, where people can swarm to the work like bees, where it is needed, and not be constrained by twentieth-century limitations of functional or departmental silos, or even permanent contracts.

Ways of working, such as those lauded in manufacturing during the Profit wave, are deployed widely in software development and are spreading into the office environment. Agile teams and lean start-up methodologies will be the norm. New phrases such as scrum (and the job "scrum master"), two-week swarming sprint processes, and squads (a new word for super-teams) are already emerging in some businesses. Many companies are urgently "digitising" back office functions, seeking to utilise algorithms, bots in place of people, or cobots working alongside people.

So, flex working will be the underlying employment trend during the Paradox wave. Career fluidity will mean that people will need a much greater sense of personal purpose to effectively navigate their own career journey.

But, as with all levels, the Paradox wave's inherent contradictions will ultimately accelerate its failure.

Organisations, faced with so much volatility, will want to optimise their own flexibility. We already saw in the Profit wave how the use of agency or third-party labour provision exploded in factories and shops. To drive down costs and ensure complete flexibility, many factories and retail outlets stopped employing people directly – a step back in time to the early "gangmaster" days of the Industrial Revolution. Amazon has established several ways of working for the company. The lucky ones are considered core employees, well looked after in geographic head office locations. The rest may work for Amazon flex, on call, when needed, but not paid when not – no pension, no sick pay, no security. Or, alternatively, they may work for Amazon via one of its partners. In logistics, we see the stressed out DPD driver, running up and down streets, driving like a bat out of hell, working to a clock, and penalised for non-delivery.

Sports Direct in the UK became infamous for their use of extensive zero-hour contracts, where employees are literally on call. Even when they were not being paid, they still had to be on call. It's hard to justify the term "employees" in such situations.

And this type of flex is not just impacting lower-paid jobs; it's coming into middle-class office roles too. Companies such as Catalant and Forshay provide project and professional people on call to flex up for projects. These people are often highly paid professionals and want to work this way because it maximises their freedom and choice. In the past, however, these people would have been on a payroll somewhere. Now they work for many organisations, moving in and out of the workplace on projects that interest them and where they can deliver value.

As the Paradox wave progresses, companies will need to overcome many polarities, including the thorny one of flex and security. Leaders who don't operate from a truly Paradox wave will talk about changing the world for the better, while at the same time seeking to set up working arrangements that barely pay a minimum wage. Such inauthenticity or inability to manage polarities will become increasingly apparent.

Of course, in any polarity, one side of the polarity is not all bad. Some employees may prefer flex working for the freedoms it offers, especially those that can command high project-based salaries. But the downsides of the flex pole, experienced by workers with limited negotiating power or choice, will occur if flex is seen in isolation of the security pole. It is possible to enjoy flex *and* security, but if these polarities are mismanaged we experience the worse of both worlds, namely little security and little flexibility. If this happens, then engagement levels plummet, undoing all the inclusive, high purpose-based benefits of the previous People wave.

If polarity management, which is a crucial new capability that emerges in the Paradox wave, is not understood, then the mangled attempts to manage flex security polarities will push governments to legislate not only on labour conditions, but also pay and potential exploitation. Such legislation may itself impair further progress, particularly if it is not informed by Paradox thinking.

The most progressive companies will anticipate such collapses and confusions to reinvent employment that works for the individual and the company.

Reinventing the employment model

In July 2018, *The Economist* ran a futuristic story of what life might be like in 2028.[40] In it, an imaginary person called Eva Smith receives an email on 13 October 2028 in which she is told that a corporate shake up means that all jobs below C-suite level are to be reclassified. All those impacted will no longer be employees and will instead work for the company as a "dependent contractor." At first glance, this scenario may feel scary. The article acknowledges as much, and goes on to describe a variation of the gig economy that goes way beyond the uncertainty people experience as a result of that model in the People wave.

Is this the likely future?

In the Paradox wave, tensions will inevitably arise between core and periphery, insourced and outsourced, flex and security. But high-functioning Paradox leaders will manage such polarities. We will see increasing intergenerational issues, both in society and the workplace. The younger generation will become more resentful as the employment proposition their parents enjoyed – pensions, redundancy payments, and secure contracts – are no longer available to them. But again, such tensions will inevitably spur business to create new models of employment or even new models of governance.

The key HR intervention in the Paradox wave will be around reinventing employment models so that flex comes with security. The companies that will survive past the 2020s, as the digital wave irrevocably changes the corporate landscape, will be those that have followed the people practices of HR 5.0 and HR 6.0.

We will need to move to models of employment that will enable people to move seamlessly between fixed and flex employment. A flex employment model that enables sabbaticals, where people have security and can get mortgages and start families. An employment model that has "management trainees" and "apprentices" at all ages – not just the young. An employment model for the 100-year life.[41]

In the Paradox wave, we will increasingly see organisations establish "employment platforms" for internal and external "job" advertising and filling. These platforms will use AI to match people and roles, and organisations will gradually begin to develop multiple employment arrangements to accommodate all needs. There will be flex contracts agreed directly with organisations (not through brokers, who will by then be disintermediated by AI), and there will be "project-based" consultancy-style contracts for one-off or irregular "events." Many contractors may prefer to use these direct vehicles, avoiding the complications of managing their own companies. There will be core/permanent contracts, but now designed with the ability for people to regularly move between fixed and flex.

Most of these initiatives will only come online fully in the Planet wave (see Chapter 7). However, in the Paradox wave, organisations will be working with their people and chief productivity teams to ensure they have an "employment platform" with appropriate matching AI up and running.

Employee relations

The Paradox wave, examples of which already exist, is witnessing the first steps to the true democratisation of the workplace. In public walks of life, democracy and the "will of the people" is seen as the primary reference point for legitimacy. And yet it is still apparent that the workplace is one of the few places where effective dictatorships still prevail. But this is changing.

When she first entered 10 Downing Street, Theresa May captured this feeling when she called for employee representatives on the boards of directors. Capita, the UK outsourcing king, has now allocated two elected seats on its board for employees.[42]

In the Paternalistic wave, the employee voice was subsumed to the Paternalistic leader. During the Power and Process waves, the employee voice was uniquely represented by trade unions and works councils. In the Profit wave, the ubiquitous employee survey came on the scene as a way to gauge employee sentiment or at least give the impression that the leadership was seeking employee input. In the People wave, employees were often given more say as a way of empowering the workforce and ensuring agility. The Paradox wave will see the continuation and integration of all these initiatives.

Companies, pressurised for profit margin, will no longer be able to afford hierarchical levels of supervision, with the corresponding checking and monitoring. Speed of response will require trust, and trust can only really develop when people are listened to and feel as though they have a voice and are being heard and respected.

Teams already have end-to-end responsibility for decision-making and will deploy this responsibility far more effectively than before. The nature of meetings will change radically, with new techniques replacing the Victorian age meeting structures taken for granted today. The boss will no longer have the last say – the team will. Decisions will be inclusive and integrated, taking all views into account. In addition, we will see an increased use of crowdsourcing, employee "hackathons," and other "direct democracy" approaches to open up to more "voices" and enhance engagement as workplaces inevitably democratise.

In the Paradox wave, trade unions will become part of company networks, perhaps becoming a key hub. They will provide professional advice to their members, even acting as agents to place people. They will sit on company boards, elected as designated employee reps. It's likely that the law will increasingly specify this type of representation at the board level. In 2018, the UK government passed an amendment to the Companies Act of 2006, specifying that boards of directors must either nominate a board member who will "be the employee voice" or have processes in place to demonstrate they are considering the employee voice. This came into effect from 1 January 2019, and is further evidence of the legislative push to democratise the workplace.

Works councils will become less procedural and come to represent a collection of teams as much as a "representative" body – the company works council becoming the forum for teams to "unblock" and hold strategic-level leaders directly to account for business performance.

Reinventing the company

As we progress into the late 2020s, a greater reckoning is likely to arise.

It will become apparent that companies in established, mature markets, still governed via the traditional "joint stock approach," will be unable to attract, retain, and energise employees. As they then seek to manage costs in the traditional way, they will regress to traditional hierarchies, back to old solutions from past waves. It will echo the Paternalist to Power transition, when the paternalists could not afford Paternalism and dividends anymore, and cut costs, causing the reaction that led to the Power wave.

Companies not in a growth phase will find themselves increasingly constrained by the need to meet shareholder demands for increased margin and increased dividend, meaning that they will not be able to afford to invest in the new models of work outlined above. Old-fashioned mergers and consolidations will also be tricky. How can you merge effective networks? How can you consolidate companies with no employees?

Once everyone has networked, competitiveness requires an investment in people and the network – having leaders at the core who are master integrators and are putting people and the magic of multiple connections at the heart of the business endeavour. To do this, as a joint stock company – quoted and traded on the stock market – you will need growth. Without growth, joint stock companies will struggle to compete at all.

Joint stock companies date back to Elizabethan England. They were the revolutionary technology of the day, enabling for the first time real capital accumulation through limited liability. The ability to raise funds on a stock market, ensuring that investments were always liquid, increased capital flows all around. Company shares have, over the years, become one of the key investment vehicles for savings, making up major parts of trusts and pension funds. First, the joint stock company powered empires, then the growth of capitalism, and has proven to be the primary wealth creation vehicle in history to date.

But Queen Elizabeth I died in 1603. Maybe it is time to evolve beyond a 500-year-old innovation?

In the 2020s, unless there is fundamental change to the shareholder value model, new-style companies simply won't list on the stock market. Instead, they will crowdfund to raise capital – and again, this is already happening. Founders who want to do things differently while protecting themselves, the business, and the ethos from the shareholder trap many in the People wave found themselves in will simply opt to have no shareholders.

There is likely to be a resurgence of co-ops, such as the Mondragon Corporation in the Basque region of Spain, or forms of business governance where workers "own" the company, such as the John Lewis Partnership or Riverford Organic Farmers. Mutualisation, killed off in the Reagan, Thatcher, and Bush eras, will rise like a phoenix from the ashes, as increasingly organisations resolve to provide services to members, as opposed to profits to shareholders.

Already, some established companies are exploring B Corp status. Certified B Corporations meet the highest standards of verified social and environmental performance, transparency, and accountability.[43] B Corp represents a new type of corporation that uses the power of business to solve social and environmental problems.[44] Ben & Jerry's, a subsidiary of Unilever, have pursued this option, as have Danone – where it's US business has declared itself a B Corp, and the concept is being aggressively championed by CEO Emmanuel Faber.[45]

If a company is growing, then a public offering and stock market listing may be the best business structure for them. Where a company is in mature markets, moves to B Corps or co-ops may be the better route. This will avoid the consolidation phase and allow the companies to focus on their offering and develop their reach via their networks, rather than their bottom line. They will still be subject to market discipline, and could therefore still become bankrupt, but they will not be subject to hostile takeovers and asset-stripping for a quick buck.

The move to mutualisation could also provide a solution to the failings of the privatised utilities. During the Profit wave, it made sense to open utility corporations, such as telecoms, electricity, and water, up to investors to invigorate the industries. That profit motive has, however, tipped into the negative aspects of the Profit wave, where shareholders are crowding out the needs of the wider community.

Mutuals, subject to market discipline, should be encouraged to enter these markets and compete with the large ex-national champions. Already, we see this happening with local governments borrowing from the Process wave and setting up their own mutual power companies. Hull City Council used to own and run their own white telephone boxes. These types of mutuals would once again be the perfect strategic vehicles for an accelerated development of renewable energy, for example.

What's especially interesting about the Paradox wave is that we will see much greater advocacy for government again. Again, the seeds of this shift are already being planted by various people, including prominent economist Mariana

Mazzucato[46] and commentators such as Michael Lewis.[47] The neoliberal capitalist view of the late twentieth and early twenty-first centuries will wither and die under demonstration of its profound failure – the notion that inefficient states and the consequential need for business brains in the public sector will be exposed for the myth that it is – although, sadly, probably not before significant damage has been done to the public sector and governance infrastructure, especially in the US and potentially the UK post-Brexit.

While many political leaders are operating from first-tier binary world views, there are pockets of resistance inside government who are still doing enlightened things, which should give us all hope. The same is also true in business – leaders who would normally be hamstrung by shareholders flying under the radar to enact or facilitate a more enlightened way of operating. It is these people and these initiatives that represent the cutting-edge thinking that will gather momentum to become the new leading edge. In the Paradox wave, everything appears to be getting worse and better at the same time! This can be disconcerting, but it's a positive sign that a real breakthrough is imminent.

Evolution from HR 6.0 to HR 7.0

HR 6.0 will bring huge benefits to any company that reaches it. Any leader or employee who does the work individually and collectively to climb the developmental ladder to the HR 6.0 world view will see further and be capable of far greater insight and innovation. They will be able to handle complexity. This is just as well given complexity is set to increase exponentially.

But HR 6.0 is still relatively rare in individuals, society, and business. When we encounter Paradox leaders, they can appear aloof and uncertain to those who are not operating from that vantage point. They can appear to overcomplicate things and make it difficult for others to follow their thinking. As with all stages of development, eventually even the Paradox wave will fail. This is likely to be because they try to make too many changes too quickly and can't explain their plan to the majority who have yet to reach the same expanded second-tier level of development. We saw this clearly with Barack Obama. Obama is a Paradox leader, but he was often misunderstood, especially by those operating from earlier world views. His actions were perceived as weak, whereas they were often nuanced because he understood that nothing is binary, nothing is certain. Obama is a sophisticated thinker, capable of holding competing truths without rushing to a simple solution, however popular that solution may be. He is able to see the truth in many world views and seek to integrate them into a more complete solution. A Paradox leader knows that there are always multiple sides of the story and multiple consequences. Given that there are very few leaders operating at this level, Paradox leaders will almost always be ousted by a regressive leader from an earlier wave who promises certainty – hence, Donald Trump.

This is part of the paradox – from the outside looking in, the Paradox leader looks to be considering everything, and therefore unfocused. Such efforts can be misinterpreted as desperate or dysfunctional, whereas if the leader has genuinely reached the Paradox wave, be they a CEO, HR professional, or politician, they are able to see the relevance and merit of all the previous waves for the first time. Their apparent lack of focus is the Paradox leader considering many options from all the previous waves and trying to determine which would best suit that situation. The result often appears to be a mishmash of all strategies from all the different waves, which can be confusing for others.

It's likely that Paradox wave leaders may struggle for a while until enough people are suitably comfortable with the contradictory and confusing nature of this wave.

In fact, it is likely to be the individualistic uncertainty of HR 6.0 that will trigger the move to a more inclusive focus on the planet, and hence the emergence of HR 7.0 Planet. Are we seeing glimmers of that with the school strike for climate protests by youngsters around the world[48] and the Extinction Rebellion[49] events of 2019? The fear, as environmental activist Paul Gilding points out, is that it may already be too late.[50] He speculates that sometime in the 2020s, our financial system will come under enormous strain as increased climate events undermine insurance companies.

But hope is not lost.

Notes

1 Walters N (2017) Whole Foods CEO John Mackey Says Amazon Deal Only Took 6 Weeks: "It Was Truly Love at First Sight," *The Street*, www.thestreet. com/story/14186201/1/7-important-facts-we-just-learned-about-the-amazon-whole-foods-deal.html
2 Wilber K (2000) *The Marriage of Sense and Soul: Integrating Science and Religion*, Broadway Books, New York.
3 Onita L (2018) Marks & Spencer to Axe More Stores as Sales Tumble, *Evening Standard*, www.standard.co.uk/business/marks-spencer-to-axe-more-stores-as-sales-tumble-a3983196.html
4 Herrera AV and MacFarquhar N (2019) Russia Warns U.S. Not to Intervene in Venezuela as Military Backs Maduro, *New York Times*, www.nytimes.com/2019/01/24/world/americas/venezuela-news-maduro-russia.html
5 Mayer C (2018) *Prosperity: Better Business Makes the Greater Good*, Oxford University Press, Oxford.
6 Watkins A (2016) *4D Leadership: Competitive Advantage through Vertical Leadership Development*, Kogan Page, London.
7 George B (2017) The Battle for the Soul of Capitalism Explained in One Hostile Takeover Bid, *CNBC*, www.cnbc.com/2017/03/24/kraft-heinz-unilever-battle-threat-to-capitalism-commentary.html
8 Massoudi A and Fontanella-Khan J (2017) The $143bn Flop: How Warren Buffett and 3G Lost Unilever, *Financial Times*, www.ft.com/content/d846766e-f81b-11e6-bd4e-68d53499ed71
9 Barbarians at the Plate (2017) 3G Missed Unilever but Its Methods Are Spreading, *The Economist*, www.economist.com/business/2017/02/25/3g-missed-unilever-but-its-methods-are-spreading

10 Daneshkhu S (2017) Unilever Chief Now under Pressure to Deliver on Reforms, *Financial Times*, www.ft.com/content/a2f1fe90-f792-11e6-bd4e-68d53499ed71

11 Barbarians at the Plate (2017) 3G Missed Unilever but Its Methods Are Spreading, *The Economist*, www.economist.com/business/2017/02/25/3g-missed-unilever-but-its-methods-are-spreading

12 Laloux F (2014) *Reinventing Organizations: A Guide to Creating Organizations Inspired by the Next Stage in Human Consciousness*, Nelson Parker, Brussels.

13 Ratcliffe S (Ed) (1994) *The Little Oxford Dictionary of Quotations*, Oxford University Press, Oxford.

14 Wilber K (2001) *A Theory of Everything: An Integral Vision for Business, Politics, Science and Spirituality*, Gateway, Dublin.

15 Watkins A (2015) *4D Leadership*, Kogan Page, London.

16 Kegan R and Laskow Lahey L (2016) *An Everyone Culture: Becoming a Deliberately Developmental Organization*, Harvard Business Review Press, Boston, MA.

17 Watkins A (2014) *Coherence: The Secret Science of Brilliant Leadership*, Kogan Page, London.

18 Watkins A and Wilber K (2015) *Wicked and Wise: How to Solve the World's Toughest Problems*, Urbane Publications, Kent.

19 Dhawan E (2012) Gen-Y Workforce and Workplace Are out of Sync, *Forbes*, www.forbes.com/sites/85broads/2012/01/23/gen-y-workforce-and-workplace-are-out-of-sync/#3ec15d9d2579

20 Chester E (2002) *Employing Generation Why: Understanding, Managing and Motivating the New Workforce*, Tucker House Books, Boulder, CO.

21 Bradford N (2018) The Mind: Engineering the Future of Human Possibility, *TEDx*, https://tedxbeaconstreet.com/videos/the-mind-engineering-the-future-of-human-possibility/

22 Strogatz S (2004) *Sync: The Emerging Science of Spontaneous Order*, Penguin, London.

23 Robertson BJ (2015) *Holacracy: The Revolutionary Management System That Abolishes Hierarchy Portfolio*, Penguin, New York.

24 Trademark of HolacracyOne in the US.

25 Robertson BJ (2015) *Holacracy: The Revolutionary Management System That Abolishes Hierarchy Portfolio*, Penguin, New York.

26 Johnson B (2014) *Polarity Management: Identifying and Managing Unsolvable Problems*, 2nd edition, HRD Press, Amherst, MA.

27 Rifkin J (2015) *The Zero Margin Cost Society: The Internet of Things, the Collaborative Commons, and the Eclipse of Capitalism*, Palgrave Macmillan, London.

28 Vadera S (2018) Oliver Wyman Forum: Leadership Disrupted at Tate Modern, www.oliverwyman.com/our-expertise/events/2018/nov/oliver-wyman-forum-leadership-disrupted-uk-event.html#OliverWymanTeam

29 Tourish D (2013) *The Dark Side of Transformational Leadership*, Routledge, London.

30 Becker BE, Huselid MA, and Ulrich D (2001) *The HR Scorecard: Linking People, Strategy, and Performance*, Harvard Business School Press, Boston, MA.

31 Ashkenas R, Ulrich D, Jick T, and Kerr S (2002) *The Boundaryless Organization: Breaking the Chains of Organization Structure*, Jossey-Bass, San Francisco, CA.

32 Collins J (2001) *Good to Great: Why Some Companies Make the Leap and Others Don't*, Harper Business, New York.

33 Dunbar R, Barrett L, and Lycett J (2007) *Evolutionary Psychology*, One World, Oxford.

34 Watkins A (2014) *Coherence: The Secret Science of Brilliant Leadership*, Kogan Page, London.

35 Ormerod P (2012) *Positive Linking: How Networks Can Revolutionise the World*, Faber & Faber, London.
36 Burt RS (2005) *Brokerage and Closure: An Introduction to Social Capital*, Oxford University Press, Oxford.
37 Mishra D (2017) *Tacit Knowledge Transfer in Inter-Organisational Networks: A Social Network Analysis of Formula 1*, PhD, Bath University, https://purehost.bath.ac.uk/ws/portalfiles/portal/187905646/Final_Thesis_PV_.pdf
38 Dyer JH and Nobeoka K (2000) Creating and Managing a High-Performance Knowledge-Sharing Network: The Toyota Case, *Strategic Management Journal*, 21: 345–367.
39 Vanhaverbeke W, Duysters G, and Noorderhaven N (2002) External Technology Sourcing through Alliances or Acquisitions: An Analysis of the Application-Specific Integrated Circuits Industry, *Organization Science*, 13(6): 714–733.
40 The World if ... (2018) If Companies Had No Employees: Run, TaskRabbit, Run – July 2030, *The Economist*, www.economist.com/the-world-if/2018/07/07/run-taskrabbit-run-july-2030
41 Gratton L and Scott A (2016) *The 100-Year Life: Living and Working in an Age of Longevity*, Bloomsbury, London.
42 Robert L (2018) Capita Invites Its Workers to Join Board for £65,000 a Year, *The Times*, www.thetimes.co.uk/article/capita-invites-its-workers-to-join-board-for-65-000-a-year-rbrkhw0mk
43 Information on Certified B Corporations, https://bcorporation.net/
44 Ben & Jerry's website, www.benjerry.com/about-us#5timeline
45 Print Edition (2018) Choosing Plan B: Danone Rethinks the Idea of the Firm, *The Economist*, www.economist.com/business/2018/08/09/danone-rethinks-the-idea-of-the-firm
46 Mariana Mazzucato website, https://marianamazzucato.com/
47 Lewis M (2018) *The Fifth Risk: Undoing Democracy*, Penguin, London.
48 BBC News (2019) Schools' Climate Change Protests, www.bbc.co.uk/news/topics/czmw21ewkzqt/schools-climate-change-protests
49 Green M (2019) Extinction Rebellion: Inside the New Climate Resistance, *Financial Times*, www.ft.com/content/9bcb1bf8-5b20-11e9-9dde-7aedca0a081a
50 Gilding P (2011) *The Great Disruption: How the Climate Crisis Will Transform the Global Economy*, Bloomsburfy, Sydney.

7 HR 7.0

The Planet wave (2030+)

In *Star Trek*, Dr McCoy famously said to Captain James T. Kirk, "It's life Jim, but not as we know it."[1]

Remember when we said there would be fewer jobs with the rise of digitisation, AI, machine learning, roboticisation, and automation. Well, scratch that, as McCoy might have said, "There will be jobs, Jim, but not as we know them!" That is providing we can deliver HR 6.0 and develop enough senior leaders or employees to second-tier thinking. If we set up organisations that can truly integrate profit, people, and purpose to manage the resulting paradox, we will successfully make the transition to the Planet wave.

At this world view, not only can we protect the planet and all the species that share it with us; we can also reverse at least some of the damage we've caused, and while doing so access the abundance we hinted at in the Introduction.

In truth, if we make wiser choices, there will be no shortage of jobs for the human race:

- We have ageing populations in much of Europe, Japan, North America, and China – care and healthcare will need to expand. We will need to pay more time and money to literally start looking after each other – and value those who do.
- As Africa and South Asia grow, infrastructure investment will increase. We are already seeing a bit of this with the Chinese Belt and Road Initiative – more will follow.
- In the West, the infrastructure we built in the 1950s and 1960s (when we were poorer than today) needs to be renewed and rebuilt. This is especially pressing in the US.
- As the consequences of climate change increasingly cause problems, housing will need to be retrofitted to deal with the changing weather patterns.
- Our thirst for entertainment and knowledge will grow. Ease of access via streaming services will enable the monetisation (or remonetisation) of traditional media as media companies and educational establishments globally scale using something similar to the Netflix model.

- As 3D printing scales, everyone will become a producer and manufacturer, leading to further P-waves of innovation. We may see greater personalisation driven by people making their own products – not quite a return to "cottage industries," but communities of producers capable of revitalising retail and their own localities.
- The "collaborative commons" will grow as we seek to lease what we need when we need it rather than own it. This shift in demand will further drive the move to zero marginal cost, as we discussed earlier. We will end up in some sort of "collaborative capitalism" as people and companies operate in a much more networked fashion. There will still be fiscal discipline, so companies can still go bust, but the system will work in a much more distributed rather than centralised fashion. This is likely to include the monetisation of personal data in that sharing economy.
- We will also be exploring a future life among the stars, building a moon base – not just for the sheer adventure of it or because we've destroyed the planet we currently live on, but because it represents an evolution of who we are.

In fact, there is likely to be a boom in jobs tasked with saving the planet – hence, the Planet wave.

The first glimmers of Planet

Our individual and collective progress through the various P-waves always starts with the individual. Each of us is growing up and waking up to the reality around us at different speeds, at different times, in different ways, and through different cultural contexts. The process is not linear; we make progress and regress, and make greater progress again. We are all making this journey together, whether we realise it or not. Some are evolving and actively seeking to develop themselves beyond the traditional boundaries of school and university, and others are happy to stay put at an earlier world view – certain that the way they see the world is accurate and everyone else is wrong. As more of us make the journey, each P-wave hits a critical mass where that wave is the dominant world view of society. Given time, the development starts to impact other areas of human activity such as business and politics.

Right now, the Planet wave doesn't really exist to any great extent in business. We are, however, already seeing it emerge at the individual level and in parts of society. For example, a growing number of people now accept the reality of climate change and our role in it, and are actively doing what they can to address *their* impact on the planet. In 2017, *Blue Planet II*, presented by Sir David Attenborough, was aired for the first time. The impact was astonishing. An online search behaviour study found that there was a surge of interest in plastic recycling following the programme's finale, with online searches for the term increasing by 55 per cent. There was also a hike in engagement with environmental non-profit organisations, with the Marine Conservation Society seeing a 169 per cent jump in website visitors and the World Wildlife Fund (WWF) experiencing a 51 per cent increase in web traffic.[2] *Blue Planet II* is largely credited with bringing the plastic problem to public awareness.

The innovative capability that comes online in the Paradox wave is already bringing forward amazing solutions to that very problem. For example, a 25-year-old entrepreneur in Indonesia, where many people buy small quantities of food or personal care products in plastic sachets, has invented an alternative using biodegradable seaweed; a surfer from Sydney has invented a "seabin" to collect plastic from rivers, where half the plastic entering our oceans originates from; and a 24-year-old guy from Holland has invented a large Pac-Man-type device, powered by solar energy, that roams the oceans gobbling up plastic.[3]

The biggest challenge to these and many other incredible inventions is the current business model. In truth, unless we change the game from just shareholder value to something more sustainable and inclusive, then business will not adopt these technologies. For example, many businesses, because of the pressure to deliver profits, will not abandon plastic. They will not ensure their plastic is recyclable or invest in recycling until they are forced to do so by consumer pressure or government legislation.

Conservation and renewable energy are inevitable. They have to become the default option because fossil fuels are finite, and even the fuel we have we can't use up without destroying the planet in the process. Jeremy Rifkin has already predicted a boom in jobs tasked with building renewable infrastructures.[4] We will see a rise in new-style energy and logistics companies riding the wave of the renewables boom.

These companies are likely to be mutual, co-ops, or some form of governmental corporations, tasked to save the planet and not make a loss, rather than make a profit and perhaps save the planet. They are likely to be the network organisations of the type described in Chapter 6.

If we manage to minimise the impact of climate change and put people and planet at the centre of what we do, the age of automation will not be something we should fear, but something we should welcome. Automation may actually end up taking the drudgery out of everyday life, something John Maynard Keynes predicted in 1930 in a paper called 'Economic Possibilities for Our Grandchildren'. In it, he suggests that, following a:

> temporary phase of maladjustment due to technological unemployment [the automation we are seeing now] for the first time since his creation man will be faced with his real, his permanent problem – how to use his freedom from pressing economic cares, how to occupy the leisure, which science and compound interest will have won for him, to live wisely and agreeably as well.[5]

Now, isn't that a really exciting purpose statement for the HR/people profession?

Planet-based leadership

In the Planet wave, leadership swings back to a focus on the collective again – hence, the ultimate inclusivity of Planet itself.[6] There are already leaders operating at this level, but they are very rare in mainstream business. Instead, they tend to be driving movements or non-profit organisations, or scattered across many commercial contexts, often unaware of each other. They are rarely running traditional business – yet.

Most are busy trying to build their influence at scale, not for the ego reasons common among Power leaders, nor for the financial gain sought by Profit leaders, and not even because they are taking responsibility for addressing the paradoxes seen by leaders from the previous HR 6.0 P-wave. Instead, they seek to create greater influence because that is what is required to move everyone forward. They naturally lead beyond their authority and look for ways to convene the best thinkers to change outcomes.[7] But they have a different way of approaching this. They are not interested in creating more "think tanks" populated by competitive or combative experts claiming to think unthinkable thoughts. Rather, they look for sophisticated thinkers who can genuinely collaborate and set aside their own egos for the benefit of the whole.

Planet-based leaders focus on long-term system balance. They seek ways to create cultural or societal change for the benefit of all people while trying to avoid being too prescriptive or sounding patronising (something that is often misattributed to them).

The Paradox leader can appear distant and disconnected. Others may struggle to follow their train of thought. In contrast, the Planet leader has transcended that constraint and is normally more engaging, has crafted a much more compelling narrative, and seeks inclusive participation from all. Like the Paradox leader, they are second-tier thinkers and recognise that everyone has value and useful insight to offer, but they are normally more skilled at eliciting that value from others.

Second-tier leaders are able to move up and down the levels and communicate with people according to the other person's world view rather than broadcasting from their own. This means they can be extremely effective communicators, capable of bringing disparate people together and delivering complex solutions, often working with a sophisticated, motivated, and integrated team.

Planet leaders consider everything. As such, they may appear distracted or disinterested. Nothing could be further from the truth. They are profoundly engaged with humanity's struggle and are possibly the most passionate people on the planet. It's just that they are thinking about completely different data sets and seeking to see the situation from all available perspectives. Their goal is balance. Rather than rushing to one polarity, Profit or Planet, they are seeking both – a way to bring prosperity to the many while also protecting the planet and all the species that call it home.

The Planet leader knows that there is no "one answer" to any challenge, especially in a world that is increasingly complex and interdependent. We face an innumerable number of what are known as "wicked problems" – these are problems that share common characteristics. A wicked problem is multidimensional, has multiple stakeholders, multiple causes, multiple symptoms, multiple potential solutions, and is constantly evolving.[8] Wicked problems include things such as climate change, poverty, and inequality. There are no easy answers to these challenges, and yet those still stuck in first-tier thinking often believe there are. Wicked problems require equally wicked solutions. In other words, the solutions that we come up with to these fiendishly challenging problems must also be multidimensional; they must address the concerns of multiple stakeholders and treat the multiple causes and symptoms. There will always be more than one solution, and those solutions must take into account that the problem itself is changing, so the solutions must also change over time. Leaders from any of the first-tier world views – Paternalistic to People – don't think in those terms and are very unlikely to construct those type of solutions. The Planet leader can, and to a lesser extent so can the Paradox leader.

Teams at HR 7.0: fellowships

Leadership teams at HR 7.0 focus on society. They consider how the team's actions can create influence beyond the market and industry in which they operate and look at the impacts on society at large. When they meet, the team's conversation is no longer about the business per se, but about global trends. They realise that the deeper they understand the macroeconomic issues and how they relate to market activity, the more likely they will be to deliver the transformations they seek. These teams prefer to think of themselves as "stewards of change" rather than leaders. This is not false humility; it is just a completely different way of conceptualising the commercial task than is normally considered by most leaders. In fact, they don't even think of themselves as a team in the traditional sense, but more of a broad fellowship in service of a wider cause.

HR 7.0 fellowships have moved beyond the flushing out and integrating multiple perspectives characteristic of HR 6.0 teams. Their advantage comes from working out how to apply such insights in a more nuanced and productive way that can "move the dial" for everyone. Much less time is wasted in debating minor points. Individual leaders readily surrender their views for the sake of the whole. This ability to surrender is based on the pursuit of the wisest answer, regardless of its source, and an understanding that momentum is key. All answers are continually honed as part of the journey forward, so there is no need to dig in and defend a set position.

There is a maturity and fluidity in team meetings characterised by easy interpersonal dynamics, creativity, and high speed of alignment. The level of respect each team member has for each other is profound, and the trust is so strong that trust has largely disappeared as an issue. Trust is just present strongly and quietly without ever needing to be spoken of.

Emerging HR and people practices

In the Planet wave, we will no longer have separate people and team managers. HR people, as we know them today, may still be required at the core of organisations, but they will be managing employment platforms via the "chief productivity office" or services platform. HRBPs will have disappeared.

Come the third decade of the twenty-first century, when the Planet wave is likely to gather significant momentum, we will see an echo of the days at the start of the Industrial Revolution whereby entrepreneurs provided facilities and then "gangmasters" organised the labour and delivered the product. These circumstances required no HR. They were their own HR – deciding when to work, what to deliver, etc. But in the 2030s, it will be materially different. This time, the "gangmasters" will not be tyrannical Power leaders, but second-tier leaders. They will be orchestrating empowered teams or networks of people (many organised as mutuals or co-ops) to achieve end-to-end tasks within the overall network.

Hours worked will be fluid, with people being paid for their labour in a much more flexible way. This formal contracted work will probably top up a modified version of universal basic income (UBI), which has already been trialled in some parts of the world.[9] Some form of UBI is already thought to be inevitable as jobs disappear as a result of automation and technological advance. Elon Musk and Mark Zuckerberg have both stated they believe such an approach is valid and also holds the key to tackling inequality.[10]

People are likely to work no more than six hours a day – something Lord Lever advocated back in 1906! However, they may well spend significantly more time engaged in unpaid collaborative efforts that improve their communities and social architecture.

Companies will be driven more by crowdsourcing processes – both financially through crowdfunding but also in terms of crowdsourcing their employees via their "employment platform."

Businesses will come to represent "teams of teams," to use the phrase of General McChrystal's book.[11] Teams will vary in size, from 10–12 up to the Dunbar number of 150.[12] They will come together to achieve a task and disband to partner with others elsewhere – just as McChrystal described his way of organising his troops in Iraq.

Those still working at the core of companies will find they are guiding crowds of committed people. Because the rules of engagement will have changed substantially, so will the quality of relationships across the business. There will be much less need for engagement surveys and trust-building exercises. Interpersonal tensions will be far less common.

HR 7.0 Planet today

Like HR 6.0 Paradox, HR 7.0 Planet is a wave for the future. However, we can already see instances of the cutting-edge ideas, interventions, and methodologies today that are likely to become mainstream tomorrow. Specifically, we will see the internal networks of organisation expand and integrate into external networks of like-minded organisations, glued together by common purpose and a commitment to the planet.

We will also see the development of real democracy in the world of work. This will eliminate old-fashioned hierarchical thinking and drive truly "bottom-up" operating models.

These developments will underpin radically different models of employment, the 40-hour/40-week/40-year model becoming obsolete. Diversity of employment forms will flourish, with people's needs to sustain themselves over the 100-year life being well and truly met.

We unpack these potential developments in more detail below.

The networked org Mark II

In HR 6.0, organisational networks reach to the boundary of the company. In HR 7.0, the company boundary itself becomes much more semipermeable. Networks inside and outside the company will be widespread. The relationship between larger organisations and the constellation of "suppliers" they used to be connected to will move from a supplier dynamic to a partner dynamic. Procurement will morph into a relationship, with contracts outlining commercial and relational expectations, which will then be proactively managed by both sides for mutual benefit and development.

In fact, business leaders will focus specifically on network health as this will become a critical key performance indicator (KPI). They will be brokers rather than generalists, "flexing in" and deploying a range of specialists – psychologists, nutritionists, anthropologists, etc. – to work with teams and wider networks to ensure connection, integration, and added value at the interfaces. The simplest analogy we can give to bring this alive is to look at the world of sport.

When we were young, football teams were trained by an ex-pro – often with a cigarette hanging out of his mouth – and training consisted of a lot of running, with injuries treated by a cold, wet sponge.

In contrast, Gareth Southgate, manager of the England football team, took a "people and team development manager" to the 2018 World Cup, as well as a whole team of specialists in support.[13] No cold, wet sponge in sight. Prior to the World Cup, one of us (AW) spoke to Gareth about the importance of creating a shared sense of identity within the squad, and one that reflected his views on how they should play.

The same will happen in business too. Business leaders will orchestrate and broker interventions at key nodes in the organisation's network and beyond. People and team performance or development managers are likely to become "development consultants," employed as part of the wider network as deep specialists in diverse disciplines such as medicine, politics, or social sciences. Such "development specialists" may well flex themselves working or advising many companies, rather than being simply dedicated to one organisation.

It may be that the evolved networked organisation will become intimately connected to other players in their sector in a more federated set of corporations. This approach would take the best learning from the success in Asian countries during the Process wave of chaebols – large family-owned business conglomerates in South Korea, but applied from a more advanced world view and for different people-focused goals. The future may hold some type of federated companies where businesses join forces and cooperate but remain separate organisational entities. This would only be possible if the purpose of those federated businesses is societal – delivering service while protecting the planet at the same time. Federated business would never be allowed under the current shareholder value model. Imagine Proctor & Gamble joining forces as a federated company with Walmart – if the purpose was to increase profit, it would never be allowed. But if their collaboration helped rid the world of single-use plastic faster and more effectively, they may very well get a licence to operate in radically different ways.

Even now in Asia, this more collaborative style of business is the norm, in contrast to the more dog-eat-dog approach of the West. This is largely because Asian companies start from a different cultural norm; they are much more collaborative by nature, whereas Western culture tends to start from a more individualistic perspective.

It is worth pointing out, however, that in many Asian businesses, this operating style is still predominantly Process wave in terms of principle and discipline. Their cultural bias towards the collective may allow them to embrace the People wave and onwards to the Planet wave, and there are certainly glimmers of the "system balance" of the Planet wave, but they have not yet broken through as to how to really make it work in a complex business environment.

Many Asian companies look at the West and recognise that the Profit wave is not the ultimate answer. But equally, many get stuck between the older Process wave in their fear of what embracing the Profit wave may do to their highly valued cultural and face-saving social norms.

We wonder whether these Asian businesses may remain stuck in the Process wave indefinitely until they embrace the greater individual freedoms and personal reward that's needed as a stepping stone to the second tier.

Crowdocracy

In HR 7.0, with its networked organisational model, a completely different decision-making process will become the norm, namely Crowdocracy.[14] The old hierarchies will have gone. People will be linking together because they choose to, not because they must.

Crowdocracy embraces the upside of Holacracy from the Paradox wave while also honouring the benefits of all previous decision-making approaches from HR 1.0 Paternalism to HR 5.0 People – all of which have their place. Crowdocracy seeks to take the integrative horsepower – and its ability to deliver a 10 versus 0 Holacratic outcome – and scale it, creating very high levels of alignment between many people inside its networked organisations.

Crowdocracy is not some fanciful utopian dream; it is already possible because of three realities.

First, there are now enough human beings who are capable of handling much greater degrees of complexity. Globally, between 1 and 2 per cent of the population are now operating at the second tier.[15] However, among certain influential populations, such as business leaders, the figure is closer to 10 per cent.[16]

Second, technology has exploded. What we can do today bears almost no resemblance to what we could do even a few years ago. In his seminal essay "The Law of Accelerating Returns," futurist, Ray Kurzweil states:

> There's even exponential growth in the rate of exponential growth. Within a few decades, machine intelligence will surpass human intelligence, leading to The Singularity – technological change so rapid and profound it represents a rupture in the fabric of human history.[17]

We are living through that rupture right now, and it offers us an unprecedented opportunity to revolutionise the workplace. Finding out what employees thought and felt about decisions used to be difficult – at best, it was represented via a trade union or an annual employee engagement survey, popular in HR 4.0. But we now have access to sophisticated social media platforms, open-source software, and mind-numbing data collection, storage, and analytic capabilities.

Third, and perhaps most surprising of all, by opening up the decision-making process to *all the people*, we will generate much better solutions than relying on a small number of "experts." This goes against everything we have been conditioned to believe. We have been educated by experts to believe that we need experts to educate us. In fact, our entire educational system – whether school, university, or corporate learning curves – is built on this idea that without expert guidance, we can't solve problems. We turn to experts when we are stuck in school, in science and medicine, in the legal system, and in organisational life. When mistakes are made, we often believe this is down to a lack of expert advice, misinformation from people who are not experts, or insufficient access to the right type of experts. We are so attached to this idea that the mere thought of not consulting an expert seems like an oxymoron.

Clearly, seeking advice from those that know more about a subject than we do is a wise course of action, despite the anti-expert sentiment of earlier waves. However, there is now significant evidence that it is possible to generate much better-quality answers by mining the "wisdom of the crowd." This is now a well-proven phenomenon in social science.[18] At the heart of collective intelligence is a "mathematical truism." If we ask a large enough group of diverse, independent people, including but not exclusive to experts, to make a prediction or estimate a probability, and then average those estimates, the errors of the individual will be cancelled out by the collective. Each person's guess has two components: information and error. Subtract the error and we're left with accurate information. What's especially encouraging about Crowdocracy is that we can already see the seeds of this revolution in the narcissism and rejection of experts we are witnessing right now as the People wave fails. Crowdocracy, using tech platforms, will integrate those diverse opinions, rather than polarise them, to create much wiser answers to the wicked problems we face.

During the Paternalism wave, even up to the early years of the Profit wave, it was possible for one person or a small group of reasonably intelligent, experienced people to make more right decisions than wrong ones, but that is simply not the case anymore, and it certainly won't be the case in the Planet wave. The speed of change and the complexity of the situations and challenges we face, together with the proliferation of knowledge and data, mean those days are long gone. Even if we sacked every business leader on the planet and made their re-employment dependent on whether they were operating from a second-tier world view, they still wouldn't make better decisions than *everyone* can make. No one person is ever as smart as all the people.

The suggestion that everyone is smarter than a bunch of experts seems particularly counterintuitive as Britain lurches through crisis after crisis following the EU referendum and David Cameron's disastrous decision to reduce the complexity of the EU down to a binary vote. But the mess of Brexit only highlights the fact that for everyone to be smarter than some experts and for the wisdom of the crowd to emerge, we need four conditions to be in place. If these conditions are not in place, then the crowd will produce the unholy mess that Brexit has created in Europe.

The first of these conditions is "independence of thinking." Each person must be able to contribute their views on a topic without worrying about how such thoughts may be perceived. There must be "psychological safety," to use the current parlance. This is why wisdom can emerge more swiftly on a tech platform, especially if there is semi-anonymity. When people are in a room together, interpersonal dynamics can inhibit wisdom emerging. This can be due to senior people talking over more junior contributions, or charismatic leaders making others feel they can't contradict them. People who may have had a significant contribution to make often feel deterred from making it because they don't want to contradict their boss or someone they perceive to be more important. This phenomenon is a massive problem in Asian cultures, where people will simply not speak up for fear of offending someone more senior or creating a loss of face for another team member. In Asian cultures, social cohesion often trumps commercial insightfulness.

The second condition that must be present for wisdom to emerge is diversity. Diversity is so important in business not because diversity delivers social equality, although such a benefit is admirable, but because diversity means wisdom. If you have a monoculture in your business where everyone operates from largely the same world view, then you are unlikely to innovate much or create new ideas to existing problems. And of all the different types of diversity, probably the most powerful is diversity of values and maturity. Surface physical characteristics such as ethnicity, gender, or sexual orientation are probably poor proxies for the diversity of mind that creates wisdom in the crowd. A room full of diverse people who work effectively together will always come up with better answers than a room full of experts.[19]

The third condition that facilitates the wisdom of the crowd is devolution. This means only the people who are affected by the decision are involved in the decision-making. All too often, when the decisions are centralised, they are made by people who do not suffer the consequences of those decisions. This doesn't create any feedback loops and results in poorer-quality answers. This has certainly been part of the dynamic at play in the EU, and is one of the reasons that in many EU countries there is significant unrest with "faceless bureaucrats" making decisions that affect the lives of people a long way away from Brussels. Crowdocracy limits participation in decisions to those affected by those decisions.

The fourth and final condition that must be present to ensure crowds develop wisdom, not stupidity, is integration. In James Surowiecki's original book, he suggested this fourth condition was aggregation.[20] We strongly disagree with that suggestion. Aggregation is a sort of averaging, and averaging often leads to a "lowest common denominator dumbing down" of an answer. Integration delivers the opposite. Integration requires all perspectives to be embraced to find a higher whole that transcends but includes all views – not in some unhappy compromise or mediocre exclusion to force-fit an answer into a process, but rather a deep understanding of each view so they can be effectively embraced.

The representative forums of companies today – works councils and employee consultation forums – will increasingly be supplemented by the voice of the crowd. The forums will provide a means of ensuring the four conditions can be put in place, and the "crowd" will then do the rest.

If these four conditions are present in an organisation, then with careful guidance the organisation can start to operate in a more Crowdocratic way. Companies will be able to deploy Crowdocracy software on their "platforms" to continually seek feedback, opinion, inputs, and ideas from their wider networks of teams and people. Such software is already available.[21] This will be how organisations will unlock the wisdom of their crowds, particularly when many people may be working in remote geographic locations. The geographic dispersal of workers will accelerate and the current trend for hot-desking in communal spaces across a city, so familiar in the tech sector, will become the norm. It is unlikely that many co-workers will share any one physical office location in the Planet wave. Office space will become part of the collaborative commons model, being leased by flex employees as required. Today's office will become tomorrow's Crowdocracy platform.

The future

To look ahead at what the world of work might be like in the Planet wave, let's go back to Eva Smith and what her life might be like if we make the transition and embrace HR 7.0.

As a 22-year-old, Eva is still studying – she intends to get a PhD in her field of interest, as deep expertise in multiple areas is now key to employability. She wants to work in a flexible manner so she can complete her PhD over three to five years.

She contracts with "People Corp." They engage her on a series of specialist projects, pay her the going rate for that role, ensure she is enrolled in social security schemes, and as she has joined them through their own "platform" – rather than via an agency – accrue on her behalf 15 per cent of her total earnings (the normal agency fee) in a fund that can be cashed out in the future. Eva's government have in fact set up a central trust to manage these employee fund banks.

This works well for Eva and People Corp, but then at 27 Eva wants to marry. Her and her partner both want to buy a house and need a secure mode of employment to access mortgage facilities. As she has worked well with People Corp, she now looks for a more "traditional" employment relationship – one with a full-time contract – working at the core of the company's network.

People Corp have no such roles, but "Network Corp" do. She joins Network Corp, transferring her employee fund accordingly. She chooses as part of her total reward to place some of her earnings into her employee fund to access at a later date. She then works for Network Corp until she is 32 and decides to have children.

To care for the children, Eva decides to cash out some of her employee fund and take extended maternity leave. Her partner does the same, enabling the family to bond together in their child's early years.

At age 35, Eva decides she would like to return to the world of work, but would prefer a few years of flex while her children are still young. Network Corp cannot accommodate, but People Corp can, so she returns to People Corp and once again replenishes her employee fund.

At age 40, Eva is again ready to commit to the core of a company network. Planet Corp offer her such a role. Again, she accrues and transfers her fund. Unfortunately, Planet Corp go into receivership and Eva is made redundant. Her employee fund has, however, ensured that she has accrued the equivalent of a traditional "redundancy payment," so she is able to move on without too much pain.

She finds alternative work in another network company, but at age 55 decides she wants to return to academia. By then, the employee fund accrual enables her to take a year or two to retrain.

Fresh from college at 57, Eva decides she will now consult and sets up her own company. This is a bit scary as there is no accrual into an employer fund anymore, but she is her own boss and can live off the profit of her company.

By the age of 70, Eva wants to slow down. She dissolves her company and offers herself back to the flex market. She works on and off for ten years before retiring at 80 to enjoy the last 20 years of her life. Her employee fund – plus the profits from her company and investments – just about stretch to fund this. Her kids are well established in their own lives.

Of course, this may sound all very well for a young professional like Eva, you may say. But what about Fred?

Fred is 55 and worked in a factory for 25 years as an unskilled worker. He cannot draw a state pension until he is at least 67, and he fears his employer will make him redundant soon because of automation. How will Fred bridge his years from 55 to 67?

Fred could flex too. Factories currently make heavy use of temporary labour to manage down costs and ensure they can flex as needed. Fred could transition to the flex crew. He could opt to take a redundancy lump sum if he has a pension, draw that down early, and top up his lifestyle as a flex employer at his old factory as needed. Once again, when working flex, he could accrue 15 per cent into his employee fund, so compensating any pension drawdown. If his employer has no flex opportunities, they would use the wider network to find Fred work as and when.

The difference from a 55-year-old being made redundant today versus one being made redundant in the near future is likely to be that the company takes responsibility for ensuring flex opportunities, retraining, or pension flex – not the state or a labour agency.

Companies could do this because they are now at the centre of extended networks, able to bring together consortia and communities of cooperation. These flexible networked options put people's needs on a par with a company's needs. They deploy the new networks to find solutions for people at all stages of their lives. They are potentially no more expensive than using agencies today, where the 15 per cent agency fee goes to the employee instead of the agency.

Clearly, it will never be as easy as described above. Jobs will start to change in nature, skills will become obsolete, new skills will become needed, and automation will reduce demand. It is therefore likely that governments will need to enact legislation to enable such a transition.

There has been a lot of talk in the last few years about the need for universal basic income (UBI), but fears that it could encourage apathy and loss of purpose dog the debate.[22] We suspect that the whole idea of UBI is a forerunner to a much more flexible employment model that involves all sectors of society. It is likely that the wisdom of the crowd will develop better answers to the issues that UBI is designed to address.

As flex employment increases, governments will also need to legislate so that flex workers have the rights to the minimum or living wage and receive holiday and sick entitlement. This will, of course, increase costs. Clearly, there will be a need for higher levels of government expenditure. This may be funded in part by people working longer and earning more through flex employment opportunities, but it will also require a tax rethink. Unless governments can act together across borders to implement a Tobin tax − a tax on all spot conversions of one currency into another (unlikely within the next ten years) − more taxes will need to come from property, inheritance, and digital sales rather than increasingly illusive profit.

Taking a wider view, this P-wave will also see the most significant evolution of human consciousness since the birth of most modern religions around 2,000 years ago.

The world of the Planet wave will not be some sort of utopia. It will simply be a world where the things we argue and get upset 'about will be different from "economics."

In the Planet wave, we will need to address issues such as those recently posed by Henry Kissinger:

> What will become of human consciousness if our own explanatory powers are superseded by A.I. and Societies are no longer able to interpret the world they inhabit in terms that are meaningful to them? How is consciousness to be defined in a world of machines that reduce human experience to mathematical data, interpreted by their own memories? Who is legally responsible for the creations of AI?[23]

There will be new controversies. Social measurement systems, such as those currently being developed and deployed in China, are likely to be a source of resentment. There is something troubling about measurements of a person's individual social capital (reputation), not least because of who decides the measures, but these types of data-based assessments and analysis are on the way. On the one hand, the argument will be that if you don't do anything wrong, you have nothing to fear, but the definition of "wrong" depends on world view and it can also be used to restrict civil liberties and freedoms − something that many fought so hard to secure. And then there is the issue of who owns or can use the data − we are already wrestling with these moral challenges.

Some people may resist the inclusiveness of Crowdocracy, which will increasingly be deployed to supplement representative democratic forums. Some people will resist this, and debates will rage about "comparative governance."

Whatever the future holds, there is already plenty of evidence that we are on the edge of a significant breakthrough in human development. More people will make the leaps to the next world view and a higher level of consciousness. Of course, this will continue to be a point of tension in society as people work off different world views, causing misunderstandings and potentially conflicts.

We will enjoy a renewed focus on human development. This emphasis on measuring and driving elevated levels of vertical development will finally deliver the much talked of but rarely witnessed transformation of business.

The purpose of work will no longer be to provide for physical needs; it will be providing for developmental needs "from the cradle to the grave." Where the baby boomers of the 1960s enjoyed cradle-to-grave welfare, in the Planet wave we access cradle-to-grave development.

What next?

Although there are tentative signs of a new world view emerging, it is so far away from business as we understand it today that we needn't worry about it. Besides, if the function currently known as HR can help enough people to make the transition from first-tier thinking to second-tier thinking so they reach Paradox and Planet, the world will be profoundly transformed.

As the "Sherpas" of this alternative future (the other potential future is extinction), the HR profession must start today. We must take a lead in creating this new business landscape, setting up new business models and governance to help create a "networked society," advocating for employee funds, rights for flex workers, flexibility in pension drawdown, incentives to mutualise or establish co-ops, and assisting governments to establish effective reskilling and lifelong apprenticeships. The HR function will need to be at the forefront of research on the different forms of universal basic income, which will likely be needed to underpin the whole system. There is much to do.

Our final chapter explores what we must do, and where we might start.

Notes

1 Star Trekkin' Wikipedia page, https://en.wikipedia.org/wiki/Star_Trekkin%27
2 Hayns-Worthington S (2018) The Attenborough Effect: Searches for Plastic Recycling Rocket after Blue Planet II, *Resource*, https://resource.co/article/atten borough-effect-searches-plastic-recycling-rocket-after-blue-planet-ii-12334
3 Ramaswamy C (2018) Drowning in Plastic Review: A Rallying Cry to Ditch Plastic, but Is It Too Late? *The Guardian*, www.theguardian.com/tv-and-radio/2018/oct/01/drowning-in-plastic-review-a-rallying-cry-to-ditch-plastic-but-is-it-too-late
4 Rifkin J (2014) *The Zero Marginal Cost Society: The Internet of Things, the Collaborative Commons, and the Eclipse of Capitalism*, Palgrave Macmillan, London.
5 Keynes JM (1930) Economic Possibilities for Our Grandchildren, *Essays in Persuasion*, https://assets.aspeninstitute.org/content/uploads/files/content/upload/Intro_and_Section_I.pdf

6 Author Marianne Wiliamson on Her 2020 Bid for President, Reparations, & Colin Kaepernick, *YouTube*, www.youtube.com/watch?v=ap9mMSd5axs

7 Middleton J (2007) *Beyond Authority: Leadership in a Changing World*, Palgrave Macmillan, New York.

8 Watkins A and Wilber K (2015) *Wicked and Wise: How to Solve the World's Toughest Problems*, Urbane Publications, London.

9 Henley J (2018) Money for Nothing: Is Finland's Universal Basic Income Trial Too Good to Be True? *The Guardian*, www.theguardian.com/inequality/2018/jan/12/money-for-nothing-is-finlands-universal-basic-income-trial-too-good-to-be-true

10 Reynolds M (2018) No, Finland Isn't Scrapping Its Universal Basic Income Experiment, *Wired*, www.wired.co.uk/article/finland-universal-basic-income-results-trial-cancelled

11 McChrystal S, Collins T, Silverman D, and Fussell C (2015) *Team of Teams: New Rules of Engagement for a Complex World Portfolio*, Penguin, New York.

12 Dunbar R, Barrett L, and Lycett J (2007) *Evolutionary Psychology*, One World, Oxford.

13 Saner E (2018) How the Psychology of the England Football Team Could Change Your Life, *The Guardian*, www.theguardian.com/football/2018/jul/10/psychology-england-football-team-change-your-life-pippa-grange

14 Watkins A and Stratenus I (2016) *Crowdocracy: The End of Politics*, Urbane Publications, Kent.

15 Wilber K (2001) *A Theory of Everything: An Integral Vision for Business, Politics, Science and Spirituality*, Gateway, Dublin.

16 Watkins A (2014) *Coherence: The Secret Science of Brilliant Leadership*, Kogan Page, London. Laloux F (2014) *Reinventing Organizations: A Guide to Creating Organizations Inspired by the Next Stage of Human Consciousness*, Nelson Parker, Brussels.

17 Kurzweil R (2001) The Law of Accelerating Returns, www.kurzweilai.net/the-law-of-accelerating-returns

18 Surowiecki J (2004) *The Wisdom of Crowds: Why the Many Are Smarter Than the Few*, Little Brown, London.

19 Surowiecki J (2005) *The Wisdom of Crowds*, Random House, New York.

20 Surowiecki J (2005) *The Wisdom of Crowds*, Random House, New York.

21 Everyone website, www.everyoneintheworld.org/

22 Goldin I (2018) Five Reasons Why Universal Basic Income Is a Bad Idea, *Financial Times*, www.ft.com/content/100137b4-0cdf-11e8-bacb-2958fde95e5e

23 Kissinger HA (2018) How Enlightenment Ends, *The Atlantic*, www.theatlantic.com/magazine/archive/2018/06/henry-kissinger-ai-could-mean-the-end-of-human-history/559124/

8 Surfing the P-waves of progress

In the 1970s, Robert Redford starred in a film called *The Candidate*. It glamourised the journey of a "no-hope" Californian Senate candidate. After the fast-paced thrilling drama and eventual win, Redford's character turns with trepidation to his campaign manager and asks, "What do we do now?" It's a fitting question here too.

As we have discussed throughout this book, we are on a (r)evolutionary journey, surfing the P-waves of progress, from Paternalism, to Power, to Process, to Profit, to People, to Paradox, and hopefully to Planet. Each wave brings progress. Each wave delivers some substantial benefits, but all of them inevitably fail. However, the failure itself is part of the evolutionary process, necessary to create the transformational energy for the next evolutionary leap forward.

All journeys start with a single step. But in order to be able to take that first step to a new, more sophisticated P-wave, we must first ask ourselves which P-wave our organisations are operating from right now. The path from one P-wave to the next varies considerably depending on the current starting point. To help you identify your dominant P-wave, we have created a diagnostic assessment, the Complete Organisational Maturity Scan (http://complete-coherence.com/methodology/), which is briefly summarised in Table 8.1.

Of course, no organisation operates wholly from one P-wave; different teams, functions, or geographies within the business operate from slightly differently evolutionary waves. One of the biggest determinants of which P-wave the HR systems and processes are running from is the developmental maturity of the senior leadership group. This top-down influence, in turn, sets the cultural norm for the organisation. If enough organisations raise their game to the next P-wave, then they can influence society at large. The impact of societal development on organisational life and HR practice is not just one-way; both can influence each other. We are arguing that the opportunity for the future of HR is that if HR can help change business, HR can help change the world.

First, work on maturity

Imagine you are the new HR director of one of the world's most powerful multinational corporations and you have been invited to meet the executive

Table 8.1 P-wave summary

	HR 1.0: Paternalism	HR 2.0: Power	HR 3.0: Process	HR 4.0: Profit	HR 5.0: People	HR 6.0: Paradox	HR 7.0: Planet
HR Job Titles	Welfare Officer/Safety Officers.	Industrial Relations Officers/Employee Relations Officers. Management Development Managers.	Personnel Officers.	HRBP. HR Expertise. HR Services.	People Development Managers. Chief Productivity Officers/Services platforms.	Chief of Staff/Productivity Officer/Services platforms. People & Team Performance Consultants.	Line managers replace core people development leaders – curating expertise as needed. Routine activities covered by platforms which provide an ecosystem for multiple employment models.
Day-to-Day HR Activities	Focus on welfare, safety and facilities. Most time spent on transactions – recruitment, HR admin, payroll, etc.	Managing conflict between owners and workers, includes union avoidance in some geographies. Management development.	Codifying rules, employee record keeping, payroll, hiring and firing. Management development and reward and remuneration.	Human resource management organised along Ulrich model of (HRBP/expertise/shared services). Outsourced shared services in places.	People Development Managers work alongside core HR service organisations. Expert roles integrate into management or if junior into services platform.	HR integrates into a cross functional Chief Productivity office providing a platform of services to one or many organisations in a network. People development activities specialise.	Line managers replace core people development leaders – curating expertise as needed. Routine activities covered by platforms which provide an ecosystem for multiple employment models.
Pay and Reward	Piece rates. Non-wage benefits.	Collective bargaining.	Fixed pay based on job evaluation. Each role thoroughly assessed and ascribed a value. Non-wage benefits. Defined benefit pensions.	Reward more based on individual contribution (bonuses). Share awards and long-term remuneration. Defined contribution pension schemes.	Emergence of total reward-employees can decide how to distribute total reward– fixed, variable, non-wage, health insurance, short term, long term.	Total reward approach broadened to enable flexible employment models.	Rise of flexible employee, flexible benefits, accrued time banks. Paid by project not job.
Training Approach	'Sitting with Nellie' – learning by watching someone else.	Apprenticeship schemes/systemic professional training.	Work study, deconstructing each task and optimising each process. Work	Skills training supplemented by attitude/cultural and	Focus on individual needs, purpose and employability.	Focus on collective/ purpose and lifelong development.	Focus on collective societal development needs and lifelong development.

(Continued)

Table 8.1 (Cont.)

	HR 1.0: Paternalism	HR 2.0: Power	HR 3.0: Process	HR 4.0: Profit	HR 5.0: People	HR 6.0: Paradox	HR 7.0: Planet
Appraisal & Performance Management Systems	Silent monitors/line-based measurements. 'Father-figure' or supervisors enforce day to day performance.	Role or job-based performance system. Pace dictated by machine or process.	study instruction manuals. Job or role-based performance system. Pace set by process or work study.	'transformational' training. Individual focused reward. Attitude assessed as well as results. Annual 'Rank and Yank' assessments	Learning versus development better differentiated. Annual reviews re placed by more regular project reviews Collective performance management linked to people and purpose. 360 feedback. Rating systems replaced by immediate feedback.	Situational. Defined by business model and other relevant variables.	Performance management withers away as extended cross-sector working emerges. People work for the planet not an organisation.
Culture	The business is operated as a family for the family.	Business is a clash of interests – 'Us and Them'. Hierarchy of control based on military model.	Work to rule and compliance culture. Process is the reference point. Hierarchy of control on professional model.	Performance culture. Empowered people and teams to work end to end – speed of decision making. Hierarchies supplemented by cross departmental teams.	Purpose becomes a driving force. Diversity and inclusion become important. Network organisations and agile working emerge.	Understands diversity is about inner values. Along with polarities, paradoxes and complexity plays as commercial advantage. Functions disappear. End to end units emerge – scaled via shared 'platform' Orgs.	Evolutionary. Organisations integrate into networks across sectors.
Dominant Organisation Development Theory	'Father' knows best. Trust the father-figure leader.	'Management right to manage' Functional organisations. Clear silos and 'turf'.	Scientific Management or Taylorism, TQM. Functional, product or geography focused organisations.	Team working/ QWL. Matrix organisation with leads for product or geography and product.	Matrix dissolving. Seeking to integrate product, geography and product as equals. Use of 'double hatted' or integrated roles.	Networks enable shared capability within sectors, building clusters and innovation platforms. Modern chaebols.	Cross-sector network. Planetary and social outcome focus enable buying/ selling alliances.

Leadership Style	Father figure or pairing rules for everyone for the company's own good.	Charismatic leadership. Lead from the front. Control-base, management hierarchies.	Technocratic leadership. Do the right thing in the right way. Rules not opinions determine approach. Value professional managers/specialists.	'Transformational' leadership with focus on productivity and profit.	Inclusive, purpose-orientated leadership. Renewed focus on purpose, people and wellbeing.	'Nelson Mandela' of the business world'. Second tier thinkers. Complexity embraced.	Network leaders. Working cross sector and beyond personal authority to effect global change.
Teams Style	Individuals operate pre-team. Often in family units or specialist groups.	Battling experts. Cross functional conflict evident (may be hidden). Briefing and counter-briefing common as is IR conflict. High use of third party agency labour.	Dependant experts. Rules help integrate plans. Leader adjudicates disputes. Management by objectives.	Independent achievers with a mission statement as a uniting focus. Uniform goals via performance management systems.	Interdependent achievers value team diversity. Collaboration to anticipate and resolve issues. IDM process and balanced scorecards deployed.	Diverse pluralists integrate diverse views. Skilled use of IDM and mindfulness in meetings. Social goals included in target deployment.	Integrated pluralists integrate ideas from inside and outside. Scope of leadership crosses sectors and boundaries. Goals primarily societal.
Employee Relations Strategies	To look after people. Conservative approach to change. Duty of care.	Power wins. Charismatic leaders battle for control. High incidence of industrial action Employee voice starts to organise but is resisted by management.	Procedural agreements provide the 'Rules'. Compromise preferred for dispute resolution. Co-determination may be prescribed by law. Employee voice via representative structures.	Direct to employee communication. Transformational leaders seek to convince through compelling narratives. Employee voice via employee surveys.	People-focused approach Purpose initiatives integrated into ER approaches. Co-invention and use of hackathons and crowdsourcing. Emphasis on employability, reskilling and upskilling.	Co-created change. Agile ways of working. Greater individual ownership of employee relationship.	Agile approaches complemented by trade unions or employee representatives as brokers and change agents – key nodes in the organisation's wider network of companies.

board. You are greeted in an expansive, industrially chic reception area by an impeccably dressed assistant who is clearly extremely bright with a warm, easy manner. The two of you chat as the assistant escorts you up to the top floor of the corporate headquarters. You are mesmerised by the amazing view over the city skyline as you alight from the opulent lift and wonder whether you are in some futuristic movie about to meet the lead actors. Large and impressively carved doors are opened as you are presented to the executive team, only what you encounter completely rocks you back on your heels. Around the table are ten children, varying in ages from 8 years old to a couple of pubescent 14-year-olds. You look quizzically at the assistant, who confirms this is indeed the executive board and whispers, "Good luck" as he quietly closes the door behind you.

Of course, we are not implying that all multinationals are run by children; rather, we are pointing out the fact that while we may look at an individual and see a grown-up adult human being, their level of ego maturity may be stuck at a much earlier stage of development. We see this in business all the time – power battles in the board room, "toys out of the pram" episodes, tantrums, bullying, and all manner of activities that would not be out of place in a school playground. We see the same behaviour in adults but fail to appreciate that the cause is the same – lack of maturity.

Sometimes this lack of maturity manifests as egocentric narcissism[1] or hubris.[2] Donald Trump is famously quoted as telling one of his biographers, Michael D'Antonio, "When I look at myself in the first grade and I look at myself now, I'm basically the same. The temperament is not that different."[3] Apparently, he was quite proud of the fact, and clearly viewed this consistency as a strength. But we are not meant to stay the same person we were in the first grade, and we certainly shouldn't be the same person if we have access to the nuclear football!

Once HR recognises that the maturity of the leader and the leadership group is the primary determinant of whether an organisation evolves to the next P-wave, they must look much more closely at how to develop their leaders.

Mature leaders can embrace the upside of each wave and are adept at handling the dysfunction of that wave when it eventually emerges. They take steps to address the dysfunction and work with the issues that arise, enabling a new P-wave to form, folding the positive characteristics of the preceding wave into the business.

Immature leaders will seek to embrace the upside of a wave but will often distance themselves from the inevitable dysfunction that emerges in that P-wave. They often go into denial, seek to lay blame elsewhere, either internally or externally, and may attempt to retrace their steps, regressing to a point where the business was "working well."

The temptation to retrace one's steps is understandable. The drive to return to a simpler time can be overwhelming, but it's normally a mistake. As

American scholar H.L. Mencken once said, "For every complex problem there is an answer that is clear, simple, and wrong."[4] Seeking to regress to an earlier P-wave is clear, simple, and wrong, and it is an approach born out of naivety and immaturity. It's likely that we witnessed this wrong turn in the UK with Brexit and the vote to leave the European Union. Much of the voter analysis showed that the majority of voters who voted to leave were from an older demographic.[5] It may have been that these voters were increasingly uncomfortable with what they viewed as a loss of control and the escalating complexity of the world. They were harking back to a nostalgic notion of Britain that never even existed. The reality, however, is that the world is simply too complex, too connected, too interdependent, and no last-gasp attempt to create Empire 2.0[6] will change that. In fact, just two years after the Brexit referendum, demographic shifts would have delivered a "remain" verdict. Even assuming that everyone who voted the first time voted the same way the second time, the death of elderly voters and the eligibility of younger voters would shift the result.[7]

The same occurs in business when an immature leader seeks to retrace their steps to an earlier P-wave where business was simpler, profits higher, and bonuses almost certainly bigger. Even if a leader could somehow turn the clock back, it is impossible to simultaneously regress society politically, economically, socially, technologically, environmentally, and legally (P.E.S.T.L.E). The world in which a simpler approach to business could work does not exist anymore.

Our ability to recognise ego maturity as a commercially critical phenomenon and to take active steps to increase the altitude in this line of development can disproportionately improve our lives and the returns we achieve. It can increase our ability to drive transformation in our business because it allows us to proactively break down silo structures, change behaviour, increase our ability to manage complexity, and increase our ability to facilitate stakeholder collaboration and communication. It also increases our perspective and makes us less reactive, more perceptive, and emotionally aware. We tend not to get so worked up about the inevitable ups and downs of business life, which can in turn alleviate stress and fatigue and improve our well-being and quality of life.

Recent research suggests that the more sophisticated and mature a leader is, the greater their ability to drive organisational transformation.[8] A typical 14-year-old child has the physical, emotional, and mental capability to function in an adult world. If there is no "burning platform" or strong need for us to mature further, we are likely to experience arrested development and stay locked at the maturity of an early teenager, or even younger, despite our advancing chronological age, even into later life.

Most people leave school or university thinking that their intellectual development and maturation is largely finished. But in our early twenties, we have only achieved the most basic levels of ego maturity, from baby, to child, to physical adult. The move from immature adult to mature adult is, however, where nearly *all* the magic happens. Society and the law consider an 18-year-old to be an adult, and yet an 18-year-old is hardly the kind of adult that you want running a complex multinational organisation responsible for thousands of people's lives and livelihoods. They may look physically mature on the outside in their early twenties, thirties, or even forties, but on the inside they may still be "stuck" at the maturity of a 14-year-old.

There is no doubt that we scale various "learning curves" at school, university, through apprenticeships, or in our early career, but we are far from developed. What is required is a concerted effort to elevate our internal maturity to match the external sophistication of the world around us. Unfortunately, this rarely happens. But it is this internal, invisible work that will deliver the necessary vertical development of the "I" quadrant that holds the key to unlocking a vast reservoir of human potential. It is also an essential ingredient in 4D leadership, which we discussed in Chapter 6.

There is rich academic literature on how adults can continue to mature throughout their lives. There have been many significant contributions from the early developmental theorists, such as Jean Piaget,[9] Lawrence Kohlberg,[10] and Jane Loevinger,[11] to more recent luminaries, such as Ken Wilber,[12] Robert Kegan,[13] Eliot Jacques,[14] Kurt Fischer,[15] Susanne Cook-Greuter,[16] William Torbert,[17] and Clare Graves.[18] All of them describe some aspect of vertical adult development from a slightly different perspective. For example, Cook-Greuter explores how the ego develops over time given the right conditions, and how this relates to identity and the sense of self.[19] Torbert's "action logics" look at how those stages play out in business,[20] and his collaborations with Cook-Greuter have been especially insightful when looking at behaviour.[21] Graves' model, which we've drawn on as a basis for the P-waves, explores individual and collective values or world views.[22] Wilber has offered the first ever complete integration of all these perspectives, and provides the most comprehensive map of adult development, covering many lines and levels, including the evolution of awareness or consciousness itself.[23]

While brilliant, many of these developmental theories never make it out of the world of academia, and they almost never reach the areas that desperately need them, such as business, government, and politics. This must change if we are to stand any chance of making the transition from one P-wave to the next, especially in the game-changing transition from HR 5.0 People (end of the first tier) to HR 6.0 Paradox (start of the second tier).

Doing the work necessary to develop the ego maturity line of development is some of the most potent work any leader can do to step-change commercial and organisational capability.

Cultivating our ego maturity can transform the internal, subjective world of "being" and add significant verticality in the vital dimension of "I." It can also yield serious competitive advantage because this work massively increases cognitive sophistication, which allows us to more effectively manage the escalating complexity and intensity of modern business (this is critical to have any chance of moving beyond HR 5.0 People to embrace second-tier thinking at HR 6.0 Paradox onwards). If we are to prosper and genuinely thrive in an environment that is constantly and rapidly evolving, often littered with complex wicked problems, we need to expand our awareness and ego maturity to raise the calibre of leadership exponentially.

That said, ego maturity can be a controversial topic to discuss in the C-suite, and one that can be met with hostility and resentment (a fact that only serves to illustrate the dire need for us to address this internal line of development). No one enjoys having their maturity questioned, and yet everyone in business, especially those in influential positions, must have their maturity questioned if we are to successfully transition from one P-wave to the next. The key is to consider maturity as simply a part of our identity that can – and should – evolve as we develop as adult human beings. Many skilled HR practitioners may therefore use terms such as "the inner game" or other terminology appropriate to their own P-wave, rather than the term "ego maturity," to get around this issue.

Approaching transition

As a leader, whether a CEO or HR professional, if we want to progress from where we are now to where we want or need to be, we must work on our ego maturity, regardless of the level of sophistication or the P-wave we find ourselves in right now.

While development of our ego maturity is necessary, on its own it is insufficient for an organisation to "wave-surf" to the next P-wave. We need to develop the whole leadership group within the business so we can create a platform on which successful transition can be built. Each leader must recognise the basic rules of vertical development, namely:

1. They must have the courage to confront their own development and the development of others.
2. They must recognise that they cannot skip a wave. They must develop through each wave individually and collectively in order to transform the organisation from one P-wave to the next.
3. They must acknowledge that they can only lead the transition to the P-wave they themselves operate from, but not beyond. A leader must be at least one wave beyond the employee base to be able to lead the organisation to the next P-wave.
4. They must be multilingual, in developmental terms, so they can communicate the benefits of the next evolutionary P-wave in the language of the current P-wave.
5. They must embrace and implement the HR practices associated with the next P-wave.

Courage to confront

Every P-wave fails eventually. Such failure is a vital part of the evolutionary process. Each wave eventually becomes outdated or begins to creek under the strain of a changing environment or escalating complexity. Whether a cursory assessment of the P-waves summarised in Table 8.1 has convinced you that you are currently in the Power wave, or whether a more thorough assessment using the online diagnostic (http://complete-coherence.com/meth odology/) has pointed to the Profit wave, if you want to facilitate change you must have the courage to confront the dysfunction of the level you currently operate from.

One of us (ND) has visited many factory complexes in the developing world operating from HR 1.0 – deeply Paternalistic. Many are now incredibly inefficient because they have never made the transition from HR 1.0 Paternalism to HR 2.0 Power. The leadership are overwhelmed by the challenges of fast-changing market conditions and do not recognise that the world has moved on around them and that Paternalism is, for them, no longer a viable business model in that geography. Yet they can't bring themselves to have the difficult but necessary conversations with the workforce to scale back the overly paternalistic interventions. Instead, they hire additional temporary workers on precarious working conditions in an attempt to maintain competitiveness. But they feel conflicted because the paternalistic, family-focused caring initiatives for existing employees and management seem to be failing as a motivational strategy. The results remain poor, leadership is dysfunctional, and there are accusations of hypocrisy, which inevitably leads to a toxic working environment.

Transition from any P-wave to the next requires the courage to confront the dysfunction of that wave and honestly face the challenges it is creating in the business. It is the willingness to have the fierce conversations that can move the business forward,[24] and it only happens with leadership maturity.

We have listed below the key issues that leaders are likely to face at the transition points between each of the P-waves. Having the courage to confront these issues when they arise is key to the transition process. Denial will only lead to regression and escalating dysfunction.

Courage to confront HR 1.0 Paternalism

Signs of dysfunction of HR 1.0 include denial, where leaders are clinging on to the illusion of "family" while gradually eroding the benefits employees receive. There is often "unrest" in the workforce, a sense that something isn't working. The workforce begins to think that they are being "kept in the dark" and decisions are being made without consultation. They are increasingly dissatisfied that they have no say. At the same time, the paternalistic bosses become restless. They sense things are changing and they start to mourn the loss of a close-knit family vibe. Trust seems to be evaporating. The bosses feel that they are taken for granted or that their care for the staff is going unappreciated. Both sides begin to realise that there are sides where there used to be a family. There is a sense of things spiralling out of control and a lack of direction.

So, in an attempt to maintain control, paternalistic bosses may appoint "insiders" or unofficial "family members" to re-establish authority. But this loss of control and lack of direction is critical for the next level to emerge.

If you are witnessing these behaviours, then the leaders must be encouraged to confront the need to end Paternalism and move to a more direct leadership approach to business. This means accepting that a paternalistic approach to labour relations is no longer credible. It is necessary to work with the workers or employee representative groups directly to face the tensions that have arisen head-on. It is wise to identify and appoint leaders from within the workforce, rather than unofficial "family members," to provide some direction and maybe even to enable effective bargaining and progress to occur.

Courage to confront HR 2.0 Power

If the management of your organisation is stuck in a head-on battle with the trade unions, with leaders claiming their "right to manage" is being under-mined and union reps stuck in bargaining dogma, then you are likely feeling the effects of dysfunction at HR 2.0.

In HR 2.0, the battle between management and unions commonly reaches a stalemate. The greater control and directional power seized by management to overcome the failure of Paternalism now creates significant resistance in the workforce. In a desire to drive the business forward, management can drift into a dictatorial stance. This naturally meets resistance, and the staff increasingly feel "told" what to do. This creates passivity in some and belli-gerence in others.[25] If the belligerence is well organised by the trade unions, then the stage is set for a full-scale power battle between the two sides.

As with all power battles, it takes courage to de-escalate the conflict. This courage can be shown by either side, but often the responsibility sits more with management. Management must rise above the emotional turbulence of the conflict and find some higher principle that both sides can agree on to break the impasse. They may need to offer some guarantees to the workforce and put some rules in place to prevent any abuses of power. If they are smart, these rules will rub both ways, creating more stability for them as well as the staff. Rules on employee relations are particularly critical at this juncture.

Courage to confront HR 3.0 Process

With the development of rules and the emergence of a more predictable envir-onment for both sides to operate in, there is often a period of stability before the wheels start to come off in HR 3.0. What often emerges is an over-reliance on the process that worked to diffuse the previous conflict of HR 2.0. When ten-sions emerge, the first thought is to put some process or rules in place to manage the conflict. But this no longer works for two reasons: first, there are already way too many processes that have crept into the system; and second, the tension is often more complex and less amenable to simple rule-making. The dysfunction of HR 3.0 lies mainly in an ever-increasing generation of new rules to try to "control" an ever-changing environment. The "predict and control" mindset, much loved for its stability, simply can't cope with the increasing variety and opportunities that are emerging in every area of the business. The process has become more important than the result.

Leaders need to confront the bureaucracy and excessive rule observance. Ironically, "simplification" programmes often themselves create more bureaucracy. The way out of this rule-based stagnation is to give greater freedom and empower people through increased individual accountability. Such a move may require a more courageous approach to reward and remuneration. Pay policies may need to be reviewed to create the right motivational environment. Governments must play their part and reduce the red tape that may be constraining entrepreneurialism and small business development. Governments also need to take a pragmatic approach to investment, spend taxpayers' money wisely, and create a stable economic environment for the Profit wave to emerge. No one is owed a living. Liberating the individual and the organisation sets the foundations for growth.

Courage to confront HR 4.0 Profit

Once the early boom of the Profit wave has subsided, the downside of the Profit wave, like all waves before it, eventually emerges. The drive for unrelenting financial growth as the sole focus spawns an excessive competitiveness as businesses aim to beat each other or acquire each other. This can create an obsession with cost, and ultimately an ever-increasing "race to the bottom."[26] Many companies institute continual cutbacks on employees and customer service. These are typical signs of a business trapped in the dysfunction of HR 4.0.

Leaders in HR 4.0 must have the courage to confront the excessive focus on growth and profit. They must become intolerant of greed and corruption, acknowledging that the purpose of organisations is to serve society and a wider stakeholder group rather than just return cash to a few shareholders. Long-term commercial sustainability necessitates less obsession with short-term quarterly profiteering. Leaders must challenge commoditisation and consolidate business futures through purpose-driven offerings, even if it means lower average profit margins. There needs to be an opening up to other views of the world and the role of business in society. To break through to the next wave, there must be greater emphasis given to the "WE" dimension to bring it to a level of importance previously reserved for the "doing" dimensions ("IT"/"ITS").

Courage to confront HR 5.0 People

The more inclusive operating models of the People wave will fail, despite all the benefits they deliver to a larger number of stakeholders. This is because the forces of evolution are unstoppable, and since the world will continue to become more complicated, so the way we think about organisations will also need to evolve. If business leaders refuse to embrace the paradox that emerges during the failure of the People wave, they will remain stuck in the dysfunction of HR 5.0. They must have the courage to take the hard decisions to adjust margin and financial expectations.

One of the critical dilemmas that emerges as HR 5.0 fails is that leaders must confront the paradox of purpose versus profit. The emphasis on people and purpose embraced at HR 5.0 to transcend the failures of HR 4.0 Profit is often seen not as an evolution, but as a contradiction. The paradox is that both can be achieved at the same time. In fact, there is now good evidence that companies that are purpose-driven can achieve higher profits than those that are purely commercially driven.[27]

Another paradox that needs to be addressed is that the inclusion of more people in the decision-making process often reduces the effectiveness of the decisions made. This is because, left to their own devices, a group of very smart people often dumb down and generate some extremely average answers. Realising that democratic process is flawed, leaders in HR 5.0 try to include more voices to increase the dwindling engagement that democracy ultimately creates. But there has been little innovation of the process of deciding, so "groupthink" kicks in and outcomes are increasingly determined by single figures in a group by dint of their role or status. Paradoxically, this means the desire for greater inclusivity reduces the number of voices in the group, resulting in much poorer-quality outcomes. To break free of the swamp in HR 5.0, leaders must change the decision-making process used in their organisations.

A third paradox that occurs as the dysfunction of HR 5.0 grips the business is that despite people being more focused on relationships, strong connections are often lacking. Leaders need the courage to tear down the siloed walls of the organisational structure and facilitate networks within the company. This is where 4D leadership is needed and must be developed.

Courage to confront HR 6.0 Paradox

To be honest, if you are operating from HR 6.0, you are already light years ahead of most businesses. Congratulations. But even this exalted altitude cannot escape the laws of evolution, and just as with every wave before it, the Paradox wave will also fail. Since it is currently so rare in corporations, there is not much data on how and why the Paradox wave fails, but fail it eventually will. One of the main reasons the Paradox wave fails is because it fails to engage the people below who are still operating from earlier evolutionary waves. The primary task at HR 6.0 is to effectively connect and communicate with earlier waves. Leaders at this level often have a sound intellectual understanding of the importance of systems and networks and much greater flexibility in communicational style and language, but paradoxically the problem is still effectively connecting with others. We often say that the "WE" dimension of human experience is the "final frontier," meaning it is the most difficult of all three dimensions ("I," "WE," and "IT") to develop.

Leaders at HR 6.0 must confront consumerism and seek to replace consumers with the concept of citizenship. This means addressing head-on the need for more diverse and people-centred business governance structures and explaining this in terms that earlier waves (represented by traditional shareholders) can not only understand, but agree with. In their attempt to "simplify" the complex nature of the world, Paradox leaders will often overcomplicate their explanations – partly because it is, in reality, very complicated solving wicked problems.[28] Paradox leaders must clearly articulate not just the vision of a better world, but how everyone gets there and flourishes in this world.[29] We must seek to replenish – not consume – the planet's resources, work in harmony – not competition – with each other, and enjoy our collective gifts of diversity and abundance. Paradox leaders must explain how the "circular economy" works and subordinate all economic activity to planetary sustainability. Such leadership is truly integral across all dimensions, providing new insights and levels of awareness.

"Plus one" principle (POP)

Moving individuals, groups, and whole businesses from one P-wave to another is not easy. It's also not fast and can take serious developmental effort. But the rewards are significant, as are the disadvantages waiting for those who refuse to evolve upward.

An immature leader may seek to miss out some P-waves and jump straight from Paternalism to People, but a mature leader knows this is not possible. We must move through the waves one at a time. We can only ever progress one wave above the wave we are currently operating from. If you have identified that your business is operating at HR 1.0, then you can only move the business to HR 2.0. Once that transition has been made and the benefits of that wave have been reaped, it is then possible to move the business to HR 3.0, but it is not possible to move from HR 1.0 to HR 3.0. Besides, even if it was possible, it's not smart. Each wave brings with it profound benefits over the previous wave. Jumping waves would simply mean you miss out on those benefits that are necessary to cumulatively build a platform on which to create even greater success. Without an understanding and experience of each wave, that platform would be unstable. Any interventions that seek to jump levels will fail.

Again, we see this in politics and the "culture wars" that exist right across the world. In the West, we look to developing countries and imagine their woes could be solved with a spot of capitalism (essentially HR 4.0). But often these countries, or at least part of these countries, are operating from an evolutionary stage even earlier than Paternalism – survival. They are not concerned with business; they are concerned with finding enough food today to feed their children. Or perhaps a country is in the grip of a dictator or dysfunctional Power leader. Moves are made to dislodge that individual, but without the instillation and embrace of the Process wave, the action is doomed – think Iraq.

Evolve to the point of the leader

The leader of any P-wave transition needs to operate from the wave they are seeking to move the organisation to or beyond. An HR 2.0 leader can move an HR 1.0 Paternalism collective or business to HR 2.0, but their own developmental level or world view will stop any transition beyond that.

It follows therefore that the higher the P-wave of the leader who is determined to shift the centre of gravity of the business, then the better able they will be to facilitate that transition (see Table 8.2).

Communicate in the right language

If the leader is operating from HR 5.0 People but the business is predominantly operating from HR 1.0 Paternalism, the People leader must demonstrate maturity and set aside their natural People-focused tendencies and appear to the business as an aspirational HR 2.0 Power leader, speaking the language of HR 1.0, so that he or she can move the collective from HR 1.0 to HR 2.0.

A leader needs elevated emotional maturity to take any system forward because they can't progress that system beyond the wave they are operating from themselves. But if they are too far ahead, they need that depth of maturity to be able to put their own world view and natural tendencies to one side to communicate and behave for the good of the collective journey. Often this will feel alien to the leader, but it is absolutely critical to land the right message and encourage the collective to make the transition to a new P-wave.

When a mature P-wave transition leader, whether the HR director or CEO, has a much deeper understanding of the subtlety of their own value system and

Table 8.2 What leader can transition what P-wave transition

	HR 1.0 to HR 2.0	HR 2.0 to HR 3.0	HR 3.0 to HR 4.0	HR 4.0 to HR 5.0	HR 5.0 to HR 6.0	HR 6.0 to HR 7.0
HR 7.0 Leader	•	•	•	•	•	•
HR 6.0 Leader	•	•	•	•	•	○
HR 5.0 Leader	•	•	•	•	○	○
HR 4.0 Leader	•	•	•	○	○	○
HR 3.0 Leader	•	•	○	○	○	○
HR 2.0 Leader	•	○	○	○	○	○
HR 1.0 Leader	○	○	○	○	○	○

the strengths and weaknesses that their own world view brings to bear, they can explain themselves better and improve communication.

One of us (AW) did some work with the UK government department responsible for distributing social payments to single mothers from a low socio-economic background. The incredibly caring individuals (largely operating from HR 3.0 Process and HR 5.0 People) had worked diligently on creating a beautiful website full of pictures of smiling people and floral designs. They had worked hard on simplifying the message for their target audience, not least because part of the problem was that the people entitled to these payments were not claiming them. But it made no difference. Payment uptake did not improve. Why? Because there was still a communication problem.

Once we had explained the value systems (which correspond with the P-waves), these civil servants realised they had created a website that would be best appreciated by those who were also operating from HR 5.0 People – in other words, people like them. It was very inclusive in its narrative and caring in its imagery, but the focus and language didn't suit the target audience. Worse still, they realised that not only was the message way off base, but most of the people they wanted to reach wouldn't even be able to access a computer, let alone the internet. Their target audience were barely surviving (operating below even HR 1.0 Paternalism), and the only way to connect to them would be through a community outreach programme, probably involving some sort of event with coffee for mothers and free clothes for babies and toddlers in their local communities. Even at the event, it would be pointless handing out leaflets; the participants, usually women, needed a face-to-face explanation. Armed with the crucial value system insights, they changed their entire communication strategy and the uptake of the payments improved significantly. Why? Because the leaders were able to demonstrate enough understanding of the issues and enough maturity to communicate with the target audience in *their* language rather than their own.

Most people communicate based on their own value system rather than tailoring their message to suit the value system and world view of the intended recipient. They do this primarily because they don't realise that there is a different way to communicate based on values. This is partly an information issue and partly a maturity issue, because even once we recognise the difference, it takes a willingness to adapt in order to land the message, and that requires maturity. Table 8.3 outlines some of the key things a transition leader should think about when customising their message to different world views.

A mature leader recognises that the collective may be at an earlier P-wave and is willing to explain the shift in terms and a language that the employee base understands. An immature leader will be much less flexible and unlikely to be anything other than who they are. They see any variation to their natural expression of their own P-wave as inauthentic weakness. In truth, it is a considerable strength because it ensures that the message is received by the people who need it in a way that makes sense to them, and therefore encourages engagement and progress to the next P-wave. This adaptability is a representation of the sophistication a leader operating from a higher P-wave must bring to the change process.

Table 8.3 World view language customisation

World view	Goal of dialogue	Style wanted	Preferred language
HR 7.0 Planet (second tier)	Harmony	Unfolding	Missionary
HR 6.0 Paradox (second tier)	Learn and develop	Exploration	Variety
HR 5.0 People (first tier)	Be included	Inclusive dialogue	Sensitive
HR 4.0 Profit (first tier)	Achieve outcomes	Data-driven	Pragmatic
HR 3.0 Process (first tier)	Get to the truth	Structured, clear process	Honest
HR 2.0 Power (first tier)	Cut through	Direct and fast	Simple
HR 1.0 Paternalism (first tier)	Feel safe	Welcoming	Friendly

Communicating the shift from HR 1.0 to HR 2.0

To effectively lead a Paternalistic culture to the Power wave, it is necessary to "sell" the benefits of that Power wave in Paternalistic language. Thus, the clarity of direction that Power leaders use to cut through the commercial noise must be couched in HR 1.0 language. As such, their passion and friendly narrative should focus on how a little hierarchy and a clear vision will allow everyone to work together more effectively and bind everyone to each other strongly to ensure the survival of the business. As such, the business (and family members inside) will be better protected against the changing environment outside.

Communicating the shift from HR 2.0 to HR 3.0

To help people make the transition from a Power wave to a Process wave, the leader needs to show up as a living demonstration of the best of HR 3.0 – measured, loyal, principle-based, and seeking to do the right thing. The benefits of the Process wave must be positioned in a way that the Power advantages of such a transition are clear. Process-based initiatives should be explained simply and in a way that cuts to the crux of the issue quickly. If you can explain how the introduction of a slightly more rigorous process will speed up the operation and allow the business to capture more market share or become more dominant, then you will win the hearts and minds of the Power collective.

Communicating the shift from HR 3.0 to HR 4.0

To help the shift from HR 3.0 to HR 4.0, the transition leader must entice the collective with the benefits of the Profit wave. Specifically, they should emphasise the inherent value of the Profit wave, namely the ability to deliver results and personal reward. But the promotion of self-interest must be explained and discussed in HR 3.0 terminology – in this case, how greater freedom and individualism is in everyone's interest and drives the wealth of all economies, and therefore societies, forward. Explaining a focus on share-holder value can be "the right thing to do" in terms of evolving the way the business is conducted. In addition, point out how success and achievement will still require clear structures and rigorous process.

Communicating the shift from HR 4.0 to HR 5.0

When evolving from the Profit wave to the People wave, the transition leader needs to demonstrate the positive traits of the People leader – inclusivity, sensitivity, and a greater appreciation for all the stakeholders. They will need to reassure the more competitive outcome-focused individuals that the key metrics and dynamics that "made the market" will remain in place to drive continued success in the future. A People leader who can share the mounting evidence that corporate social responsibility agendas are delivering elevated financial results for the businesses will enable Profit-focused colleagues to embrace this more inclusive approach. Inclusivity initiatives can be positioned around their pragmatism in light of changing consumer demands. Embracing everyone in a targeted way will ensure better results and greater achievement.

Communicating the shift from HR 5.0 to HR 6.0

The shift from People to Paradox requires the transition leader to be more innovative and open to multiple perspectives so they can more effectively integrate the best of all views. The explanation of the move from HR 5.0 to HR 6.0 must be done sensitively with acute understanding of the people involved. Dialogue needs to be inclusive and fair. Initiatives should be couched in terms of taking care of the people in the business and defining how they allow the business to realise its purpose.

Communicating the shift from HR 6.0 to HR 7.0

The transitional leader wishing to move a business operating at HR 6.0 to HR 7.0 must demonstrate the best of HR 7.0 – a willingness to see a much bigger picture than just the company, an awareness and care for all people, all systems, and the planet. Any initiatives must, however, be positioned in HR 6.0 terms. So, the far-reaching benefits must emphasise the new thinking and how things link to each other. Leaders should explain how the business needs to "hack" old, outdated systems for a better, more inclusive, and beneficial future.

Embrace and implement the HR practices

The leader at any P-wave wishing to move the collective on to the next P-wave must also embrace and implement the HR practices of the next

P-wave. These are summarised in Table 8.1. There needs to be demonstrable evidence of the change in the business, and this can be made visible through the HR practices. As ever, linking these practices to the strategic intent of the business is key. They need to drive the improvement that is accessible through the wave.

Who should lead the transition?

By now, it might be obvious who is best suited to lead the transition from one P-wave to the next, bearing in mind that the collective will only ever be able to advance to the level of the leader and that transition can only happen sequentially one wave at a time. The leader, whether CEO, HR director, or work group leader, seeking to transition any collective must be operating from the destination P-wave or above.

The decision about who can lead that transition successfully can be assisted by applying the "4A filter." Any leader should be assessed against these criteria:

1. *Aptitude*: What evidence is there of skill sets? How many different models does the leader use? Is the leader attached to a single model or do they integrate multiple perspectives and a range of practices? Their ability to integrate multiple views testifies to the sophistication of their ability. A brilliant leader will naturally come with an extensive kitbag, a back catalogue of experiences that suggest they may have a very broad range of capabilities that they can bring to bear. The critical factor is not that they can tick lots of experiential boxes, but rather that they can make nuanced use of such skills and experiences by integrating them into a coherent narrative that is useful to the collective and move the centre of gravity in the group or business from one P-wave to the next.
2. *Amplitude*: What scale have they worked at? Have they worked all over the world in multiple markets and multiple geographies? Have they experienced several economic scenarios and market conditions? Can they lead at the C-suite and the factory floor? Are they equally comfortable with a diversity of cultural values, financial backgrounds, age ranges, sexual orientations, etc., or have they been restricted to leading just one or two types of people? Working across multiple fields is not a checklist. What matters is why the leader was working across multiple fields, and whether they have compared the insights from these multiple fields to more deeply understand the nature of variance to create a more powerful ability to transition from one P-wave to the next. Someone who flourishes in a diverse environment is more likely to have a greater amplitude.
3. *Attitude*: How good are their social skills? Are they emotionally intelligent, literate, and well managed? Are they easy to get on with? Do they radiate warmth and enthusiasm? Would you enjoy spending time with

them away from the transition journey? Are they interested in the individuals in the business as human beings, or are they just tools in the business? This dimension comes with a warning. It is easy to be fooled by a veneer of niceness and sociability. Many a company has been taken in by a socially skilled leader with little behind the facade. Look deeper for evidence of genuine concern and proof of emotional depth.

4. *Altitude*: What level of sophistication do they bring? If you had to weigh the "four As," then this would be the most heavily weighted. Has the leader got real depth, or are they just retelling a well-known story they have taken off others? Do they have something fresh to say about the human condition and how to effect a positive change? Most importantly, do they understand the difference between vertical development and horizontal learning, and can they operationalise this difference? What distinctions do they make, and what level of nuance do they work with? Do they understand multidimensionality across the quadrants of "being" ("I"), "doing" ("IT"/"ITS"), and "relating" ("WE")? Altitude takes a leader beyond simple description of phenomena to the ability to transform the future.[30]

When HR professionals are thinking about how to develop the people around them or step-change the capabilities of the executive pool, and who is best placed to lead the transition from one P-wave to the next, they must think in terms of a development journey. Vertical development is not a one-off or annual event. Facilitating development is much more like planning a trip to the moon than a cross-country road trip. The former will increase the altitude, and therefore the vantage point; the latter simply changes the scenery. When designing a cross-quadrant vertical development journey, the first step is to ascertain who is operating from where and how are they connected to everyone else in the business. The Leadership Values Profile (LVP), discussed in Chapter 5, and organisational network analysis (ONA), discussed in Chapter 6, can be useful diagnostic tools in this regard. If a leader with suitable altitude exists in the business, they can be the transition leader. If such expertise doesn't currently exist in the business, then as HR professionals you need to focus on the developmental journey of the leadership or consider buying that expertise in. When assessing a consultant or coach, however, the same "4A filter" should be applied to ensure you select the right transitional partner.

HR call to arms

While it is vital to understand what drives the transition from one P-wave to the next, it is equally important to understand what interventions can support the transition process. Table 8.1 summarises the key changes that can be made to HR organisations, systems, and processes to further underpin the P-wave journey. In Chapters 1–7, we hope we have brought these examples to life.

Business must evolve. We have spelt out the challenging business landscape ahead. There are significant benefits for every company, society, and for humanity, but each P-wave comes with a new level of complexity. The P-waves we are moving into now represent a level of complexity that business has never witnessed before. The only way to flourish is to evolve business and move through the P-waves. This active transition requires emphasis on the individual and collective developmental journey of everyone in the business, especially the C-suite leaders. The goal should be to ensure that as many of the business executives as possible reach HR 6.0 and beyond.

As HR 5.0 People continues to grapple with the paradoxes of cost pressure and purpose, as HR 4.0 increasingly realises that the old capitalist model needs to be reinvented, smart business leaders, shareholders, and other commercial stakeholders are all calling for change.[31]

Traditionally, HR change has followed change in business and society and has sought to adapt its practices to meet the prevailing P-wave's needs and aspirations. This reactive outlook itself must change.

We must step forward as HR people leaders to illuminate the path to a better business future for everyone, where we solve our economic problems while improving the human condition. We must help create a future where we measure gross national happiness as well as gross domestic product, something to which Robert Kennedy alluded decades ago:

> The Gross National Product measures neither our wit nor our courage, neither our wisdom nor our learning, neither our compassion nor our devotion to our country. It measures everything, in short, except that which makes life worthwhile.[32]

A future where we leverage technology, renewables, and a zero marginal cost society to ensure all can flourish. A future of the "collective commons" and sharing over ownership, which can in turn lead to a place where we focus on ourselves and each other as human beings, not money and possessions.

This is going to mean taking a proactive role in directing how business changes, and providing interventions – most crucially, leadership developmental interventions – that enable that change.

It's time to lead – we can change the workplace and change the world.

Notes

1 Farbrot A (2014) Narcissists Picked as Leaders, www.bi.edu/bizreview/articles/narcissists-picked-as-leaders/
2 Garrard P (2013) Dangerous Link between Power and Hubris in Politics, *The Conversation*, http://theconversation.com/dangerous-link-between-power-and-hubris-in-politics-20169
3 Syracuse A (2016) Donald Trump Is a Mother's Nightmare, *Time*, http://time.com/4187658/donald-trump-is-a-mothers-nightmare/

4 Mencken HL (1920) *Prejudices: Second Series – A Collection of Essays*, Kessinger Publishing, Whitefish, MT.
5 Whitely P and Clarke HD (2016) Brexit: Why Did Older Voters Choose to Leave the EU? *The Independent*, www.independent.co.uk/news/uk/politics/brexit-why-did-old-people-vote-leave-young-voters-remain-eu-referendum-a7103996.html
6 Olusoga D (2017) Empire 2.0 Is Dangerous Nostalgia for Something That Never Existed, *The Guardian*, www.theguardian.com/commentisfree/2017/mar/19/empire-20-is-dangerous-nostalgia-for-something-that-never-existed
7 Kentish B (2018) Leave Voters Dying and Remainers Reaching Voting Age Means Majority Will Soon Oppose Brexit, Study Finds, *The Independent*, www.independent.co.uk/news/uk/politics/brexit-leave-eu-remain-vote-support-against-poll-uk-europe-final-say-yougov-second-referendum-peter-a8541971.html
8 Rooke D and Torbert WR (2005) Seven Transformations of Leadership, *Harvard Business Review*, http://hbr.org/2005/04/seven-transformations-of-leadership/ar/1
9 Piaget J (1972) *The Psychology of the Child*, Basic Books, New York.
10 Kohlberg L (1981) *The Philosophy of Moral Development: Moral Stages and the Idea of Justice*, Harper & Row, London.
11 Loevinger J and Le Xuan Hy (1996) *Measuring Ego Development (Personality & Clinical Psychology)*, Psychology Press, New York.
12 Wilber K (1995) *Sex, Ecology, Spirituality: The Spirit of Evolution*, Shambhala Publications, Boston, MA.
13 Kegan R (1982) *The Evolving Self: Problem and Process in Human Development*, Harvard University Press, Cambridge, MA.
14 Jacques E (2002) *The Life and Behavior of Living Organisms: A General Theory*, Praeger Publishing, Westport, CT.
15 Fischer KW (1981) *Cognitive Development*, Jossey-Bass, New York.
16 Cook-Greuter SR and Miller ME (1994) *Transcendence and Mature Thought in Adulthood: Further Reaches of Adult Development*, Rowman & Littlefield, London.
17 Torbert WR (1991) *The Power of Balance: Transforming Self, Society, and Scientific Inquiry*, SAGE, New York.
18 Graves CW (1970) Levels of Existence: An Open System Theory of Values. *Journal of Humanistic Psychology*, 10(2): 131–155.
19 Cook-Greuter SR and Miller ME (1999) *Creativity, Spirituality, and Transcendence: Paths to Integrity and Wisdom in the Mature Self*, Ablex Publishing, Stamford, CT.
20 Rooke D and Torbert WR (2005) Seven Transformations of Leadership, *Harvard Business Review*, https://hbr.org/2005/04/seven-transformations-of-leadership
21 Cook-Greuter SW (2002) A Detailed Description of the Development of Nine Action Logics Adapted from Ego Development Theory for the Leadership Development Framework, *Next Step Integral*, http://nextstepintegral.org/wp-content/uploads/2011/04/The-development-of-action-logics-Cook-Greuter.pdf
22 Graves CW (1970) Levels of Existence: An Open System Theory of Values. *Journal of Humanistic Psychology*, 10(2): 131–155.
23 Wilber K (2000) *Integral Psychology*, Shambhala Publications, Boston, MA. Wilber K (2017) *Religions of Tomorrow*, Shambhala Publications, Boston, MA.
24 Scott S (2002) *Fierce Conversations*, Piatkus Books, London.
25 Martin R (2003) *The Responsibility Virus: How Control Freaks, Shrinking Violets – and the Rest of Us – Can Harness the Power of True Partnership*, Basic Books New York.
26 Rifkin J (2015) *The Zero Margin Cost Society: The Internet of Things, the Collaborative Commons, and the Eclipse of Capitalism*, Palgrave Macmillan, London.
27 Kimmel B (2018) Return on Trust: The "State of Trust" 2018, https://trustacrossamerica.com/documents/index/Return-Methodology.pdf. Eccles RG, Ioannou

I, and Seraeim G (2014 revised) The Impact of Corporate Sustainability on Organizational Processes and Performance, www.hbs.edu/faculty/Publication% 20Files/SSRN-id1964011_6791edac-7daa-4603-a220-4a0c6c7a3f7a.pdf

28 Watkins A and Wilber K (2015) *Wicked and Wise: How to Solve the World's Toughest Problems*, Urbane Publications, Kent.

29 Anthony S and Schwartz EI (2017) What the Best Transformational Leaders Do, *Harvard Business Review*, https://hbr.org/2017/05/what-the-best-transformational-leaders-do

30 Kegan R and Laskow Lahey L (2016) *An Everyone Culture: Becoming a Deliberately Developmental Organization*, Harvard Business Review Press, Boston, MA.

31 Edgecliffe-Johnson A (2019) Beyond the Bottom Line: Should Business Put Purpose Before Profit? *Financial Times*, www.ft.com/content/a84647f8-0d0b-11e9-a3aa-118c761d2745

32 Kennedy RF (1968) Speech at the University of Kansas at Lawrence.

Index